The Culture of Hope

A New Birth
of the Classical Spirit

Frederick Turner

THE FREE PRESS

New York   London   Toronto   Sydney   Tokyo   Singapore

The Free Press
A Division of Simon & Schuster Inc.
1230 Avenue of the Americas, New York, N.Y. 10020

Printed in the United States of America

printing number

1 2 3 4 5 6 7 8 9 10

Library of Congress Cataloging-in-Publication Data

Turner, Frederick
    The culture of hope : a new birth of the classical spirit /
Frederick Turner.
        p.   cm.
    Includes bibliographical references and index.

    ISBN: 1-4165-7685-1
    ISBN-13: 978-1-4165-7685-3

    1. Postmodernism—United States.   2. Arts and society—United
States—History—20th century.   3. Semiotics and the arts—United
States.   I. Title.
NX180.S6T87   1995
700'.1'0309730904—dc20   94–45343
                                                                      CIP

Contents

A Note to the Reader

Contemporary works of cultural criticism often carry an impressive freight of footnotes referring to the unchallenged authorities in the field. Even when they deny the validity of authorship and text, as is so common today, they are meticulous in citation and bibliography. This book does the opposite: though it indeed acknowledges many writers, thinkers, and artists as authorities, and treats many texts as sacred, it relies upon no authority but its own; and it comes into the world naked of any scholarly apparatus, but for an annotated list of recommended readings at the end. If the reader finds anything here that is convincing, whether by its logic, by its accordance with fact, or by its imaginative truth, let that be the warrant for the rest. The references to authors and books in the body of the text indicate an indebtedness to them, rather than an attempt to subdue the reader with the eminence of my sources. In these days of on-line bibliographic databases, the careful scholar should have little trouble tracking down my intentionally brief citations.

In various parts of this study I have used passages that are substantially unchanged from earlier books and essays of mine, though at the same time this work probably breaks more new ground than any other prose book I have written, and the synthesis of the whole is more comprehensive. Rather than give a lame paraphrase when I could not put it better, I felt the most honest thing to do was to repeat myself when the argument required the recapitulation of an earlier idea. Those readers who know my work will, I hope, be able to see those passages in a new light, and through them to understand certain connections of thought among my writings.

Chapter 1

The Culture Wars

The Sickness of the Arts

This book is for those who have been shaken out of themselves by art, who have felt a piece of Mozart's *Magic Flute* reach out and grab them by the heart, who have seen the grave look on Flora's face as she steps out of Botticelli's *Pimavera* the way the gods always do, lit by a light too powerful to be quite shown; for those who have heard a line of Shakespeare so that it rang again and again in their ears—"Not mine own fears, nor the prophetic soul/Of the wide world dreaming on things to come." All great art leads us beyond anything we have ever known; this is as true now as it has ever been. Art is culture communing with itself and generating a new spring, like the flowers of Botticelli's painting cascading from the mouth of April; it is the prophetic soul of the wide world. It is not authoritarian but infinitely vulnerable; all you have to do is to stop listening or watching or reading and it goes away. The grand modernists—Matisse, Joyce, Stravinsky—all knew this; but their successors today (and alas, those who oppose the successors too) have forgotten. It is my contention that our "high" or "academic" or "avant-garde" culture is in a state of crisis. This crisis is not a healthy one, but a sickness unto death, a decadence that threatens to destroy our society.

1

The symptoms of the crisis are well known. A few years ago art collectors were paying large sums to a certain artist for sealed and labeled cans of his excrement; recently the artist decided to eliminate the middleman and sell the collectors their own excrement instead. A dead Mexican pauper's head was sawn in two, and the two halves exhibited in profile, kissing each other. In the 1993 Whitney biennial show, which is supposed to represent the best contemporary art being produced, crude racist slogans directed against people of European descent vied with a pile of simulated vomit and photographs of private body parts for the delectation of the connoisseur. Completely blank canvases are solemnly exhibited and sold; the Tate exhibits an empty gallery as a work of art. In avant-garde music, melody is studiously avoided; a Slinky toy is portentously dropped off a piano at a concert otherwise devoid of sonic content; various contrivances are devised to produce entirely random combinations of sounds. In performance art, performers execute sexual acts on stage, maim themselves by a variety of means including high-powered rifles, and engage in lavatory activities with strong political messages. The strangely misnamed "language poets," whose hallmark is that their poems do not make any kind of sense, are the present rage. Architecture has graduated from modernist brutality to deconstructivist nausea.

This catalog of abuses is a familiar litany. To complain in this way is to adopt the traditional position of the "straight man," the bluenosed bourgeois who is the butt of all avant-garde sarcasm, the poor benighted philistine harrumphing at what he does not understand. But I am not the first to warn the public that our culture is sick and needs cure. In *The Culture of Complaint*, Robert Hughes gives a partial diagnosis. He argues that the great artistic ideals of modernism are still valid, but have been lost in a welter of claims for artistic attention by neglected minorities or oppressed groups, to the extent that the prestige of art has become a consolation prize to mollify the politically or economically unsuccessful. In his periodical *The New Criterion*, Hilton Kramer has made much the same point. Earlier, in *The Culture of Narcissism*, Christopher Lasch blamed what he saw as the moral flabbiness and cultural decadence of our times on the cult and psychological condition of narcissism. Allan Bloom, in a more complex argument, has rooted the malaise in the philosophical, political, and cultural failure of the central ideas of romanticism—a tragic failure, given the grandeur of its hopes, but one whose deepest symptom is the contemporary incapacity for tragedy itself, for that tragic love of life which accepts that it must be painful and unfair. Roger Kimball's *Tenured Radicals*, Martin Anderson's *Imposters in the Temple*, Arthur Schlesinger, Jr.'s *The Disuniting of America*, Robert Alter's *The Pleasures of Reading in an Ideological Age*, and David Bromwich's *Politics by Other Means: Higher Education and Group Thinking* all deal with the same problem, with special emphasis on the failure of the academy. Dana Gioia, in *Can Poetry Matter*, has focused on the decline of poetic standards and the withering away of the audience, due the neglect of craftsmanship and traditional form. Christopher Clausen, putting poetry in a larger cultural and philosophical context, has argued that poetry damaged itself by resigning its cognitive function, its claim to a kind of knowledge. E. D. Hirsch has addressed the problem in terms of the decline in cultural literacy. David Griffin, in several books, has argued that the deconstructive postmodernism of recent decades is but another manifestation of the deadening and unspiritual legacy of modernity. The neo-Marxist social critics, like Frank Lentricchia and Frederic Jameson, have made similar points about our predicament, blaming what they call the commodification and fetishization of "late capitalism." There is surprising unanimity that something is rotten in the state of our culture. However, the diagnosis differs each time, and usually no cure is offered, except for the vague injunction to desist from what we are doing and return to the path of virtue. In this book I shall try to combine the diagnoses into a larger picture of our sickness, and prescribe a real cure, one which treats our mind and imagination as well as our behavior.

Players in the Culture War: Left, Right, and Radical Center

Avant-garde leftist artists and intellectuals see the culture war as an assault by evil fascistic conservatives upon the freedom of artistic expression, an attack based on patriarchal white Western values. In order to defend these values the conservatives are attempting to regulate the National Endowments and censor art. The conservative insistence on standards, quality, and excellence is, according to the avant-garde position, just code for racist and sexist bigotry, covering up the continuation of economic and social privileges for rich and powerful elites. In contrast, the avant-garde sees itself as being the vanguard of social change, encouraging economic and cultural justice and a new world of equality, caring, universal self-esteem, and self-fulfillment; thus their art serves as a way of exploring new forms of sensual experience, new conceptions of the self as dissolved or disseminated, and nontraditional forms of social and personal relationships.

Conservative right-wing critics of the arts see things differently. They look at the horrors of the inner cities, the devastation of the family, the collapse of personal self-discipline and psychological health, widespread sexual promiscuity, declining rates of educational achievement, rising drug use, crime, and violence, and blame the nationwide decay of moral fiber and cultural morale. The culprits, they believe, are the avant-garde artists and intellectuals who encourage sexual license, ethnic separatism and fragmentation, and life-style experiments, at the same time ridiculing self-discipline, virtue, Judeo-Christian values, the traditional family, and the moral and rational tradition of the West. They suspect there is an artistic establishment that has deliberately censored wholesome and up-lifting forms of art. Conservatives feel that if the current fashion of nega-tivism were not supported by the National Endowments and by the major private foundations, it would lose what audience it has; whole-some family art would arise, the nation could rebuild itself, there would be universal prosperity, clean safe streets, an educated public, and a re-vival of people's sense of meaning and purpose in their lives.

If you identify with either one of these camps, the conflict is insoluble except by total victory—that is, by the disappearance or forced reeduca-tion of the enemy. However, a third side is emerging, one which recog-nizes the valid ideals on both sides of the conflict but approaches art and culture in a very different way. This third side, which I call the radical center, sees that the avant-garde and the conservatives share certain metaphysical and philosophical assumptions, inherited from the nine-teenth century, concretized in the polarization between Left and Right, and frozen in place by an esthetic and evaluative vocabulary that no longer corresponds to our best knowledge about the world. Those as-sumptions are the reason, not only for the ideological impasse, but also for many of the real problems of the contemporary arts, such as its des-perate crisis of originality, its failure to find an audience, and its isolation from vital intellectual currents in the human and natural sciences, reli-gion, technology, and the environmental movement.

Perhaps the best way to point out the differences—and the potential for reconciliation—among the three positions is to give a brief description of each.

What is value, where does it come from, how ought it to be distributed? What is the nature of the physical universe in which value exists? Is art fundamentally orderly or disorderly? What is the nature, if any, of the human beings who make and experience art? What should art's attitude be to traditional forms, genres, and crafts? What is art's relationship to the Western tradition, and what is that tradition? What is the role of art with regard to social improvement and social progress? What constitutes social improvement or progress? Who is the chief enemy of art? What is the chief evil? What should be censored, if anything? What is the chief value of art?

The artistic Left, that is, the established avant-garde as it has persisted in various forms since the early nineteenth century, still accepts the view of value implicit in traditional "scientific" economics: that there is a limited stockpile of natural value. This stockpile roughly corresponds to the thermodynamic order remaining in the accessible universe, and it is running down through the increase of entropy—the "shrinking pie." The Left believes that this natural value can be extracted from nature only by painful labor, and that it is distributed among human beings either through coercive control by a ruling class/race/gender, or through liberating struggle against that control. The conservative Right shares this view of value, but with different emphases. Natural value is a diminishing stockpile that is distributed by the Invisible Hand of the market, a just process that cannot be disrupted without economic damage. Social value is the recognition of natural value in the context of consumer demand and scarcity.

The radical center holds a very different view of value. In agreement with many fields of twentieth-century natural science, ranging from evolutionary theory to chaos theory, it believes that value is continually created by the natural universe, that it is not a shrinking pie, and that human beings can share in and accelerate the growth of value through work which may be delightful, if disciplined. Value of this kind should circulate freely where it is needed. The present market system of capitalist economies is a linear and clumsy attempt to imitate the more subtle processes of true value-creation, but though it is our closest approximation to date (much closer than any socialist system) it is transforming itself as our technology enables more perfect and multidimensional forms of communication. As machines take over the drudgery, the labor basis of value is being replaced by an information basis of value; and this in turn will be replaced, perhaps, by an emergent kind of value which is hard to define but as a kind of embodied grace.

If the universe is, as both the avant-garde and the conservatives believe, an ordered system that is gradually running down and becoming more disordered, what is the role of art? The Right believes that art should help maintain and preserve the order of the past against the ravages of dissolution and cultural decline. Order may be tyrannical, but it is all we have; quality and standards cannot be detached from bondage. The avant-garde, on the other hand, observes that natural physical order, which is the only kind it recognizes as not an illusion of political hegemony, is deterministic and opposed to human freedom. Thus the only course for art to take must be that of disorder, of constant dissent, disruption, and rebellion against order; we are free only if we can perform a gratuitous act with no sense or reason. Modernist and postmodernist artists have sought in the name of freedom, which they value above all else, to incorporate a larger and larger element of the random, irrational, and unintelligible in their work, so as to break the shackles of deterministic order. The fact that in so doing they are in their own terms furthering the decay and collapse of the physical universe is either ignored or silently celebrated with a dark glee. There is a curious correspondence between this view and that of nineteenth-century industrialism, that was willing to ravage the natural environment to increase human power.

The radical center, however, has seen that evolution—a concept now extended by scientists to cover not just biology but the whole of the physical universe—is productive of novel forms of order. Chaos theory tells us that beautiful "attractors" can underlie apparent chaos, and that highly ordered systems can, through iteration, feedback, and the mutual communication of all their elements, generate entirely unpredictable emergent properties. Thus the order of the universe is neither running down nor deterministic, and the strict distinction between order and chaos, vital to the Left and the Right, is invalid. For the radical center art can, from the strictest traditions and severest order, derive unexpected and profoundly original visions and perspectives. At the same time the most heterogeneous and unlikely elements can be mixed together to produce, out of an apparently wild disorder, a classical synthesis that can rival and even surpass the achievements of the past, if those elements are permitted a consistent and thoroughgoing process of mutual feedback.

As for the human artist and human audience, both the avant-garde and the conservatives find themselves shackled by eighteenth- and nineteenth-century notions of nature as a deterministic machine. Conservatives tend to accept the idea that the body is a machine like the rest of the universe, and that we have a human nature that determines our station in life, but that we also have an immaterial soul that is preserved in its free state by religious observance and the willing acceptance of duty and service. Apologists for the avant-garde have a harder time dealing with the human body, agreeing only in the nonexistence of the soul. Some accept what they imagine to be the body's mechanical limits but wallow in them. An example would be the "desiring machine" theory of human nature as proposed by Deleuze and Guattari. Some, like the French feminists, except the human body, especially the female body, from the constraints of nature, regarding it as uniquely polymorphous and liquid. Others, like Feyerabend and Foucault, deny the whole edifice of science, and thus its findings about human nature, as a socially constructed illusion designed to keep the lower orders in place. Still others, like Sartre in *The Flies*, reject the body itself as part of nature's conspiracy of bondage.

For the radical center, human nature does indeed exist; however, our nature is not a limitation of our freedom but the very source of it. The body and brain evolved through a marvelous feedback between biological and cultural evolution; and the evolutionary imperative that drove the process was the development of greater powers of learning, adaptation, personal communication, creativity, and freedom. Freedom is what our bodies were designed to produce, if they are properly taught, disciplined, loved, and nurtured by a culture that has not forgotten its roots. Freedom is not a condition but a unique personal achievement, reached through submission to one's culture's best traditions and one's body's demand for training in what it does best. The rest of nature is only in various degrees less free than we are.

In this view our biological nature is designed to exist within a cultural context that is in the broadest sense *classical*—by which I mean centered upon the values of truth, goodness, and beauty. Both the Right and the Left would disagree. The conservative Right regards human nature as essentially fallen, selfish, and individualistic. Our life in a state of nature is nasty, brutish, solitary, and short, said Hobbes, and only the authority of social rules backed up by profound moral and cultural sanctions, and the miracle of the market that transforms individual selfishness into collective welfare, can save us from ourselves. For the Right, Western culture, a pure European civilization deriving from Jerusalem, Athens, and Rome, is unique in having brought to a classical state of excellence the cultural and economic wisdoms, together with the Judeo-Christian morality, that best control and channel human nature. The avant-garde Left, on the other hand, regards human nature as infinitely malleable, so that it can be easily "constructed" by society. Western civilization has distorted and stunted that nature—or constructed it so as to profit the powerful white male elites—in a way that is uniquely reprehensible, leading to such atrocities as the Holocaust, colonialism, racism, sexism, and widespread economic injustice.

In its rejection of the idea of human nature, and the closely related concept of classical standards of excellence, the Left is paradoxically at odds with those very non-Western cultures that it professes to prefer. The artistic productions of the radical Left tend to be either indifferent to technique and craftsmanship or blatantly in violation of them. The irony here is that any real "third world" artist, embodying the traditions and training of an ancient culture, would find the work of these new avant-garde multiculturalists incompetent, ludicrous, or disgusting. There is much more in common between, say, baroque Italian and Maori art than there is between Maori art and the Whitney biennial. It is Mozart and Shakespeare, not John Cage and Karen Finley, who are universal.

On the other hand, the Right seriously underestimates the extent to which classical Western art has always contained a profound critique of its own society, along with an equally profound endorsement of the fundamental values of humankind. Just as in tribal village societies the rituals of life crisis and seasonal change always contain a "liminal" period within which the ideals and symbols of society are reevaluated, so the rituals of Western art, whether the history plays of Shakespeare, Mozart's *Marriage of Figaro*, or Goya's etchings, become a space within which a thoroughgoing assessment of European norms can take place. As with content, so with form and technique: it is not enough just to repeat the past. The classical genres of art—landscape painting, epic, tragedy, the sonata form, and so on—only come alive when they are stretched to accommodate new material, hybridized with other genres, or deepened by an unprecedented twist.

The radical center contests the very terms "Western" and "classical," pointing out that what is called Western culture is already an amalgam of hundreds of wildly different cultures from Asia, Africa, and Europe, one which has found the knack of listening to and absorbing other cultural values. Much of what is called Western, including science, democracy, reason, classical art, and the achievements of religion in ritual practice, ethics, mysticism, and spiritual psychology, is the creation and property of the whole human race. Europe played the leading role in the great synthesis of human cultures that has been going on for the last four thousand years; but it was by no means an exclusive role. Many cultures throughout the world, even before trade or conquest brought them into the converging mainstream of the major civilizations, achieved classical excellence in some field or other of art, government, philosophy, cuisine, ritual, healing, and so on; these achievements share certain deep structural and thematic characteristics wherever they occur. There is what I am calling a "natural classicism" in human arts that is based on culturally universal art forms and genres. Poetic meter, musical tonality and scale, visual motifs, techniques of visual representation, mythical stories, and so on, have deep neurobiologically based grammars, as does language itself, that are common to all cultures. It is only by training in a tradition which activates our innate propensity for these grammars that a budding artist, and a budding audience, can be liberated into their human heritage. It may not matter much which of the great classical traditions—the Chinese, the Hindu, the European, and so on—is chosen as the basis of such training, but one would be wise to choose the most humanly comprehensive one available, and a great world artist should attempt to master and synthesize several of them.

The radical center rejects the ethnocentrism of the Right, but it also rejects the demonization of the West by the Left. Any careful reading of history will show that every human group is capable of atrocities and injustice, as of magnificent and original contributions to human welfare—the larger and older the group, the more of both. Slavery, colonialism, and the sexual division of labor were not the exclusive invention of the West; indeed, the West has in fact been a leading force in the abolition of slavery, the economic enfranchisement of the masses, and the liberation of women.

These issues bring us to the matter of social progress and the role of art with respect to it. The Left believes that art should serve social progress, be its mouthpiece and interior decorator, so to speak. What constitutes social progress is defined in theory by the people, in practice by political leaders and theoreticians, but in any case not by artists. Its general goals, as viewed by the Left, are the liberation of the individual from all constraints of tradition, rule, custom, and control; these constraints should be replaced by an education that will enjoin absolute equality among all persons, complete acceptance of all differences, and total noninterference by any person in the life of another. All value judgments (other than positive ones which can be shared among all, like grade school valentines) are hurtful and should be avoided, except when describing—negatively, of course—members of traditional authoritarian groups.

Conservatives see art in two roles: as harmless entertainment that helps us temporarily escape the responsibilities of the world, or as the anointed propagandist of traditional religious, moral, and social values. For the Right, social progress is a dubious concept, though conservatives may embrace technological and economic improvements as long as such innovations do not sap the moral fiber of the nation. Art can maintain standards and discipline the will and intelligence of the young; it can also show how social inequalities are just and rational and for the benefit of all. Art, like a constitutional monarch, should stay out of important political and economic decisions, though it may provide emotional justification for decisions already taken.

The radical center sees art as the only place where the new concepts essential to real social progress can germinate and gestate. Current political struggles, where well-meaning people find themselves locked in bitter disagreement, are usually insoluble in their own terms. If negotiation or logic or the application of legal or moral rules could solve them, they would not be problems. It is only art that is able to leap out of the terms of the debate, find new ground and new values, and provide a common vision toward which the contestants can strive. Thus art must be committed to no existing political program or party, though imaginatively it must be able to empathize with all such programs. The radical center is not particularly interested in issues of power and equality; it knows that power is transient, superficial, and corrupting, and that equality is a noble legal fiction, valid in the political realm but meaningless everywhere else. Art is like play in that it exists in a world of "as if"; but it is also a training ground and experimental test bed for more mature moral and political conceptions. Though the deep genres and themes of art are traditional, they have a vitality and eternal generativeness that makes them the only final resource against the ossification of social roles and the hardening of political dogma. Art tends to question any conventional axis along which people could be judged either equal or unequal; it exposes the desire for inequality as power-seeking, and the desire for equality as gnawing envy, mediocrity's ressentiment against excellence. What constitutes progress for the radical center is the continuation of the natural evolution of the universe in a new, swifter, and deeper way, through the cooperation of human beings with the rest of nature, bringing conscious intention and organized creativity to the aid of natural variation and selection. Evolution in these terms is a spiritual and mysterious process. This evolutionary process is one in which there are honorable roles for technology, for natural conservation, for art, and for economic development.

The Left and the Right resemble each other in setting up enemies that must be defeated if the promised era is to come. Most obviously, their enemies are each other. But they also propose less tautological villains, and when they do, profound contradictions appear in their positions. The Left, especially the artistic Left, hates and despises the middle class, or what is now generally called the dominant group in society; of course, it is that very group which tends to produce left avant-garde artists. The Right hates and despises the indolent poor, criminals, and outsiders in general. But without the beggar or mugger in the street, the racial or sexual or cultural Other, the right-winger would be hard-pressed to maintain his or her own identity.

For both the Right and the Left shame is the greatest evil, to be denied at all costs. The shame of our human condition is not just that we are animals with a digestive system, a sexual means of reproduction, and an irreducibly cruel and exploitative economic relationship with the rest of nature and with each other. It is that we also have a conscience and spiritual consciousness that can judge us for these things and compare us unfavorably with ideals and good examples. Both Right and Left are united in their endorsement of censorship; what is to be censored is the shameful and the shaming. The Right wishes to censor the sexual and mammalian/primate aspects of our nature; the Left wishes to censor ideals of cultural and moral excellence that would make any viewer feel ashamed of him- or herself. As for the radical center, it does not believe in censorship at all, though it does believe that wicked, ugly, and lying art ought to be roundly subjected to public criticism. The Right displaces the shame of our human condition, often murderously, onto the social, racial, or sexual Other; the Left denies the shame of our condition and seeks to be shameless, but scapegoats the middle class, often murderously, as the source of shame.

"Beauty" is a natural and organic term that nevertheless embarrasses us because of the way it mixes our emotional, physical, and intellectual responses. For the radical center, one of the most important things that all great human art does, especially religious and theatrical performance, is conduct us through the acknowledgment and recognition of our shame to the epiphanic experience of beauty that follows and grows out of such recognition. The inhuman architecture of Mussolini, in which shame is banished, attempted to frustrate that process; so too do those avant-garde works of art which attempt to deaden our sense of shame by denying the validity of our reaction against obscenity, and replace the shame with political scapegoating. This combination of denials, right and left, has paralyzed the contemporary arts. The radical center in the culture war seeks a renewal of beauty and is not ashamed of the term; it also defends its position by a thoroughgoing analysis of critical theory in the light of new developments in human and natural science.

Thus one final way of defining the differences among the Left, the Right, and the center is in terms of the highest value to which art can attain. The Left believes in the sublime, that is, it denies shame by breaking all the boundaries and distinctions that make shame possible. Either it rejects the moral judgments that make our biological and economic predicament painful and problematic, or it denies that predicament altogether as a socially constructed illusion devised by the conservative regimes of power and knowledge. Left-wing sublimity always gravitates in the end toward the ultimately ugly, for it is only there that we will no longer be shamefully challenged by what is better than the worst in ourselves. The Right believes in the pretty; it denies shame by exporting to the outside all the unpleasantness and smell of our lives, leaving an art that is entirely proper and devoid of embarrassing challenge. Its final state is the terminally bland.

The radical center believes in the beautiful. It accepts the shame of our conscious existence as animals in an ecological and evolutionary context, and as perpetual amateurs in a world in which fairness and luck, justice and mercy, the earned and the given, cannot be disentangled. The radical center resists alike the rightist tendency to slacken beauty in the direction of the merely pretty, and the leftist tendency to slacken beauty in the direction of the merely sublime. Beauty is the most nonutopian of all ideals, and is the only one which can tolerate the existence of tragedy as an irreducible component of being.

The New Movement

There is at present a growing number of artists in various fields who have begun to embrace the new paradigm of the radical center, and who will one day be seen as the pioneers of the next major historical phase in the arts—as Dante, Petrarch, Giotto, and Piero were for the Italian Renaissance, as Blake and Wordsworth were for English romanticism. The contemporary establishment finds them threatening, but they are preparing their Armory Show, their Preface to the *Lyrical Ballads*, their *salon des refusés*, their Defense of Poetry.

There is a new movement afoot throughout the arts; the question is how to define it. What makes definition especially difficult is that the new movement is at once so widespread, so little reported, and so disconnected. We do not have a cultural capital like London or Paris in this country. The movement has arisen spontaneously in a variety of "fields" and "disciplines," in part as a reaction against academic modernist conceptions of field and discipline; the divisions and boundaries themselves have hindered communication among people and ideas. And so it might be especially helpful to develop a hypothetical vocabulary for talking about the movement.

One crude way of defining the movement is in terms of a return to classical forms, genres, and techniques in the arts. In "serious" music we can cite a disillusionment with seriality, the twelve-tone row, and atonality, a renewed interest in worldwide folk music, a search for the deep pan-human roots of melody, and a focus on the immediacy of performance, improvisation, and the context of audience and performer.

In visual arts we find a strong return to representation, to landscape and the figure, a rejection of the hegemonic modernist authority of abstraction, and the beginnings of a revulsion against the idea of art as the ideological enemy of ordinary human life. In poetry there is a wave of renewed interest in poetic meter and in narrative, a questioning of the role of poetry as therapeutic private expression, and a return to the great public themes of enduring human interest. In theater the influence of ethnodrama and "magic realism" have combined with a recovery of the classical canon to cause a partial breakdown of the barrier between serious theater and popular theater. In fiction there has been a swing toward storytelling and "moral fiction," and a tendency to absorb the formal and stylistic experiments of modernist fiction into a more traditional narrative fabric; we can, once more, identify characters and plot, and theme and setting. We are in a great age of film, and though we are distracted by the enormous consumption of hyped schlock, there is now also a large audience for an art that is superbly crafted and plotted, visually subtle, and thematically classical. In dance there is a return to story and to representation, and a convergence of mime, dance, tableau, and kinetic sculpture.

Two terms have been used for the new movement in the visual arts: "romantic realism" and "classical realism." Although these names give a vague impression of what such art looks like, they are misleading in crucial ways. The term "romantic" is perhaps intended to evoke the emotional appeal of such work; but it also carries the misleading impression of intellectual shallowness and moral license, whereas the new art is, at its best, informed by profound thought, philosophical inquiry, and severe ethical and spiritual concerns. The name also suggests a historical connection with the romantic period, which was precisely the time when virtue, reason, and esthetic discipline began to come under systematic attack. "Realism" does not entirely fit the case either, because the new art does not make a fetish of reproducing gritty reality. When appropriate, the new art is exact and gritty; and when not appropriate, it is not. One can always see what the new art is a picture—or a sculpture—*of*; but realism is not quite the right word. Perhaps "representationalism" would be closer; but the new art seems often to strike through toward truths and entities that have never had a visual appearance in the first place, and thus can neither be photographed nor imitated by pictorial representation. Certainly the new movement would reject the iconoclasm of postmodern theory, with its "problematizing" of representation and the image. "Classicism" seems right, but it contains its own traps. The new movement is not simply a return to ancient European ideas. It recognizes that classicism is not an exclusively European property, but a miracle that has happened many times throughout the world in a variety of societies, ranging from hunter-gatherer bands through priest-and-pyramid cities and feudal warrior-states to mercantile empires and industrial democracies. Ancient classicisms have proposed fixed and perfect ideals that never change. The new classical spirit sees the world as evolving into a richer and richer mix of physical and spiritual complexity.

Some examples of the artists of this movement in the visual arts are the painters David Ligare and Cynthia Krieble, and the sculptor Frederick Hart. Even as "postmodern" an artist as the earthworks sculptor James Turrell is in much the same spirit. In architecture I would cite especially Christopher Alexander, and in architectural criticism Michael Benedikt; in this field, because of the practical requirements of livability and physical integrity, art could never depart too far from the classical, and the modernist Louis Kahn is very close to the ideal.

In poetry there are two highly vigorous movements that represent at least part of the radical center paradigm: "the new formalism" and "the new narrative." The new poetry breaks modernist rules established since Edgar Allan Poe condemned the long narrative poem, and dares to tell stories, often gripping and fascinating ones, in verse. "New formalism" refers to the revival in poetry of poetic meter, verse, and rhyme. Modernist critics of the new formalism have suggested that it is elitist and un-American, but have been staggered by the rejoinder that it is free verse that is confined to a small group of European-influenced cognoscenti, while meter and rhyme are the normal forms for blues and jazz lyrics, country and western songs, mariachi, Broadway musicals, and rap. Several poets use both meter and narrative, and the two movements combined are called "expansive poetry," a phrase coined by the poet Wade Newman. Expansive poetry is expansive in the sense that it attempts to wide the scope of poetry beyond the short, free verse, imagist, private,

existentialist lyric poem that has become the norm in late modernist letters. It is also expansive in that it feels free to recover past modes and genres of poetry, and presupposes an expanding and evolving universe, in
which new forms of order can grow out of the old, and where freedom
can consist not just in wrecking traditional kinds of order, but in creating
new ones. Leading practitioners of "expansive poetry" include Jack Butler, Julia Budenz, Frederick Feirstein, Jane Greer, Tim Steele, Christopher
Clausen, Charles Martin, Annie Finch, Brad Leithauser, Dana Gioia, Paul
Lake, Gjertrud Schnackenburg, Robert McDowell, and Dick Allen.

In fiction there has been some recognition of the bankruptcy of postmodern fictional self-consciousness, and a call by such wise writers as
John Gardner, Anthony Burgess, and Tom Wolfe for a storytelling that is
moral, organically related to its past, and realistic. But the predicament
of the novel is somewhat different from that of the more esoteric arts.
Modernist avant-garde fashions could not vitiate the novel's popular appeal. Postmodern fashions such as the "new novel" were so unpopular
that their products failed economic tests other arts were not expected to
undergo, and were quickly forgotten. Meanwhile one genre of fiction has
continued triumphantly to satisfy the requirements of a full-blooded and
healthy art: science fiction. Insulated by its cheerful and uncomplaining
acceptance of outsiderhood from the hothouse tantrums of the avant-
garde, it has continued to explore the mythic undercurrents of our culture, and stands as an example for the emerging artistic consciousness.

The poet and critic Kevin Walzer sees the new movement as another
variety of postmodernism, and there is some justification in his view.
That is, in much postmodern art there is a conscious reference to past
genres and modes of representation, and a new concern with significa-
tion and cultural codes. Charles Jencks has made a similar point with regard to the neoclassical flavor of some postmodern painting. But the
intent of much of what is called postmodern is to satirize or politically
discredit those past modes and genres, whereas the new movement is
more in the spirit of respectfully and lovingly grasping hands with the
great dead shamans and artists of the past. The philosopher David Griffin distinguishes between "deconstructive postmodernism" and "reconstructive postmodernism," attempting to save the term "postmodern" for
positive and creative purposes. Others, including myself, have felt that
this battle may be lost, and that postmodernism is destined, like the late

eighteenth-century "picturesque" movement, to be seen as only a transitional phase into a new period of cultural history that does not need to be labeled feebly with a modification of its predecessor's name.

James Mann, a poet, art critic, and ironist, proposes the violent name "Vandalism." His explanation is that the new movement actually overthrows two hundred years of cultural history and makes the avant-garde turn in its collective grave. He also argues that the last phase of liberation from traditional authority is to liberate ourselves from the authority of the liberators and be free to choose any style we want for our art, without regard for its art-historical correctness. This is a highly appealing polemical strategy; it remains to be seen whether its subtlety will catch on or distract from the central simplicity of the new movement's ideas. Nevertheless, Mann's proposal reminds us that artists now have an enormous opportunity to be both firmly within a great artistic tradition, and at the same time in rebellion against the prevailing esthetic authorities. If everything is new, the only really new thing is an old thing; and Ezra Pound told us, after all, to "make it new."

In music there does not seem to have been much of an attempt to name the new movement. "Minimalism" is, I believe, a misnomer; but some "minimalist" music, for instance Philip Glass's operatic and film scores, seems close to the new paradigm. "World music" carries some of the right flavor, in its seeking out of what is universal within the rich variety of human musical traditions. There are many quiet, obscure, and excellent composers who are working entirely in the new spirit, without recognition, Claudia Annis for instance. Within the popular music genres much fine work is being done by people like Laurie Anderson and David Byrne, that approaches a condition we might recognize as part of the emerging paradigm.

In the other performing arts the new trends are definitely in evidence. The "ethnodrama" of Peter Brook and others, which transfers, translates, or mixes classical performance genres from various cultures, such as Noh drama, Kathakali, and ballet, carries the same implications as "world music": there are fundamental artistic principles common to all human beings and recognizable across cultural barriers. An exciting combination of world classical traditions with natural body movement is evident in some of the new dance choreography, such as the work of Momix, Mark Morris, and Sankai Jukku. The revival of the tableau by Robert Wilson, and the revival of opera in general, challenges the modernist notion of purity and hermeticism. Wilson's handling of major philosophical and moral themes, such as Einsteinian relativity, Gandhian nonviolence, Akenaton's monotheism and the like, is a departure from the cynical and deconstructive impulse of most postmodern drama. The performing arts in general tend to be drawn back to the classical spirit by the demands of the trained body's natural grace.

Another term that has been found to describe the new movement is the apparently dull and colorless "centrist." The sculptor Frederick Hart quotes Lao Tsu: "If you stay within the center of the circle you will endure forever." Artists today are in the delightful position of living in a time when only the marginal and the extraterritorial are fashionable; thus they can follow the Taoist's maxim with a special twist, in that the only way to be truly marginal and inventive is to go directly to the center. T. S. Eliot, in *Four Quarters*, sees the divine dance at the center of the turning wheel of life; and this paradox of movement and stillness, of edge and center, can also be found in Shakespeare's ecstatic description of the beloved in *The Winter's Tale*:

> When you do dance, I wish you
> A wave o' th' sea, that you might ever do
> Nothing but that—move still, still so,
> And own no other function.

Perhaps the idea originates with Eliot's beloved Dante, whose heaven is simultaneously at the edge of the whole universe and at its center. Of course the mystical literature has known it all along: the *Brihad-Aranyaka* Upanishad places the vision of Brahman in the very heart of the seed, as the seed is at the heart of the husk.

Chapter 2

The Failure of the Avant-Garde

Faulty Assumptions of the Avant-Garde

Much contemporary avant-garde art is desperately ugly, simplistic, and unsubtle in its message, lacking in craft, skill, and technique, and thus unappealing to a mass audience—a consideration that might well give pause to its enthusiasts. However, criticism of this type is for the most part ineffective, because it does not grapple with the underlying premises of the avant-garde. If the ugliness and incompetence of much of our poetry, plastic arts, music, and performance art could be justified by being derived from certain incontestable assertions about aesthetics, the human mind, and the world, then we would celebrate such art as a bold and unflinching encounter with reality. But several major revolutions have taken place in the natural sciences since the key dogmas of modernism were proposed at the start of this century; there has been a rejection of both biological and behavioristic reductionism in psychology, and a radical revision of our old, confident role as the technological masters of nature. Let us examine how the basic tenets of avant-garde art stand up in the light of our new knowledge, and see how they have fared.

One of the fundamental assumptions of avant-garde art is that beauty is in the eye of the beholder. The avant-garde denied the classical position, that beauty is a reality in itself. They argued either that beauty is purely subjective (as they interpreted the Freudian theory of the sublimation of libido) or that it is culture-bound and reflects the economic interests of the ruling class—an argument rendered persuasive by the apparently large differences between cultures in what is considered beautiful. In the light of contemporary knowledge, however, both arguments appear to be without foundation. The popular avant-garde theory of sublimation no longer goes unchallenged. Our sense of beauty can no longer be explained as second-hand repressed libido; beauty has a perfectly good brain chemistry of its own without having to borrow from the energy resources of sexual reproduction. Research has shown that there are pan-human cross-cultural esthetic preferences, and a neurobiology that rewards all human beings for the recognition and creation of certain complex, organized, and unified patterns—patterns traditionally known as beautiful. The classical account of beauty now better satisfies the known facts than the avant-garde account. Furthermore, it is now the ruling class that supports avant-garde art, and the large mass of ordinary people that yearns for beauty, meaning, and craftsmanship—a situation that directly refutes the argument that classical standards are elitist.

Another major avant-garde assumption is that human nature is socially constructed. This argument was borrowed from the social sciences, for which it was always rather an article of faith justifying their existence, and a defense against the natural sciences, than a proved or even provable hypothesis. However, within the social sciences themselves this dogma is now under severe challenge from several directions. Behaviorism as a tenable explanation of human psychology has completely collapsed; human beings do appear to have a nature after all. Studies of newborns show that we come into the world with a formidable array of predispositions. Studies of animal intelligence reveal that we are not unique in our ways of understanding the world. Cross-cultural anthropology demonstrates how much all human groups have in common in family and kinship organization, myth, language, gift-exchange customs, etiquette, ritual, supernatural beliefs, and so on. Linguists show that we all share a deep structure in our language. Likewise, cross-cultural and neuropsychological studies of the arts reveal that the classical genres of the arts—pictorial representation, musical scale and tonality, poetic meter, narrative, and so on—are built into our makeup as human beings and cannot be lightly ignored by a culture without damage to its young and a loss of meaning and value for its adults. A natural classicism is emerging, which implies genuine canons of value in the arts. Thus avant-garde social constructionism cannot serve as an artistic justification.

A third important avant-garde premise is that all systems of meaning and value create hierarchies and that all hierarchies diminish human freedom. The first half of this dogma now seems true enough, but not the second. Even in theory the leftist hope for a totally egalitarian community is untenable, because biology shows that all living systems are organized hierarchically, from the lowest molecular levels through the cell, the organ, and the metabolic system, up to the highest levels of neural control in the individual; and through individuals, kin groups, species, and whole biomes on the collective level. The more complex and multileveled the hierarchy, the greater the opportunity for individuated behavior, free decision, and creative innovation. Similarly, close study of democratic and economic organizations reveals that the more freedom of opportunity and self-expression they permit, the more complex and multileveled the hierarchy of function. A totalitarian state is one which approaches the simplest and flattest kind of hierarchy, where one supreme ruler commands an otherwise completely egalitarian mass of ruled. A modern constitutional democracy is a highly complex hierarchy, whose complexity assures flexibility, legitimation of authority, limitation of powers, assent, and a turnover of personnel at various hierarchical levels. This seeming paradox, that hierarchy generates freedom, holds also for the family. The traditional family, with its clear lines of authority, has now been shown to create independent, healthy, and active offspring, capable of love, work, and reasoned dissent from the surrounding social norms; the unstructured and transient family tends to create weak, passive individuals, lacking in self-control, who are easily led, incapable of independent thought, and ripe for crime, self-destruction, and addiction.

Rigid authoritarian structures usually emerge when a natural and evolving hierarchy is overthrown on ideological grounds. Get rid of the complex, nonlinear, self-organizing forms of hierarchy, and simple, linear, coercive forms replace them. When one seeks for radical equality, and a total pruning of the tree of authority, one gets an Oliver Cromwell, a Napoleon Bonaparte, a Hitler, a Lenin, a Stalin instead. In recent times the egalitarian commune movement has given birth to such monstrosities as Charlie Manson and Jimmy Jones. Any of us who were involved in radical consciousness-raising groups in the sixties, seventies, and eighties can remember the oppressive atmosphere of thought control and authority, the way in which some unacknowledged leader emerged supported by a little coterie of moral enforcers and yes-men, and the bullying of the weak or independent.

Hierarchy is essential for political freedom; and the same applies to the arts. In practice, those arts that have a large popular audience usually have a very elaborate chain of command, as a glance at any display of film credits demonstrates. And it is those arts that provide the economic scope, in their varied ecological niches, for individual creativity and artistic freedom. If avant-garde art tended to attack or deconstruct systems of meaning on the false grounds that they lead to hierarchy and unfreedom, the new centrist art of the next century will tend to reconstruct meaning and value systems or create new ones, precisely in order to generate complex hierarchical systems of human interdependence which *maximize* human freedom.

Another dogma of the avant-garde art theorists is that logic, rationality, and science are part of our oppressive Western patriarchal racist system. This postmodernist dogma relies heavily on its premise, that our society is indeed oppressive, patriarchal, and racist. Let us note here that people of all races are beating down the doors to get into Western democracies and escape systems run by people of their own ethnic background; that those same Western democracies have taken the lead in providing more equal opportunities and political freedom for women; and that those regimes that criticized the West in exactly these terms have now been shown to have been the most oppressive on earth. Nevertheless, the rejection of logic and scientific rationality has the advantage that it relieves one of the responsibility of modifying one's argument so as to eliminate contradictions in it. If logical consistency has a logocentric/phallocentric bias, then logical fragmentation ("slippage") becomes a virtue. But political consequences flow from this position. One is that logical disagreements must be suppressed, lest they disrupt the harmonious atmosphere of agreement which is the intellectual equivalent of a harmonious ecology. Since rational argument can no longer be the basis of agreement, one is left only with feeling, shared experience, "sensitivity." Dissenting voices must in themselves be the sign of a criminal absence of proper feeling, must be an attempt to disrupt the ecology, and thus should be suppressed. Hence, of course, political correctness: its real motive is the protection of the idea of a felt truth that is logically inconsistent, from the reminder that it is inconsistent.

Let us put ourselves in the place of the avant-garde theorists. If we cannot use logic, what can we use to win people to our cause? Political power, perhaps, in the form of control of the press, coercion, liquidation, and reeducation camps; but it is one of the fundamental articles of avant-garde faith that the existing Western patriarchal power structure has a commanding lead in the use of force (if it did not, the whole raison d'être of the avant-garde would come into question). To attempt to oppose the establishment in the arena of coercive power is to play to one's opponent's strong suit. Much the same is the case for rhetoric: the establishment controls the value system and the media which are the arenas of rhetoric.

Another promising method may be to use the weaknesses of the patriarchal Eurocentric power structure's political system, for instance its self-justifying reliance on the popular vote. If the oppressed population can simply multiply faster than their oppressors, then when they are in the majority they will be able to outvote them and do what they like. Unfortunately this takes a great deal of time, during which there is the danger that large numbers of the oppressed will have become sufficiently prosperous to defect to the enemy, frustrating the general strategy. The ideal tactic would be to devise sociocultural mechanisms that would keep the oppressed in misery and helplessness until their numbers are sufficiently great—mechanisms such as family-dividing welfare systems, the drug trade, cultural taboos against education or, in appropriate circumstances, refugee camps and the like. But such tactics are politically very risky, and the popular vote itself cannot be relied on, because of the effectiveness of establishment propaganda. All these methods lead to despair.

Another avant-garde artistic dogma is that the only way to get anything done is by coercive power, whether expressed in oppressive violence by a reactionary elite, revolutionary acts by the disenfranchised, or legal sanctions by an enlightened ruling group. If beauty has been relativized out of existence (which is indeed the result of avant-garde theory) and if logical reasoning is, as we have seen, condemned as the property of the oppressor, the only way to persuade people is through force. Force is the more perfect, the fewer side-effects and unintended consequences it entails, the fewer reasons it needs to give, and the less it needs to disguise itself. Thus avant-garde art has tended toward more and more simplistic, brutal, irrational, and unbeautiful expressions. But in most fields of thought outside the arts and the cultural criticism that supports them, a very different theory of how things get done has begun to emerge. Force, after all, is a linear phenomenon, most perfectly expressed in one-way cause and effect. However, physics teaches us that power of this kind is absolutely and universally subject to the second law of thermodynamics, that is, it tends over time to waste itself and turn into useless heat and thermal disorder. Yet the universe has evolved into a wealth of elaborate, ordered, and beautiful forms—galaxies, crystals, life, sentient beings—and it did so by very different mechanisms than coercive power. These mechanisms, involving mutual feedback, nonlinear communication among and within whole systems, harmonic entrainments, self-referential adjustments, and subtle influences, are now being studied by chaos theorists. Thus the power-based theories of the contemporary arts and humanities are profoundly out of date and intellectually bankrupt.

One last dogma of contemporary avant-garde thought is "anti-foundationalism." A foundationalist maintains that common realities underlie the different experiences of persons, species, and forms of matter. The avant-garde espouses the position that there is no prior reality or presence or authority or transcendental signified on which to base our ideas and actions—and that one can therefore think and do what one likes.

Let us briefly list some antifoundationalist positions. One maintains that since everything we can know depends on how we see it, there is no fundamental reality (phenomenology). A second, misinterpreting Wittgenstein's dicta "whereof one cannot speak, thereof one must remain silent" and "the limits of my language are the limits of the world," maintains that since everything we say depends on how we say it, there is no fundamental reality (linguistic philosophy, deconstruction). A third points out that because everything is dependent on its context within a structure, there is no fundamental reality (structuralism). A fourth sardonically points out that whenever anyone says anything, they are naturally following their socioeconomic interests, partly crystallized into the form of cultural values, and that therefore there is no fundamental reality (Foucauldian discourse analysis, neo-Marxism). A fifth reminds us that everything that is said is said in a determining historical context, and thus there is no fundamental reality (the new historicism). A sixth insists that the psyche that says everything is an illusory construction anyway, and that therefore there is no fundamental reality (the neo-Freudianisms of Lacan, Deleuze, and Guattari). A seventh denies the objectivity of science, because science is made up of a society of persons with ideological and economic interests, and therefore there is no fundamental reality (the scientific antifoundationalism of Kuhn, Feyerabend, and Habermas). An eighth points out that whoever says anything has a sex and a gender (usually male) that irremediably distorts what is said, and therefore there is no fundamental reality (feminist epistemology). And we can now add a ninth, that maintains that all human views of reality are only human views, and that since we cannot know how Nature sees things, there is no fundamental reality: the view of the radical Greens and Deep Ecologists, such as Arne Naess and George Sessions.

Of course, the secret of all these antifoundationalisms is that they are really foundationalisms in disguise. Number one says: sensation is the foundation. Number two says: language is the foundation. Number three says: the logic of structure is the foundation. Number four says: economic power backed up by coercion is the foundation. Number five says: history is the foundation. Number six says: psychological development is the foundation. Number seven says: the sociology of legitimation is the foundation. Number eight says: sex is the foundation. Number nine says: nature (excluding human beings) is the foundation.

Once we see the implied foundationalist assertion of these views, two things become immediately obvious. One is that a sort of competition is going on between specialized disciplines, conducted in rather peculiar terms: each delegitimizes the others by asserting the groundlessness of all assertion while tacitly excepting its own point of view. It is is like contemporary political election campaigns, which do not so much assert the virtues of the candidate as the dishonesty of his or her opponent. A cynic might speculate that the motivations are not dissimilar, and that what is really at stake are tenured chairs, graduate fellowships, and full-time faculty lines (but this would be to fall into the neo-Marxist view).

The other obvious conclusion is that, stated in their positive form, these positions do not particularly contradict each other. In theory, if the candidates did not impugn each other's honesty, they might all be honest! And this conclusion might lead us, by an odd but perfectly legitimate turn of logic, to the positive assertion that *all* these implied foundations are actually foundational—sensation, language, structure, power, history, psychology, legitimation, sex, and nature—and that probably there are dozens of other foundations as well. Foundations, then, need not be mutually exclusive; and it might be particularly interesting to work out how all these foundations are related to each other. A universe crammed with partial foundations, that have not ceased to interact, and that thus leave open a huge future space where they are unpredictably going next—this is what we see if we escape the feverish loyalties of a particular ideological camp.

Since the intellectual underpinnings of contemporary avant-garde theory can no longer be maintained, it has lost its capacity to grow and develop in a way that might serve artists with animating ideas. Nevertheless, those avant-garde premises, elaborated over the last eighty years or so by modernist and postmodernist art theorists, social critics, and philosophers, are at present accepted without question by most contemporary artists, who often have only a dim and hazy half-consciousness of what underlies the doctrine, and no real notion of the evidence originally brought to prove it or the argumentation by which it reached its conclusions. Paradoxically this unconsciousness of the theoretical bases of their dogmas makes holders of this position difficult to convince otherwise, because they did not entertain it as subject to argumentative defense or refutation in the first place. Thus gifted artists, potentially capable of freeing themselves from limiting presuppositions and giving their culture the benefits of a new lease of creative life, remain cut off from the kind of radical reappraisal of reality that truly vital art demands. Theory now turns back on itself, in a dimming series of self-reflections, and no longer serves the artist.

What remains, then, for artists working in the avant-garde tradition?

One recourse is sheer talent. Many gifted avant-garde artists still find a pleasure in, and an audience for, sheer virtuosity in doing whatever it is they do. But tragically some of the very best artists have turned against their own virtuosity, as too easy, as having a suspicious tendency to produce beauty, as too human, affectionate, and good-humored to fit into their bleak view of the world. This rejection of one's own talent is a kind of self-mutilation; we see in those artists the spectacle of nature's lovely power and generosity cut off and stunted. Thus the community at large is deprived of the huge gifts that such artists might have been able to offer.

Other artists play with the remains of the traditional artistic genres and techniques, castrated of their animating metaphysics. We find poets exploring wordplay, painters who dabble in the mysteries of color and composition theory, composers who experiment with musical textures and odd combinations of instruments, novelists who lay bare the old narrative devices, and so on. Other artists even indulge their irrepressible appetite for beauty, but defang its threat to their autonomy by setting it in a context of more than usual ugliness—rather like the rapist's sad little pretense of consensual intimacy, his insistence that the victim is enjoying it. Sometimes avant-garde artists will have gleaned from their highly specialized MFA education some half-digested piece of intellectual content, which then becomes a sort of concealed skeleton key for their work. Emotion, too, can serve as a current to galvanize the body of an avant-garde artist. Contemporary art has inherited the modernist contempt for "sentimentality," but the emotions of hatred, rage, envy, ridicule, fear, sadism, despair, boredom and depression seem to have been exempted from the stigma of sentiment, and are seen as legitimate materials.

All avant-garde artists attempt novelty of conception, or execution, or both. The problem is that in the absence of the *specific* virtues of craft, beauty, intellectual coherence, and so on, the only novelty of such art must be a *generic* novelty, which is exhausted by one example of it. All avant-garde artists also attempt some version or other of the sublime, whereby the viewer is terrified or shocked or sickened by some grotesque effect of scale, disproportion, scatology, discord, or irrational disjunction. In this sense sublimity is a putting into effect as an artistic strategy of the injunction to violence. Alas, the power structure of the real world is much more effective at this than artists are; for all it takes, after all, is money and technology. Far more sublime than any hideous sculpture or shrieking discord is an open-pit coalmine or a nuclear submarine.

The Death of Avant-Garde Hope

Bereft of the nourishment that a vigorous and fertile body of science and theory once supplied, avant-garde art has begun to fall prey to despair. There have been so many momentous changes—the end of the cold war, the liberation of Eastern Europe, the economic collapse of world socialism, the replacement of authoritarian and totalitarian regimes all over the world by democratic capitalist ones, the revival of cultural and religious chauvinisms thought to have been dispelled by modernity, the accelerating change from a matter-and-labor-based economy to an information-based economy, the poststructuralist heat death of the literary, artistic, and critical avant-garde. After all these transformations, do we even know what to hope for?

Cultural despair is, of course, no new attitude or posture in the history of human thought. But until now despair has been largely the property of conservatives and, later, right-wingers. The immemorial despair of conservatives has always been that things have gone from bad to worse ever since the good old days. All we can do is hunker down in some moral bunker and try to preserve some shreds of grace, decency, and clarity amid the rising tide of chaos and wickedness. Believers in this position are part of the dead weight the world carries; they do not help to carry the world. One of the few virtues of the avant-garde Left was that at least for a while it denied that comfortable despair. Now even that virtue has gone.

The way that art changes society is through hope. Hope is what gets us out of bed in the morning, and carries us cheerfully and spontaneously through the work of the day. The brain is a feedback reward system: the feeling of hope is the reward for projected emergent features of that system. Sociological research suggests that a measurably hopeful attitude is a better predictor of academic success among students than are SAT scores. The same statistic shows up in a population of handicapped people, who are confronted not only with real grounds for despair but also social prejudice that would regard the possibility of their success with skepticism. It is not the expectation of prejudice that makes us fail, but a deficiency of the virtue of hope. The hopeful handicapped are more active and successful than the no more handicapped hopeless. In other words, hope does not need to be justified by present circumstances or rational expectations to be effective. We organize our actions according to a flexible set of stories or myths; and hope is the attractive force of every story. In this book I espouse—on new grounds—the traditional assignment of hope to a place among the three theological virtues: if faith is the affirmation of what was, and love the affirmation of what is, then hope is the affirmation of what is to come.

What is hope? First of all we must distinguish between hope and desire. Desire drives us, hope uplifts us. Hope involves an imaginative estimate of possibility, an intellectual leap into the future. We might say, crudely, that hope is the combination of expectation and desire. And of course there are many kinds of hope: private hopes and public hopes, hopes based on the human organism's desire for comfort, hopes based on the species's drive to reproduce itself, hopes based on socially con- structed desires, hopes based on spiritual aspirations. Let us review the traditional kinds of hope, which constitute the battlefield of ideological struggle as it has been waged until now.

Among our most basic private hopes are those which anticipate the satisfaction of metabolic needs and desires, for food, warmth, pleasure, sex, aggressive contestation, and rest: the desired expectations of a high- er mammal. Less self-centered, but nevertheless based upon a biological drive, is our hope for progeny, for the survival of our offspring, and its so- cial expression in the establishment and continuity of a lineage. These are the desired expectations of a member of a biological species. Then there are the private hopes we nourish that require a social world to satis- fy them, our hopes for property and possessions, for security, status, fame, power, the esteem of others: the desired expectations of private gain in terms of socially constructed prizes. The most attractive of our private hopes, though not always the most powerful, are those that con- stitute much of our spiritual world: our hopes for the welfare of those we love, for the satisfaction of personal honor, for the achievement of tasks we have set ourselves, for the peace of a good conscience, for the discov- ery of truth, for the creation of beauty. These are the desired expecta- tions of a human soul. Our public hopes fall into two categories. The first is that of social hope, the major wrestling-floor of politics: hopes for peace and harmony among nations and communities; for freedom, jus- tice, equality; for the democratic distribution of power; for universal en- lightenment. These are our desired expectations for society. The second is religious hope: for the salvation of souls, the salvation of the world, and the fulfilment of cosmic purpose. These are our desired expectations for the divine economy.

Obviously many of these hopes contain internal contradictions: satiety is both the goal and the extinction of our metabolic desires; the freedom of others awkwardly infringes on our own. And they are even more often deeply at odds with each other. Any parent knows the contradiction be- tween progeny and pleasure; any political scientist, the contradiction between equality and liberty. Sex is often at war with security, foraging with rest, love with peace, truth with status, aggression with property, salvation with the esteem of others, the divine economy with individual or even social aspiration. Different political and cultural worldviews have different constellations of hope, by which those contradictions are negated, mitigated, accepted, hypostatized, or resolved; in each worldview, different categories of hope are permitted, recommended, condemned, or reduced to invisibility. To a large extent, a worldview identifies itself by its struggle to represent certain hopes more genuinely than its rivals, by its attempts to valorize its own preferred brands of hope, and by its contestation of the legitimacy, and even existence, of others.

The traditional conservative way of dealing with these contradictions can be roughly described as follows: our metabolic hopes, for pleasure, sex, and so on, are accepted as a reality—the Flesh—but as an enemy to be fought. A genial hypocrisy permits but does not excuse them. Their internal and mutual contradictions are taken as the sign of their fallen distortedness. Through the institution of chivalry, the aggressive drive is domesticated to the service of the community; through the institution of *fine amour*, sex is tamed to the service of love. Private hopes for public gain—the World—are also accepted as a reality, but as a necessary evil, to be resisted for the many but permitted to a trained and morally excellent few, the aristocrats and mandarins who have the discernment to resolve the contradictions harmoniously. The hopes of progeny and lineage become the foundation of society. Social hopes, for political and legal improvement, for the extension of rights and liberties, are regarded as the inspiration of the Devil, are denied, condemned, and suppressed, and reduced morally to the status of ambitiousness—private hopes for public gain. Society aspires to a reconciliation of personal spiritual hopes with public religious hopes within the framework of a theological orthodoxy that resolves their internal contradictions.

Though this system worked admirably for long periods of time, its inadequacies were to destroy it. The hypocritical abuses of aristocratic privilege became too glaring to justify the continuation of a systematic monopoly of social goods in private hands. Technological and economic advance, ensured by the very stability created by the *ancien régime*, led to social hopes that could no longer be suppressed, for liberty and the Rights of Man (and later, Woman). Technological improvements created better communications and better weapons, which in turn put whole societies into close and hostile contact with each other. Conflict between different theological orthodoxies produced catastrophic disruptions, like the Crusades, the French religious wars, the German Thirty Years' War, and the English Civil War, that threatened to tear the human world apart. Church must be safely separated from state; but as soon as this was accomplished, religion lost the power to control the many contradictions within and among all other kinds of hope. Some East Asian traditional cultures were able to resist technological progress into the nineteenth century, and to find ways to reconcile different religious traditions, as Buddhism and Shinto in Tokugawa Japan, or Confucianism, Taoism, and Buddhism in China. But they were only postponing the collapse of the old system.

The liberal capitalist democratic way of handling the contradictions, what Marx called the bourgeois state, is very different. Our metabolic hopes for food, sex, and agonistic contestation, and our private hopes for social advantage, are accepted as a natural selfishness which, in a well-designed system, can be harnessed for the public good and act as an Invisible Hand to ensure prosperity and progress. Personal spiritual hopes are encouraged to flourish, but in a pluralistic milieu, without reference to an approved divine economy, and subject to the leveling demands of the marketplace. Dynastic hopes are discouraged, and the bonds of kinship either ignored or condemned as nepotism. Religious hopes are permitted without comment, but society is protected by legal means from them and from the conflicts they engender. Social hopes—equality, justice—are highly valorized and cultivated, but only when consistent with the individual's hopes for life, liberty, and the pursuit of happiness, and with religious freedom. Wide margins, by which contradictory hopes are spaced out and thus need not encounter each other, are provided by an overarching ideology of pluralism, relativism, and commonsense; and the contradictions which still occur are resolved by the market, where conflicting hopes and values are reduced to money prices and haggled to a mutually agreeable reconciliation in those terms.

This constellation of hopes has not yet totally failed, and is still a viable compromise; it has produced a world of political moderation and economic wealth. But its systemic problems are potentially as deep as those of the *ancien régime*. Among these are the domination of the

marketplace, and the consequent leveling of higher aspirations; the insta-
bilities produced by rapid economic and technological change; and the
unsolved contradiction between equality and freedom in a market-domi-
nated polity with its painful contrasts between wealth and poverty. For a
young person waking up in the morning there seems nothing in this
regime to inspire the fierce loyalties and high aspirations which the young
feel so ready for: it appears to be a base and ignoble system, compelling
the young aspirant to years of work, rewarding the money-grubber, and
discouraging the hero. Though in comparison with other extant systems
there is usually greater opportunity for all, the necessary fictions of capitalist democracy—that all persons are equal in all respects, and that freedom does not depend on discipline—make for persistent agonizing
discontent. Vitiated by democratic pluralism, the old social and religious
hopes are insufficient to control and redirect our metabolic and selfish
hopes, and reconcile their contradictions; and without the support of society at large, reproduction has become detached from family, the hope
for progeny itself has been repressed, and the family, the vital link between biology and culture, is in a state of collapse.

The weaknesses of democratic capitalism seem glaring, and its apparent hypocrisies disgusting. Thus the intelligentsia, the young, and the discontented sought a replacement. The result was the system of leftist
modernism.

Why did leftist modernism arise in the first place? Partly because of
the manifest flaws of the *ancien régime* on the one hand and liberal democratic capitalism on the other. Partly, too, because the expanded and enfranchised populations of newly educated young people in the
industrialized countries had not encountered, and tended to deny, the
contradictions within and among human hopes. They had not seen the
damage and suffering caused by those contradictions, nor had they realized the labor and ingenuity by which the existing constellations of political hope had mitigated, however clumsily and incompletely, that damage
and suffering. They thought they could do better. The left-wing modernist constellation was the result. How did it arrange its hopes?

This worldview not only accepted our biologically based personal
hopes—for sex, pleasure, leisure, and so on—but elevated them, via a
naturalist or existentialist philosophy, to the status which had previously
been held by the spiritual personal hopes. There was one exception: the

aggressive drive, which was thought to be the result of imperialistic social conditioning, and was repressed in the individual (while tacitly encouraged, under the name of class struggle, in the service of the Revolution). Any suggestion that our metabolic desires might themselves infringe upon the freedom and dignity of the person was furiously denied. (Hence, for instance, the extraordinary claim by some contemporary feminists that there is nothing sexual about rape: since it is axiomatic that sexual desire cannot be wrong, and equally axiomatic that aggression, as an evil, cannot be a natural drive, the only logical recourse must be that rape is the result of a politically indoctrinated conspiracy to oppress women.) The leftist-modernist worldview recognized, but condemned as absolutely evil, all individual hopes for socially constructed prizes, all desires for personal gain through public means. This was the sphere of alienation and commodity fetishism (Marx), the mirror stage (Lacan), voyeuristic sadism and the panopticon (Foucault), mimetic desire (Girard). The bourgeois individual was the hideously inauthentic result of these social forces, and his very thought process was hopelessly contaminated with them. The clever young person woke up doubting the very existence of personal spiritual hopes—of doing one's duty, of personal loyalty, of objective scientific discovery, of making something beautiful, of saving one's soul. These values were dangerously implicated in bourgeois false consciousness and existential bad faith, and could not be trusted. Nevertheless the emotional tone of these hopes did survive, transferred to the realm of social idealism. Likewise, the universal religious hopes were also denied, as remnants of superstition and obscurantism, or worse, as the justificatory mystifications of hegemonic socioeconomic power. Social hopes, then, were promoted to the position formerly held by religious hopes. Liberty, equality, fraternity, the end of class struggle, the dictatorship of the proletariat, the withering away of the state, social and economic justice, the abolition of all inequalities of race, sex, economic background, and education—these were the idealistic hopes that got us out of bed. Equality, not freedom, became the dominant social goal; or rather, freedom was redefined as equality.

Those hopes were given body and immediacy by the license they endorsed, for any kind of sexual adventure or sensual indulgence; and they entailed a triumphant justification for any kind of hatred, self-esteem, and violation of social rules. Such terms as "rip off" or "liberate" for stealing, "confrontation" for violent rudeness, "doing your own thing" for selfishness, and "honesty" for the heedless pursuit of one's own desires and interests, give something of the flavor of this worldview, in its worst excesses. At its best it helped bring about the abolition of slavery, improvements in the conditions of workers in capitalist countries, racial integration, generous reforms in sexual and gender roles, and valuable revisions in our attitudes toward the natural environment. Our young intellectual awoke to a delicious condition: that of being the illuminated one in a country of fools, the sighted among the blind, the ethically superior among the "pigs"; he was the prince in exile, the pure among the polluted, the spy licensed to kill, the liberated one whose every action and desire was justified by a higher purpose. The ordinary rules of ethical behavior did not apply to a revolutionary in a capitalist society; they were put on hold until the revolution came. There was a special, exquisite feeling of liberation in this.

And yet the intellectual was not totally isolated; an underground community could be recognized by certain secret signs. Within that community sex was free, unhampered by the musty old conventions of family, but sharpened and ennobled by the aura of the Resistance, by the improvisations of hiding, by the pathos of two doomed people thrown together by the vicissitudes of war. One might not survive at all; nuclear holocaust, fascist oppression, and birth control alike relieved us of any concern for our children or our dynastic future. The enormous popularity of such films as *Casablanca, Bonnie and Clyde, Easy Rider*, and *M.A.S.H.* is due in part, I believe, to these deep cultural currents. Their most extreme manifestations include the Symbionese Liberation Army, the Weather Underground, the Baader-Meinhof gang, and even, in a strange religious extension, the community of Jimmy Jones. An automatic consensus of cynical distrust, contempt, and pitiless malevolence toward the "bourgeois," the businessman, the ruling class, and one's elders cemented, as do all ritual scapegoatings, the solidarity and brotherhood of the elect.

It is this constellation of hopes that has in the last few years definitively, radically, and irreversibly failed, resulting in despair. To grasp the nature and dimensions of that failure we must make a historical excursion through the origins and development of the radical leftist avant-garde. How did we find our way from the euphoric hopefulness of 1789, the year of the French Revolution—of which Wordsworth was to say "Bliss was it in those days to be alive, And to be young was very heaven"—to the despair and cynicism of 1994?

The Rise and Fall of the Avant-Garde

The avant-garde began in the late eighteenth century, when the literate elite—the brahmin or mandarin caste of our society—found itself challenged on several fronts. Its aristocratic patronage had begun to dry up; its authority was challenged by the new caste of commercial and business leaders. With the fragmentation of religion and the decline of the established church, there were fewer benefices (the equivalent of tenured university positions) to support its existence; and its intellectual prestige was being eclipsed by that of the scientists. The birth of romanticism was thus to some degree a way of making a virtue of necessity, and celebrating as artistic independence and creative rebellion an alienation that seemed unavoidable anyway. During the romantic period and on into the twentieth century, literature and art proceeded to distance themselves from the world of commerce and technology, and to identify themselves with a fading aristocratic dream, or with a proto-fascist ideal of the Folk, or with the militant political Left. This self-alienation extended itself to a contempt for the middle classes in general, and the term "bourgeois" became the most bitter insult in the avant-garde vocabulary. Although it was precisely this class which was the potential audience for art and literature, the main source of avant-garde acolytes, and the only conduit to the population at large, the artist's explicit contempt for it provided an insurance in advance against the sting of possible rejection. The genre of the novel retained its connection with the general population rather longer than those of poetry, drama, "serious" music and "serious" visual arts, but the novel's central subject, marital infidelity, constituted a covert attack upon the kinship basis of middle-class life, while its celebration of the epiphanic insights to be derived from adultery salved the consciences of its all-too-human readers.

Organized religion had once been a secure economic niche for the intellectual brahmin caste, but once it ceased to be a reliable source of living for an educated and aesthetic person, it began to be a suitable subject for artistic and literary ridicule. The avant-garde tended to replace it with new theologies which, variously, elevated the artist into the position of

deity, borrowed the Rousseauvian idols of the noble savage or the Marxist idols of the proletariat, or, as with the Paris Symbolistes and California
hippies, sought mystical experience in drugs and the extremes of sensory
perception.

The avant-garde was irked by the prestige of science, which throughout the eighteenth, nineteenth, and much of the twentieth century relied,
for the sake of experimental purity, on a deterministic and mechanistic
model of the world. The avant-garde response was at first to embrace
this model, as in the sociological or psychological fatalism of the nineteenth-century naturalistic or realistic novel. But as the idea of freedom
hypertrophied into the only value recognized by the arts, and as writers
and artists began to feel they could not compete with scientists, the deterministic naturalism of the nineteenth century was rejected. Since nature was deterministic, and since it was the domain of science, nature
itself began to become the enemy, as for instance in Dostoevsky's *Notes
from Underground* or Hardy's *Tess of the U'Urbervilles*; or else the scientific description of nature was denied, and a phenomenological (and essentially sentimental) one was put in its place, as in Flaubert's marvelous
Madame Bovary or in the impressionist movement. This series of developments can be seen paradigmatically in the response of the visual arts to
the exact reproductions of photography: because painting could no
longer rival the exactness of the photograph, it rejected first realism, and
later, with abstract art, any attempt to represent the physical world at all.
The same process was going on in literature. From Zola and Tennyson,
who both embraced scientific fatalism, there is a clear trajectory to Alain
Robbe-Grillet and John Ashbery, who seek the truth in human subjective
experience detached, however, from a coherent narrative psyche that
might be subject to psychosocial determinants. In the universities Kant's
prophetic solution to the problem was adopted, and the split between
science and the arts was institutionalized in the curricular distinction between *Naturwissenschaft* and *Geisteswissenschaft*.

From time to time the avant-garde has seen signs of hope in the sciences, but only to the extent that science seemed to be denying its own
orderliness and rationality. For instance, artists and humanists seized on
quantum theory, and more recently chaos theory, as implying that the
universe is essentially lawless and random, and that reality is thus whatever we want it to be. Needless to say, this interpretation was a hopelessly

simplistic attempt by writers and artists to regain the upper hand, which cost some artists their own craftsmanship and logical integrity. "Aleatory" art actually abdicates the artist's freedom, often replacing it by processes that are neither random nor nonlinear, but physically deterministic. Ironically, in becoming the servant of simplistic political programs, art has in fact become much like the reductive science of the nineteenth century, whereas in its free investigation of chaotic systems, science has taken on the role once played by the arts. But unlike the sciences, within the avant-garde there is now no rational mechanism for self-criticism or for a radical revision of its own flawed premises, because it has for its own purposes discredited the very logic, rationality, and evidence by which such a debate might be conducted. There are important implications in quantum and chaos theory for the arts, but because of the avant-garde's equations between order and determinism, and between disorder and freedom, those implications were missed.

At the beginning of the twentieth century science offered little comfort to the avant-garde, but economic theory was much more promising. Marx became the essential justification for its social and political program. The adoption of Marx (together with Freud) marked the transition from late romanticism to early modernism. Marx's international class analysis seemed triumphantly confirmed by the First World War, his political ideas were embodied in the Bolshevik revolution, and his economic critique of capitalism was apparently confirmed by the Great Depression. But the Marxist triumph was short-lived. By the 1980s state socialism and state communism had failed in their own chosen arena of technological and economic progress. What became clear through their great and tragic experiment was that progress and economic health are dependent upon one central human activity: exchange. Whether the medium of exchange is gifts, as in some preindustrial cultures, or corporate stock, as in the stock exchange, or goods, services, and money, as in a market economy, or ideas, as in the free press and free academy, or even genes, as in sexual reproduction within a gene pool, exchange drives the life of the world. The Marxist slogan "To each according to his need; from each according to his capacity" was an explicit attempt to replace exchange with social justice.

Social justice is, however, essentially sterile; in its context, as King Lear puts it, "nothing can come of nothing." In that great play one of the mysteries for the left-wing critic is that it is Cordelia, the good and loving daughter, who says "I love you according to my bond," who insists on the contract, on the exchange of goods and services. She is the capitalist, whereas Regan and Goneril, the evil daughters, claim to love him in ways that go beyond base considerations of social and economic exchange, and are the ones who deal with Lear according to his need and reduce his superfluity to nothing. "O reason not the need," groans Lear as he goes mad. It is the evil Edmund who argues for social justice. The compassion for the poor that Lear discovers in himself after he has learned his terrible lesson is not a matter of social justice, but of mercy, of love, of a supererogatory recognition of value that can only, paradoxically, exist in a world of true exchange, bonds, and contracts. Shakespeare uncannily foresaw the central error of Marxism.

Such works as Dostoyevsky's *Crime and Punishment*, Conrad's *The Secret Agent*, and James's *The Princess Casamassima* examined with marvelous insight the appeal of the political avant-garde and yet warned against its moral dangers. When its program came to power, the result was the most horrible evils the human race has yet known, described allegorically in Orwell's *Nineteen Eighty-Four* and *Animal Farm*, and in actuality in Solzhenitsyn's *Gulag Archipelago*. Hitler's Germany was just another version of the same system, a fact to which the Left has always been strangely and catastrophically blind. The efficiencies of Nazism were that it concentrated the normal leftist romantic hatred against the bourgeois, the businessman, and the ruling class into the war against the Jews, that its socialism was also a national socialism, and that it resurrected the powerful energies of the dynastic drive to reproduce the species, within the social-hope context of the Master Race. It was not until the fall of the Berlin Wall that the full failure of Marxist socioeconomic ideology finally became evident. Its social hopes could not reproduce themselves, even by the most rigorous educational propaganda, into another generation. If the hated ruling class *are* the former revolutionaries, the engine of the scapegoat reflex turns its force against the Left itself, and the Left becomes the Right; it is the Stalinists who are the conservatives. If the secret agents are in charge, the only way to recapture the thrill of the Resistance is to be "reactionary" and collect icons, or, like Czeslaw Milosz, to deconstruct the grand narrative of social progress altogether.

Even the last epistemological bastion of the avant-garde had fallen. This was the argument that the West and the East, the Right and the Left, were alternate views of reality, and represented different ways of seeing, equally valid intellectually (though of course morally weighted in favor of the Left) in a world in which reality is constituted by how we see things. This was the fallback position that the liberal Western Left adopted after it became clear that the Eastern bloc was not infallible and was not even a bloc. It was accompanied by an interesting, and sometimes valuable, critique of "Western objective rationality," which indeed revealed flaws in the positivist/behaviorist fashion of the times. But in the long run the critique only strengthened and deepened Western science (because the capitalist exchange system was able to assimilate it) while it undermined the certainties of the Left. The real shock of the liberation of Eastern Europe was that even this relativist, pluralist epistemology had been shown to be simply wrong. The people who wrote the socialist and communist accounts of reality and history, it now appeared, had been voluntarily lying or coerced into lies, and there was a real truth, however foggy in places, and however open-ended and subject to evolutionary change, which underlay different "points of view." Reality and history had obdurate "points of view" of their own, which could be silenced but not eradicated by political correctness.

The economic collapse of the Soviet bloc was the direct consequence of the gigantic mistake of trying to repair the deficiencies of human exchange by abolishing it. What the avant-garde was forced to recognize was that, haphazard though they are, the compassionate love that exists in the interstices of the market economy and the fundamental trust and fellowship implicit in all trade are more reliable than any state program of distributive justice in promoting the actual welfare of people. They are more reliable precisely because they take creative risks and teach the world to grow; and because it is in the long-term interest of business to satisfy the wishes of its workers, to create wealthy consumers, and to produce the cheapest and best-quality goods with the minimum waste and cost. Business can only compete if it creates its own corrective forces, that is, workers and consumers with collective or individual bargaining power. The recent film *Schindler's List* is an eloquent illustration of the basic decency of business enterprise as against state ideology.

The avant-garde were all wrong about social progress; they thought that the same process which removed legal barriers against trade unions, minorities, women, and the poor—a process which made human exchange more efficient by bringing all kinds of interests into the market—could be used to legislate and routinize the intangible and weightless values of compassion and mercy that emanate from human exchange. As the shock wave of new wealth created by commercial technology passed through society, it created two resistance points. The first, of which Marxism was a pathological fixation, was the point where trade unions and the like needed to form in order to spread the wealth created by mass production to consumers wanting mass-produced goods. The second is where we are now, where the working class is beginning to disappear with mass production itself, and we incur obligation by supplying intricate forms of information to each other, rather than mass-producable material objects. Those who do not participate in this process become the underclass. But we cannot wave a magic governmental wand and make things better by destroying the very process of exchange and obligation itself which makes us human. We must instead buckle down to the long, tedious task of education, creative art, personal charity, scientific discovery, and technological improvement by which all people will be enabled to create and exchange the new informational goods. Such long tasks must be fueled with hope; and the hopes of socialist and communist ideology have collapsed in despair.

The would-be commissars, disappointed in the larger world of political economy, turned to literary and critical theory. Theory's main themes—deconstruction, discourse analysis, ethnic and gender criticism—were an attempt to recuperate at the level of the artistic text what had been lost in the open arena of industrial and economic achievement. Of course not all critical theory was an attempt at political sabotage. Part of the problem is that the literary/academic fashion is always about twenty years behind the leaders of it, and is a caricatured, simplified, factionalized, and negative version of what the leaders speculated and dreamed. A bold idea about literature that was not intended to apply to all aspects, periods, or genres of writing is transformed within the pressure cooker of the academic marketplace into a universal rule, a sign of belonging, and an ideological test to distinguish one's own group from the enemy within the academy or in society at large. This process is normal, and maturity brings about a subtler and more genial mixing of ideas and approaches. But today the process has been frozen by the accession to positions of academic power and eminence of a cohort of politically disappointed intellectuals. These thinkers had pinned their hopes on a left-wing transformation of society, one which would naturally have led to their own elevation to positions of influence in politics and government, with Benz automobiles and bodyguards; they would have become the Pablo Nerudas, the Melina Mercouris, the Andrés Malraux, even the Daniel Ortegas of the United States.

In the last twenty years poststructuralist critical theory has developed several branches: deconstruction, reader-response theory, new historicism, neo-Marxism, radical feminism, radical multiculturalism, deep ecology, Lacanian Freudianism, and social constructionism. The failure of left-wing economic theory and the evident triumph of capitalism throughout the world set off a frantic search for new victims, since it seemed the proletariat was happily turning into a middle class, and the underclass did not fit classical Marxist models of exploitation. Oppressed women and people of color were especially promising victim substitutes for the working masses who had defected to the side of their employers. Unquestioning adherence to these oppressed groups was the passport to avant-garde acceptance for all artists and writers. The view of the larger society these perspectives presented was of an insidiously oppressive, ruthless, and sadistic conspiracy masked by democratic window-dressing, middle-class moralism, technological hubris, and consumer advertising. Writers and artists began to see themselves as a sort of underground, as romantic vermin living in the polluted warrens of a *Blade Runner* technocapitalist wasteland, speaking for rebellious freedom as against the impersonality of scientific determinism, economic oppression, racial discrimination, male domination, and mechanistic psychology. Religion, the corporate culture, and the white patriarchy had joined in an unholy alliance to brainwash the population into sheeplike dependency on the consumerist late-capitalist system. The avant-garde writer and artist was a sort of graffiti bandit, secretly defacing the technology and advertising of the oppressor.

If the world had been as the avant-garde saw it, they might have been justified in such a posture. But remarkable developments were taking place, from which artists and writers had largely excluded themselves. Capitalist technology had created, instead of a wasteland, huge populations enjoying unprecedented wealth, education, health, and variety of opportunity, living in extremely pleasant suburbs with full access to all the riches of culture. In the technologically advanced countries the forests were coming back, the air was getting cleaner, and an environmental ethic was taking root among the middle class. The establishment itself was making good faith efforts to equalize the conditions of ethnic minorities and of the sexes, efforts so massive that they were self-defeating, creating social and economic distortions that actually damaged those they were created to assist. Religion had not gone away, but was staging an extraordinary transformation. Most exciting of all, science had patiently worked its way through to a view of the universe as free, alive, creative, beautiful, and deeply spiritual.

With a few exceptions, avant-garde artists were left high and dry. The exhilaration of the imagined liberation from narrow bourgeois views, from outmoded religious rules and superstitions, from the blue-haired ladies—those mother substitutes who maintained tradition—from deterministic science and alienating technology, had turned to ashes in their mouths. Art was cut off from nature, its own source and past; it was cut off from its audience; and it had no realistic economic place in the world. All that remained was physical sensations, which the critics, meanwhile, were steadily deconstructing as a hopelessly adulterated collection of commodity fetishisms, mimetic desires, mirror-perversions, phallocentric imagery, race prejudices, and logocentric categories. One of the subtlest forms of despair is that brought on when, in defense of an argument, one is forced to challenge the possibility of objective evidence that might confirm or deconfirm one's position, on the grounds that one's opponent has probably doctored it. Such a stance can cut one off from any reality and leave one in a state of paranoid isolation. If logic itself is impugned as the spawn of the enemy, then we find ourselves, if we are honest, progressively demolishing the structures of our own thought, until we enter a condition that might be called cognitive despair. And if we are dishonest and do not apply to our own thoughts the critical skepticism we apply to our opponent's, then we become trapped in a cynicism that might be called moral despair.

It is now becoming clear that the expectation of revolution, and thus the postponement of ordinary ethical behavior until it can be exercised meaningfully in a revolutionary society, is itself the purest of bad faith. Imagine how the theft of a public library book by a bright avant-garde intellectual might be defended in the late sixties, the seventies, the eighties, and the nineties. In the sixties it would be defended (with a broad grin) as "ripping off the pigs," or as part of a process that was already abolishing property as such. In the seventies it would be a sort of loan against the time that the working classes awoke from their brainwashed slumber and rejoined the intellectuals in the revolutionary enterprise. In the eighties it would be defended on the grounds that moral rules against theft contained slippages and erasures that signified their own absence; that as the whole world was text, there was no such thing as the theft of "a" text; and so on, in the vein made famous by Paul de Man and his defenders. In the nineties, I think that the bright young intellectual would, surprisingly, regard the theft of a library book as wrong. There is no illusion that things will be different after the revolution, and so ethical behavior cannot be postponed.

We might similarly trace the evolution of avant-garde attitudes to other cases of conscience: the abandonment of a pet cat, unfaithfulness to one's spouse, the claim that someone of another ethnic group cannot ever understand one's own ethnic experience (is this a racist claim?), plagiarism, the knowing citation of inaccurate or unreliable statistics or false or unproved scientific facts in support of one's position, or the infecting of others with a sexually transmitted disease without their knowledge. In each case the collapse of the idea of the future revolution has shown up past leftist justifications as bad faith.

The leftist-modernist constellation of hopes has failed. There will be no redeeming social revolution, that will at one blow dispel prejudice, poverty, social conflict, and privilege. To hope for it now is simply to hamper what real social progress is possible within an evolving capitalism. But this book is not just another piece of left-bashing. I cannot rejoice in the death of hope. Instead I am searching for a way in which the best elements of all systems of hope, including the Left, can be recuperated and transfigured in a larger and more generous conception. "Evolutionary hope," which I believe is an emergent idea, shaping itself slowly and inchoately in the experience of many people of goodwill, is proposed as that alternative, and as a cure for the sickness of the arts.

Hope can be re-rooted both in traditional humanistic and artistic forms of knowledge and in the new science of the twentieth and twenty-first centuries. As may already be clear, this project involves a radical transformation of our accepted rules about disciplinary boundaries and regions of discourse. When Kant proposed "culture" as a mediating term between nature and civilization, he could not have known that it would in turn become the opposite, antithesis, and antonym of nature, and that the dichotomy in turn would spawn that whole brood of academic disciplines and subdisciplines in whose toils any larger discourse is necessarily lost. We must, if evolutionary hope is to be possible, be prepared to abandon the clear borders between nature and culture, science and the humanities, technology and art, and thus to relinquish our hostility toward whichever of these we perceive as being "the other" to our own position. We must accept a ground-changing, open-ended, though classical, view of what is hoped for.

The Politics of Shame

In James Joyce's story *The Dead*, Gabriel Conroy, a middle-class provincial in colonial Ireland, finds out after a Dublin Christmas celebration that his wife Gretta had been in love with another man, Michael Furey, before their marriage. He realizes that she has never loved him as she loved her former suitor.

> A shameful consciousness of his own person assailed him. He saw himself as a ludicrous figure, acting as pennyboy for his aunts, a nervous well-meaning sentimentalist, orating to vulgarians and idealising his own clownish lusts, the pitiable fatuous fellow he had caught a glimpse of in the mirror.

We recognize this as one of the most painful emotions that it is possible for a human being to suffer. But Conroy accepts this shame "that burned upon his forehead"; he makes no attempt to deny it. Gretta reveals that Michael Furey died at the age of seventeen; she believes that he died of his love for her. Conroy's shame and jealousy are transformed into a strange humility, then pity, then an astonishing feeling of solidarity with all human beings, who are either dead or destined to die; and finally to a beautiful and epiphanic experience of the snowfall all over Ireland.

The work of a literary theorist, James Hans, and three sociologists, Helen Lewis, Thomas Scheff, and Suzanne Retzinger, has established shame as the hidden cause of much contemporary cultural damage. We can distinguish two pathological reactions to shame, straightforward repression and what is called bypassed shame. The signs of simple repression are a cycle of shame at one's own shame, rage at oneself, rage at the person who has shamed one, shame at one's own rage, and so on. The subject is flushed, inarticulate, trapped in painful emotion, and crippled in function. Bypassed shame, in contrast, is recognizable by a sudden sharp pang of shame followed immediately by a total suppression of it, covered up by glib and rapid speech, ingenious but superficial and flawed thought, a paralysis of the emotions, and a capacity for affectless and conscienceless cruelty. Both Scheff and Hans point out that shame itself, even more than shameful objects and actions, is the object of massive euphemism, repression, and denial. We deny that we feel shame, because shame is a shameful feeling to have. We would much rather feel an ennobling guilt, which we have safely internalized where nobody can see it, or embarrassment, which we can attribute to unlucky circumstances.

Modern writers like Joyce, at the height of their genius, are able to achieve a painful and provisional standoff with the shame of life. Perhaps the task would be easier in a traditional society, where sophisticated mechanisms have been developed over millennia to deal with the pain and extract from it the strange epiphanic renewal of beauty that it contains.

The foundation myths of most cultures depict some deeply shameful act at the origin of the human world. Take, for instance, the Eskimo story of Sedna and her father Anguta. Sedna marries a dog against her father's wishes; the father kills her dog-husband. On the way back a storm rises and Anguta, to lighten the boat, throws his daughter overboard; she clings to the boat and he, to get rid of her, cuts off her fingers. Or the Shinto story of how the Sun-goddess Amaterasu was shamed by her bad brother Susa-no-wo, who threw a flayed horse through the roof of her weaving-hall. Her subsequent retirement to a cave deprived the world of sunlight—as did the shamed rage of Ceres in the myth of Persephone.

Or consider the biblical story of the Fall, of the shame of Adam and Eve at their disobedience, their lies, and their nakedness; or Cain and Abel; or the shameful story of Christmas, of the infant god born between the two places of excrement, urine and feces, and laid in a manger among the brutes, because there was no room at the inn. Or in the Greek tradition the shameful story of Cronus castrating his father Uranus with a sickle, and the generally incestuous provenance of the gods. Or the shameful murder of the corn god in Amerindian mythology; or the various shameful acts of tabu murder and incest in Australian aboriginal creation myths.

These myths express the essential knot of our human predicament. The threads of that knot include: the problematic coexistence of a reflective mind with a smelly, sexed, and partly autonomous body; the horror of death; the ambiguous relationship of human beings with the rest of nature; the incestuous paradoxes of kinship and parenthood; the crimes of our ancestors against the peoples or species they displaced; the capacity to lie given us by language; and the difficulty, obligation, and anxiety inherent in the socioeconomic acts of gift-giving and dividing the fruits of the hunt. Our aboriginal human philosophy tended, with the intuitive economy of dualism, to divide the cultural from the natural. Today, in the light of evolutionary biology and cosmological science, we may be in a position to revise that ancient dichotomy. We recognize that to some extent other species share those reflexive paradoxes, and that our version of them is only an intensification, across certain crucial thresholds, of tensions inherent in the evolutionary process itself and belonging perhaps to the feedback nature of the universe as a whole. However, even if we do replace an absolute division between the human and the natural with a more continuous evolutionary gradient of increasing reflexivity, and even when we come to recognize nature as not just that which is given, but as the very process of accelerating evolution that transforms the given, we must still deal with a world in which greater and lesser levels of self-reference, feedback, intention, and freedom must somehow coexist.

And this coexistence is essentially shameful. We are ashamed about our sexuality, about how we came into the world, about how we did not at one time exist, either as a species or individually. We are thus ashamed of our parents, especially when adolescence forces on us a constant attention to the process of reproduction that originated us; and the reflexive appetite of the mind makes us at the same time seek out the nakedness of father Noah, the nakedness of mother Jocasta. We are ashamed at our bodies, which display an impure and inextricable mixture, a mutual *adulteration*, of the intentional and the instinctive. We are ashamed about eating, because, whatever we eat, we are assuming, upon the confessedly untrustworthy warrant of our own biased judgment, that we must be more valuable than what we destroy with our teeth and digestive juices; hence we naturally find the end products of eating to be objects of disgust. We are at the top of the food chain and feel an anguished and unrepayable obligation to those beings which gave up their lives for us.

We are ashamed about our economic system, whereby we define ourselves as members in good standing of our community, and thus as human beings; we are never quite sure whether we have given the right gift, or given a gift when we should not have, or not given a gift when we should; and we are shamefully anxious about whether we have been given the right gift. We are ashamed at what we have made, whether because of uncertainty about its worthiness or because of the obligation we incurred to those parts of the world we destroyed to make our new contribution to it. The institution of money, by which we extend through time and space the reckoning-up of the balance of obligation for past gifts, and so transcend the limitations of memory, is a basically shameful object of contemplation; we call lucre filthy and are always seeking ways to delegitimize our own economy, at least as it applies to ourselves. We are, finally, ashamed at our own feelings of shame, our own reflexiveness, our awareness of our awareness.

However, it is precisely in this whole area of experience—the reflective interaction at the deepest level with nature, with our origins, with our means of life, with our closest kin, with our community as an object of obligation, and with our very self-consciousness itself—that we encounter the beautiful. Thus in ways that are bearable to us because their story-nature insulates us from their direct personal application without denaturing their meaning, our myths conduct us into the realms of shame where the hot blush of consciousness—the "Blank misgivings of a creature / Moving about in worlds not realized," as Wordsworth put it— can be transformed into the delicious shiver of beauty. The severed fingers of Sedna become the beautiful warm-blooded marine mammals by which the Eskimos survive; the sun-goddess Amaterasu is lured forth from her cave by the newly invented mysteries of dance, comedy, and the mirror of self-awareness. Adam and Eve get knowledge as well as death, and give birth to history and to human redemption; Cain's descendant Jubal invents music; the infant Jesus is attended by Magi with splendid gifts. The genitals of Cronus arise from the sea-foam as the beautiful goddess of love; the corn god's golden hair waves in the wind as the silk of the ripening maize; and the pratfalls and transgressive gaucheries of the aboriginal tricksters are the source of all human arts and graces.

Shame and beauty, then, share a common root. Our myths show us how to experience the beauty we have paid for with our shame, and remind us that if we attempt to avoid or repress shame, we will find ourselves as cut off from beauty as the world was from sunlight in the myths of Amaterasu and Persephone. Both conscious joy and shame involve the emergent and aroused reflexivity, self-reference, and feedback of nature, both within and beyond the sphere of human culture. Certainly there never was an unalloyed purity in the universe; the cosmos hides its privates with a fig leaf, and, if the cosmos is the body of God, then God, coyly, hides Hers too. The blush, which Darwin saw as one of the defining characteristics of humanity, is the very condition of physical existence, and there is no way back to a time before the blush. The blush is time itself.

Many of the major institutions of traditional societies—ritual in general (especially sacrifice, but also funerals, initiations, birthing ceremonies, puberty rituals, and purifications), religious codes of behavior, customs of modesty in clothes and deportment, courtship and marriage, hereditary privilege, etiquettes of education, the traditional forms of the arts—may be seen in this light as other ways of ensuring a productive passage through shame to beauty. Sacrifice transforms a shameful act, the public killing of a living being or its substitute, through collective acknowledgement of our condition and recognition of the nature of the universe, into an experience of beauty. Other rituals similarly accept, frame, organize, and elaborate the chaotic shame inherent in death, life-crisis, birth, sexual awakening, and pollution, in such a way that we recognize the beauty that also attends those moments of embarrassing emergence and self-reference. Religious moral codes give us clear boundaries to transgress and ways of seeking beautiful repentance when we do transgress. Modesty, by explicitly concealing our animal nature, draws attention to it; the blush brings out the special conscious beauty of the face. Courtship and marriage accept and concentrate the shame of sexuality, and thus allow its strange mutually mirroring beauty, the lovely pathos of its nakedness, to be revealed.

Hereditary privilege thematizes and renders acceptable the shame of inequality, whether that inequality stems from lucky genetic differences of talent or from the luck of the social circumstances of birth and upbringing. Our shame at the relative paucity of our achievements is accepted as integral to the beauty of service to what is nobler than we. The necessary and institutionalized inequality of parent and child during the child's minority is the source of both humiliation and the most exquisite tenderness. The traditional relationship of teacher and student (one of the few other examples of explicit and prescribed personal inequality that remain in the modern world) transforms what is potentially the most murderously shameful situation of all, one person telling another what to think, into a beautiful and mutual pursuit of the truth.

The classical forms of the arts are also, in a less immediately obvious way, both reminders of our shame and revealers of beauty. The traditional pan-human artistic genres are keyed to our neurophysiological makeup in such a way as to remind us of our materiality, our mortality, the automatism of our delight, as well as the strange reflexivity of our awareness. We are embarrassed by our pleasure in rhyme, by the sweetness of melody, by stories with neat endings, by gorgeous color combinations, and by the great natural genre of representation in general. It is in and through this very corniness, this shameful twinge of natural response, that the mysterious powers of beauty take flesh and reality. Many have felt that the beauty was not worth the concomitant twinge of shame. The aesthetic severity of the modernist has its precedents: in the Hebrew prophets and the Islamic mullahs with their shame-denying injunctions against representation, in the Athenian feminists who in their destructive fury castrated the statues of the gods, in the Byzantine iconoclasts, in the followers of Savonarola who burned the Botticellis, and in those of the puritan John Knox who forbade the beauties of church decoration and ritual, and who smashed the stained glass and abolished the old church music. These movements could arguably have been attempts to renew and refresh the shame that our rituals had so beautifully *managed* that it had almost been buried and forgotten. Something rather different, I believe, has happened in the last one hundred and fifty years: the systematic cultural attempt to deny shame altogether.

It is a truism of sociology that modernity was the period during which, for a multitude of reasons—greater personal mobility, the contraction of the unit of production from the extended family to the individual worker, the drive toward political liberty, the spread of literacy, urbanization, and so on—many of the traditional institutions of preindustrial society fell into decline. Myth, ritual (especially sacrificial ritual), religion, traditional customs of modesty, courtship, marriage and family, hereditary privilege, and the traditional art forms all lost their hold upon the allegiance and imagination of the people.

Modernity can also be usefully defined as that period in which politics came to be polarized into Left and Right. Thomas Carlyle, writing about the French Revolution, was the first writer we know of in the English language to use the term "left" in its political sense, in 1837 (though *gauche* and *droite* had been in political use in France since before the turn of the century). By 1887 the left–right distinction was a regular and recognizable description of the two wings of the British Parliament.

It has been precisely since politics divided itself into Left and Right that beauty began to be rejected by artists and critics, or euphemized and denatured as aesthetics. To adapt a saying of Brecht's, there can be no tragedy either in a leftist or a rightist world. How are these events connected? How may we relate these three facts: the function of traditional institutions in accepting shame and thus releasing its mysterious twin, beauty; the decline of those institutions in the nineteenth and twentieth centuries; and the rise of the Left and the Right? Let us examine briefly the psychology of the political Right and Left, for if we consider beauty deeply we will find that it cannot endure their presence. The beautiful and the left–right political dyad are mutually exclusive. Other kinds of political affiliation, such as tribal, civic, national, or even factional loyalties (as in Dante's Florence) seem to be able to coexist with beauty; politics was regarded both by the Greeks and by the Founding Fathers of the U.S. Constitution as an activity of beautiful excellence. It is not politics in itself that is fatal to beauty, but some particular characteristic of it that has emerged in the modern world.

Let us begin with the Right. As the old ritual institutions faded and lost their legitimating and unifying power, those who, through natural talent, inherited wealth, or the effects of the last generation of hereditary privilege, had been left in favorable or leading positions in society, found themselves at an impasse. The shame of their position—their knowledge of their kinship with the beggar, the cripple, the idiot—was no longer rendered acceptable by the old institutions. The political Right arose out of a new response to shame: outright denial of that shameful kinship with the less fortunate, sometimes rationalized by the pseudo-science of Social Darwinism. If we take this turn we deny the discomfort of shame altogether and impose upon ourselves the rectitude and adroitness of the political Right, which exports to the Other both its own gaucheness and its own sinisterness. The self-righteousness of the right is implicit in the very word itself. Right is correct, unblemished, unshamed, preserving of face; it is the *Recht*, the *droit*, the dextrous, the dutiful, the adroit. It is one's due, one's right, one's proper destiny, one's portion, one's appointed *moira* or fate or slice of life. The fugitive and elusive quality of beauty avoids the right in normal circumstances not so much because of its potential for brutality but because of its breezy philistinism, its complacency, its apparent incapacity for shame. Keeping up that rectitude is exhausting, and one unconsciously resents the effort. Hence the cruelty of the Right. All the shame of one's own condition is projected upon the poor, the racial or sexual Other, the unfortunate, the Left, the left outside. Once one's own disgrace has been displaced and shifted to the margins, its stink becomes associated with the Other and is the justification of an unthinking contempt.

In extreme economic conditions when it appears that the privileges of the in-group are being eroded, as in the period of hyperinflation that preceded the rise to power of the Nazis, that contempt can turn into hysterical hatred. It is highly significant that the Nazi pathology arose in the atmosphere of shameful defeat fostered by the Versailles treaty, in which the Germans had to bend the knee to the French, whom they despised; and that it seemed to them that the Jews were the beneficiaries of the disruptive economic conditions created by the treaty. As Scheff points out, Hitler's formula of the "stab in the back" is a masterful use of rhetoric to mobilize repressed shame. Instead of sacrifice, which implicates the sacrificer in the shame of existence, the Nazis instituted the

Holocaust, which was an attempt to annihilate the source of shame. The Holocaust, as a name for these events, is thus both chillingly accurate and profoundly misleading.

Many human qualities—solidarity, hatred, dogged loyalty—can be aroused and manipulated by the promise to eliminate shame. But not beauty. Nazi ideology was accompanied by gigantic and sentimental attempts to recreate the beauties of traditional public rituals and public arts. But the torchlight parades, the monumental architecture, the *völkisch* paintings of wholesome Aryans reaping the fields, all ring hollow and do not capture the shock and mystery of beauty. The reason is that shame has been denied, not accepted and incorporated. In contrast, the operas of Wagner are beautiful precisely because, whatever Wagner's views, the shame of life cannot be alienated from his heroes and heroines and comes tragically home to roost.

Beauty equally avoids the Left, and for the same reason: its denial of shame. The *mechanism* of denial is very different from that of the right, however, and more interesting. In a society where, because of the breakdown of traditional institutions, one's fate is largely in one's own hands, and where there exist no ritual or sacrificial means of catharsis, personal failure becomes unbearable. This is why social unrest occurs paradoxically not in conditions of extreme and established social inequality, but during periods when that inequality has already lost its legitimacy and efficacy. One can no longer explain the dissatisfactions of one's life, and thus dissolve them, by reminding oneself of one's proper station in society; one has no proper station.

Leftist ideology attempts to repress and bypass the unbearable shame of personal failure, real or imagined, and transform it into pity for the oppressed. Feelings of sadistic rage and icy noble justice, which one could not legitimately feel on one's own behalf, as a bad loser, one can indulge without limit on behalf of someone else—or something else, in the case of animal rights extremists. Nothing is as pleasant as an emotion normally forbidden as wicked that is justified by the wholesome and righteous glow of altruism.

Leftists then translate pity for the oppressed, via the natural human sacrificial-scapegoat instinct, into hatred for the rich and successful. This hatred is essential and central to the leftist ideology; it is not the product of extreme and paradoxical circumstances, as rightist hatred is, but is the very heart and soul of the position, its fundamental psychological payoff and the sure sign of its presence. True pity for the poor and unfortunate, which is a real, and a most beautiful human emotion, accepts its own shame and extends to all creatures rich and poor, and makes itself felt by immediate, unpublicized, and local attempts to ameliorate the condition of others. It is incompatible with hatred. We can tell ideological pity from true pity by the killing, or the desire to kill. Once the killing starts, another feedback mechanism springs into being. Our shame at our crimes is denied and transformed into further hatred, which must be slaked by further crime, leading to further denied and redirected shame. This is the essential mechanism of the phenomenon of the Terror.

Envy, too, which is one of the immediate offshoots of shame, plays an important part in this move. Leftists are no more immune to the temptations of luxurious living than, say, TV evangelists (in fact they are often, when they get into power, sybarites and sensualists of amazing ingenuity and scope, as we may see from the life-styles of folk like Mao Tse-tung and the Ceausescus, not to mention people closer to home). The shame of the desire for goods whose very value derives from those whom we believe have shamed us, a desire for them *because* those goods belong to those who have shamed us—our reluctance to admit the mimetic desire that makes us value what they have made valuable—leads us to project upon the rich a monstrous greed and insatiable appetite that is in fact our own, the fevered product of our imagined deprivation. The established rich are often rather bored with expensive and complicated possessions that require time-consuming upkeep and protection, and sometimes lead lives of remarkable simplicity. The true gifts of wealth are empty space and empty time. It is the *nouveaux riches* who conspicuously consume, who displace the shame of their earlier poverty upon the Other. We might define the leftist as an unsuccessful member of the *nouveaux riches*. If the leftist does achieve success and wealth, the paradox of his or her position is itself a shame that must be denied, with fresh justifications for sectarian cruelty.

Many of the shame mechanisms of the Left are, as with the Right, implicit in the term "left." We have already glanced at the gaucheness, the anguished feeling of social shame which we at first deny, then transvalue, and finally even flaunt as the banner of our political correctness, the gauche transformed into the political Left. The Left is also the left out, the excluded from social communion; and it is the sinister, both in the imagination of the Right and, romanticized, in its own. The left hand is the one used in many traditional societies to wipe one's behind; it is the *linkisch*, the clumsy, the dark, the "female," the maladroit hand. In the leftist ideology all these weaknesses are gloried in, transformed into the victim's anguished defiance, and fastened upon the enemy as the consequences of his crime.

What happens to beauty in the world of avant-garde leftist ideology? The word "beautiful" is replaced by "aesthetic"—a word which came into English from Germany just seven years before the first known use of "left" in its political sense. Thus the sweet old shame of beauty could be erased in the severe and intellectual pursuit of aesthetic purity. The aesthetic carries with it a large vocabulary of technical terms whose possession protects the elect from any embarrassment. Once the aesthetic was detached from its humanity, its shame, and its mystery, it could then be turned to political uses, and political correctness—paradoxically, "rightness"—became the fundamental principle of leftist esthetics.

In attempting to counter the shame of the involuntary, the organic, the genetically imprinted in the beauty experience, avant-garde theory sometimes insists on the originality of the artist, the artist's heroic will and defiance of the natural, which rises above the merely fleshly and and organic. Another, opposite, approach is to emphasize the physical and sexual, but in a context in which moral judgments are ridiculed, and always in a way calculated to shock and pain the bourgeois onlooker, to leave the audience alienated and disgusted, with all the slime, as it were, of the artist's imagination now amusingly fastened on the observer rather than on the artist, who as the arranger of this little trick remains untouched by it. Yet another avant-garde ploy is a willful obscurity in the arts, calculated to induce a feeling of shame in the audience, reader, or viewer. The shame of the disadvantaged social misfit (who didn't understand opera, perhaps) is turned back with a vengeance upon the wretched middle-class rube, who now becomes the victim in turn.

Another way the avant-garde found to take the sting out of beauty was by abandoning, on strict rational principles, all rationality in art. Such artwork was designed to subvert the hierarchical power system of the Right—it was, as it were, deliberately *wrong*! But again it was a kind of attempt to mirror back to an imagined oppressor the shame, and thus confusion, of the oppressed; or by breaking down all distinctions to bury in a general disorder the painful difference between shame and justified complacency. Postmodern criticism, detecting shame, personalized as the transcendent signifier, even in the ideas of author, self, reader, meaning, text, and world, has proceeded to feed them one by one to its flames.

One of the most pernicious aspects of the myth of America is the assumption of an entirely new start, of New World innocence as opposed to the ancient fleshpots and bloodbaths of the Old World. This myth makes even Walt Whitman a little repulsive to those who have a true respect for history. What is pernicious about the myth is not so much its relative truth or falsehood with respect to the peoples of North America (indeed, the USA may well have cleaner hands than any other nation of comparable wealth, age, size, and power in its time) but that innocence in the sense intended might be a virtue at all. The recent celebrations of the quincentennial of Columbus's voyage to the New World, and the controversy surrounding them, are an interesting example of a ceremony which has gone wrong because of the failure of avant-garde hope. The tragedy is that it might, redeemed by the full acceptance of shame, have been made into a true ritual for all peoples of the American continents. The celebrations of 1892 triumphalistically denied the terrible cost of the European conquest, in classic right-wing fashion. The celebrations of 1992 were turned into a feast of self-pity disguised as indignation on behalf of the oppressed, in typical left-wing fashion.

This point should not be misunderstood. The genocide and enslavement of pre-Columbian peoples by the European invaders, though no different in kind from, say, the extermination of the indigenous Khoisan by Bantu invaders in Africa, or the activities of the Mongols and Tartars in Europe and Asia, or the Polynesians in the East Indies, were horrible events. But it is we, the survivors, who see them as horrible. It was partly the latent capacity to see them as horrible that enabled the colonists to triumph over the pre-Columbian peoples in the first place. The Greco-Roman humanism and Judeo-Christian conscience that combined under Charlemagne and his successors to create Christendom was not only the force that enabled modern Europe to overcome tribalism and dominate the world. It was also the origin of the idea of the Rights of Man and the reason why we can recognize the horror of what our conquistador ancestors perpetrated.

Suppose the indigenous Mesoamerican and Andean politics had continued their evolution without interference from Europe. The ancient Middle East, where pyramid/priest/irrigation/emperor cultures persisted for millennia with occasional changes of dynasty, is probably a sound analogy. The political ethics of such cultures have little of our modern squeamishness and ambiguity. They celebrate with gusto on magnificent ritual stelae their bloody victories, conquests, enslavements, and human sacrifices, and show a robust disregard for the rights of conquered peoples. At the time they were overthrown by the Spanish, the Aztecs and the Incas were themselves freshly returned from the destruction of other civilizations; their altars were not yet dry from their enemies' blood. (Indeed, part of the success of Cortés and Pizarro was that they could enlist the help of the resentful remnants of enslaved and conquered peoples like the Tlascalans.) Nor is there any historical warrant for believing that the passage of a mere five hundred years would have much sophisticated the ethics of those empires. It took at least two thousand years for the riverine civilizations of Mesopotamia, the Nile, the Indus, the Ganges, and the Yellow River to develop the more humane ideas of the Hebrew prophets, the Vedic tradition, the Greek philosophers and Roman lawyers, and the Buddhists. If the Spanish had tried, and failed, to conquer the Aztecs and Incas, and if those empires had survived into the present day, there would no doubt be splendid frescoes and bas-reliefs of the enslavement, dismemberment, and ritual sacrifice of those strange demons from the sea, unless, in our alternative history, we can imagine that the moral qualms of Europe might have come to infect them across the Atlantic. But would Europe have learnt to interpret its morality in political terms if it had not conquered America?

The irony is manifold. It is not just that it was those most beautiful images of human love, the Virgin and Christ-child, and the crucified savior, that gave the Europeans the faith and cohesion to crush the Amerindians. Nor is it only that the succeeding civilization, founded upon such atrocities, was for the first time in human history capable of repenting its past conquests. The irony is that it took those particular conquests to arouse the latent political conscience of the world, to translate the personal ethics, evolved at such cost and expense of time in the Old World, into the beginnings of a decent political morality. In other words, the true value of Columbus's journey and the conquest of the New World may be that they helped to create the very ethics that could condemn them. Certainly the wealth that they created made possible large populations of the middle class in Europe and America, that class which may be unique in giving serious thought to such matters as intercultural ethics (unless the small but important Confucian mandarinate of China qualifies). And this is for all peoples, not just "Westerners," cause for a dark and complex kind of celebration, that we are all now better able to recognize how bloody are our hands, how extravagant was the cost of our survival, and how valuable we must be, purchased thus.

Our dignity as human beings, paradoxically, depends upon the acceptance of our shame. To deny our shame is to attempt to fly away from the heavy weight of our past, to alienate ourselves from our present enjoyment of the spoils of our own or our ancestors' crimes. To make the denial is to trivialize ourselves, to declare a kind of bankruptcy that may leave us without weight but also without momentum or consequence. Without that weight we become helpless, handless, like a ghost in the real world, incapable of acting or feeling, an observer only. Our crimes are our incarnation in the world, the purchase we get on it. It is the denial of shame that is the true "disempowerment": even the most wretched inhabitants of traditional societies, laborers or sweeping women, have more dignity and power in their faces than the harried, self-righteous, paranoid living dead who have denied their shame and projected it upon others.

Nor is there any way of making restitution for those crimes, except by the full-hearted effort to make ourselves, and each other, and the human future, as beautiful and splendid and generous and creative as they can be. The people we have injured, and to whom we, as receivers of stolen goods, are indebted, are all dead and cannot be repaid, except by redeeming the promise of the human future that they must have believed in, if they in turn were properly cognizant of their own tainted past. We do not owe their descendants; and even if we did, those descendants would be ourselves, such is the marvelous mixing of human genes. We all have a bit of Aztec, Inca, black slave, persecuted Jew in us. The people who are the present inheritors of the injury have a claim, but it is a claim against dead conquistadors and dead slave-traders. The injured are likewise the descendants, and beneficiaries, of their ancestors' oppressors. Every woman today is the inheritor and beneficiary of the crimes and rapes and conquests of all her fathers, as of her mothers, and is no kin to those who did not survive to reproduce. If women are victims, every man today is the descendant of an unbroken succession of victims, and deserves compensation, if compensation were possible, which it is not. None of us is clean, and this is no excuse; our very dirtiness ties us to the earth, to life, and claims our commitment to make things better. Indeed, the brotherhood and sisterhood of humankind is precisely our companionship in crime; and we can love each other strangely as fellow-criminals trying to reform ourselves.

In this perspective art might take on a new mission, which is also its old one: to be the ritual by which we accept our shame and transform it into beauty. It means a new importance for historical art, for the subject of the family and of reproduction, for myth; and it also implies the necessity of hope, and a commitment to the future as our only way of ethically shouldering the burden of crimes we cannot expiate in any other way. Given the new science of human heredity, which confounds the old liberal notions of the individual as a *tabula rasa* to be inscribed freely by social conditioning, we must come to accept a nonutopian view of history, and acknowledge the inescapable and beautiful unfairness of life. If we come to be able to change human genes, the exercise, or even the renunciation, of this power will surely implicate us not less but more in that essential unfairness. The future cannot but be more tragic than the past, in precisely the same measure as it will be more productive of deeper and higher values. Instead of social amelioration, which seeks to impose deterministically a utopian perfection on the future, we should try for a much more subtle, *listening* posture, more that of the artist than the social planner, in dealing with cultural, political, and economic problems. Rather than to constrain a theoretically desirable result, a "happy ending," we should try to sense and bring to fruition the attractors of the future, to let the best story tell itself, even if it is a sad one.

Chapter 3

A New Cosmology for the Arts

Dissolving the Order–Disorder Dualism: Self-Ordering Chaos

The avant-garde professes to reject all dualisms as leading to the hierarchical privileging of one term of the duality over the other; however, it is itself just as prone to dualism as any other system of human thought. One of its most subtly paralyzing dualisms is the apparently harmless one between order and disorder. The idea of hope as liberation, under which we have labored for so many years, is especially liable to the corruptions of this dualism. For instance, if order means predictability, and predictability means predetermination, and predetermination means compulsion, and compulsion means unfreedom, the only way we can be free is if we are disordered. The failed hopes of the last two centuries have been founded upon a deep discomfort with the idea of order, and what are taken to be its close relatives: hierarchies, foundations, norms, and essences—even with value itself, if value is conceived of as being anything other than momentary individual preference. The logic of the duality has forced the avant-garde to choose the random, the disordered, the arbitrary, the *acte gratuit*, the unconditioned, the weightless, the unfurrowed. What, after all, were the alternatives? They could submit themselves to the Transcendental Signified, the old man with the white beard, Nobodaddy Himself, the ancestral authority figure who bars the doors against franchise, potential for achievement, free play of art, sexuality, political identity, and self-expression. Or they could accept that the world was a dead machine and human beings were merely parts of that machine, linear and deterministic. Thus they would be fated to some kind of mechanistic social order determined by the genes, by the physics of our energy economy, by economic necessity or psychological drives.

Indeed, it began to look as if the second alternative was just a new avatar of the first, that the scientists and psychologists and sociologists and businessmen and commissars who preached materialist determinism were really just the old white-bearded patriarchs and racial oppressors in disguise. Nineteenth-century psychic determinism, which had proven so convenient when it was useful to argue that there was no choice but to follow the command of desire, could also be used to sanction sexist gender roles. Nineteenth-century social determinism justified oppression, nineteenth-century historical determinism justified war, and nineteenth-century biological determinism justified ideas of racial superiority. The ramifications of this predicament were pervasive.

For instance, the fundamental problem of any natural philosophy is time. The avant-garde was faced with three difficult choices in talking about the relationship between the past and the future: one is that some external and ineffable divine will governs the relationship and makes it partly intelligible and meaningful; another is that the relationship is deterministic, and that the past causes the future in a linear and mechanical way; and the third is that the relationship is essentially random, and that any sense it seems to make is only in our perception of it. The problem with divine will is that it simply begs the question: how does *God* know what to ordain, what is good and valuable? Can God's will meaningfully be free, if its future state is only random with respect to its past? If freedom is simply randomness, is not God's will, in the absence of a further, superior divine guarantee of its validity (which would be subject to the same objection), simply autocratic whim, arbitrary in the worst sense? Would it not be worse still if God's future state were deterministically governed by His past state? How could God be free in any sense if this were so? Should we obey a God who is less free, less, therefore, of a person, than we are? This was Socrates' question: is an act good because the gods will it, or do the gods will it because it is good?

Nobody wants either a random universe or a deterministic one, for freedom and value and meaning appear impossible within them (though great philosophers in the tradition of Nietzsche have struggled to assert them nevertheless). Given the potential for abuse inherent in the deterministic position, it seemed safest to opt for a more or less random relationship between the past and the future, despite the fact that if this were the case, memory and experience would be completely useless. At least events could be individually *perceived* as meaningful and valuable. One person's perception would be as good as another's, so there could be no political repression. And then the random relationship began to look promising; the universe would be unknowable because it was fundamentally incoherent, and all science and objective knowledge could be dismissed either as irrelevant or simply the means to rationalize the political interests of the powerful. Did not quantum theory, if squeezed a little and its beautiful mathematics not too closely observed, say something of the same kind? Were not the white lab-coated ones condemned out of their own mouths?

But then, the knots and toils the avant-garde tied itself into when it tried to profess views such as these! A new sin had been discovered: involuntary hypocrisy—hypocrisy when they were most desperately trying to avoid it. When they opted for simple disorder and randomness, they were faced with the problems of how to *mean* the destruction of meaning? How to publish the discrediting of publication and public? How to achieve an institutional position, say in the University of Paris, when institutions are the legacy of the past and thus based on sadistic repression? How to attack hierarchy in a language with a syntactical tree and grammatical subordination? How to get paid for copyrights where payment must be in the coin of mimetic desire and copyright is the quintessence of commodification? How, even, to act with a body possessed of an immune system of quite military rigor, and a nervous system strikingly unified under central control? Can freedom, seriously, be the same as random or disordered behavior? According to classical physics the universe becomes more disordered over time, that is, less intelligible and less able to do work. Is freedom, then, just the human contribution to the universal process of increasing entropy? Is it the job of free beings to assist in the destruction of this beautiful ordered universe? Intention requires a highly organized brain; can the only free intention be that which would tend to disorganize that brain and disable intention itself? What becomes of responsibility if freedom is randomness? Can one take credit for good works, if there is no responsibility? Can there be such a thing as justice, for instance, if one cannot be held responsible for one's actions?

Until recently the best that the avant-garde could do with the available intellectual tools in cobbling up a reasonable account of the universe, and of personal freedom, was to devise some kind of combination between order and randomness, linear determinism and disordered noise. The title of Jacques Monod's book on biological evolution, *Chance and Necessity*, puts it well. Perhaps both the emergence of new species and the originality and freedom of the human brain could be described as a combination of random mutations and relatively deterministic selection, the *clinamen* of the random swerve and the *ananke* of the survival of the fittest, as mapped onto a genome that would record and reproduce the results.

Although evolution was clearly a fact, its precise mechanism was under heavy debate. Even here there were deep and subtle theoretical objections. One was that evolution seemed to proceed in sudden jumps, not gradually; a new species did not seem to emerge slowly but rather leap into being as if drawn by a premonition of its eventual stable form. Another was the odd bootstrap logic of species and their ecological niches. Without the right suite of species, the ecological niche wouldn't exist; but without the ecological niche, the species wouldn't. How do new niches emerge? Again, from a purely intuitive point of view even four billion years didn't seem nearly enough to produce the staggering variety and originality of form to be found among living species—birds of paradise, and slime molds, and hermaphroditic parasitical orchids, and sperm whales, and all; especially when, as was the case, the huge majority of present species only evolved in the last few tens of millions of years, and most of the major classes and phyla in the last few hundred million. Other problems, like the fact that RNA, which can be altered by the experience of an individual member of a species, can play the role of DNA in determining heredity, also confused the evolutionary picture. The genome, though for the most part alterable only at the level of the gene pool of the whole species, wasn't untouched by the life of a particular organism, but belonged to its reciprocal system.

Most disturbing of all, in the realm of developmental biology—the study of how seeds grow into embryos and embryos grow into adult plants or animals—it became clear that the process of development could not be described by a straightforward causal model. The journey by which a fertilized egg or seed multiplied and diversified itself into all the cells in all the correct positions necessary for an adult body, was not a mere following of genetic instructions embedded in the DNA blueprint, but an original and creative process in itself, which produced a unique individual out of a dynamic and open-ended interplay of cells. The miracle was that the interplay could produce something in the end remotely resembling its twin siblings, let alone its parents. It was as if the individual organism were *drawn* toward a beckoning form, and that the genes were not so much blueprints *specifying* that form as gates *permitting* the developmental process to rush to its conclusion.

Further, chance and necessity, though they were the only permissible inputs to the system of evolution, did not exhaust its description. Time, for instance, was an essential ingredient, and what was time? In the case of biological evolution, the essence of time was that it was a medium for *iteration*, for going over the same process again and again until the process itself could alter by degrees, and cross critical thresholds into new types of process altogether; even new types of *iteration* altogether. In classical evolutionary theory time was just a sort of space or quantity; but suppose iterative processes had laws of their own? Why should not time itself be altered by the change in the nature of the iteration, since iteration was its essence? Why should time be a neutral metric, when all metrics seemed to be slightly pliable according to what they measured? And those "critical thresholds," they seemed innocent, and were essential to all scientific theories, including biology. They determined, for instance, how big an animal could get and still walk on land; the ratio of its volume, and thus weight, to surface area and thermal exchange with the environment; how its digestive efficiency, the amount of forage per square mile, and its mobility were related. But where did those thresholds come from? Were they, before life evolved, *waiting* in the timeless wings of eternity to find a concrete expression in an ecosystem? Was there not a marine airbreather archetype ready to be filled by plesiosaurs, penguins, dolphins, whales, and seals according to the available genetic material?

The same kinds of problems arose if the chance-and-necessity model was applied to the working of the human brain. Just as with mutation and selection, which are, indeed, the only *external* inputs to the biological system, modernist science was clearly on the right track; but even more clearly, something was hugely missing. Maybe "nature and nurture" don't exhaust the inputs. Can it make sense to speak of *internal* inputs, or forms which *draw* an appropriately prepared human brain into a specific competence, like language? Did the ghost of Plato, whose ideal forms had been dismissed forever by materialist science, walk again? The great brain scientist Sir John Eccles has found himself compelled, by his observation of brain events that seem to anticipate the stimuli that should activate them, to postulate a detachable human Soul. The first attempts at creating artificial intelligence used purely deterministic programs. When these failed, researchers tried to "lighten" or free up the system by throwing in random elements. This didn't work, either: one ended up with just a less efficient calculator. Cybernetic neural network models of the human brain, which use iterative and nonlinear feedback processes, and whose operations cannot really be called either deterministic or random, seemed to show more promise. But there seemed to be a huge mass of endogenous laws and principles in such systems that we have hardly begun to understand, and where did they come from, all of a sudden?

The dualism of order and disorder was coming under increasing strain. But within the humanities the traditional avant-garde hatred of any kind of essentializing, hierarchizing, (biologically) determinist, transcendentally significant and totalizing Order was so ingrained that the more shaky that dualism became, the more passionately it was asserted. It may now be obvious that the problem with which we began this section, of the order-disorder dualism, is implicated in other dualisms: the dualisms of nature and humanity, of the natural and the artificial, of animals with natures and humans without natures. The problem the avant-garde was honestly trying to solve was that the only alternative to repressive order that seemed to be offered was random disorder, or on the psychological level, whim.

Suppose we were to try to specify what an escape from this dualism might look like philosophically. We would have to distinguish between two kinds of order—a repressive, deterministic kind, and some other kind that would not have these disadvantages. We would also have to distinguish between two kinds of chaos—one which was simply random, null, and unintelligible, and another that could bear the seeds of creativity and freedom. If we were really lucky, the second kind of order might turn out not to be the antithesis of the second kind of chaos; they might even be able to coexist in the same universe; best of all, they might even be the same thing!

The extraordinary turn of events—an astonishing stroke of good luck, an earnest of hope for the future—is that there really does seem to be the second kind of order, the second kind of chaos. And they do seem to be the same thing. This new kind of order, or chaos, seems to be at the heart of an extraordinary range of interesting problems that had appeared as philosophers, mathematicians, scientists, and cybernetic technologists tried to squeeze the last drops of the imponderable out of their disciplines. They included the biological and artificial-intelligence problems already alluded to; the problem of how to describe catastrophic changes and singularities by means of a continuous mathematics; the problem of how to predict the future states of positive feedback processes; Gödel's paradox, which detaches the true from the provable; the description of phase-changes in crystallography and electrochemistry; the phenomenon of turbulence; the dynamics of open systems and nonlinear processes; the observer problem in a variety of disciplines; the failure of sociological and economic predictive models because of the rational expectations and second-guessing of real human subjects; the theoretical limitations of Turing machines (in certain circumstances they cannot turn themselves off); the question of how to fit the fractal geometry of Benoit Mandelbrot into orthodox mathematics; the classification of quasi-crystals and Penrose tilings; the whole issue of self-reflection, bootstrapping, and positive feedback in general; and most troubling of all, the question of the nature of time. I have discussed several of these issues in other books, and would refer the reader to them, to the recent work of Alexander Argyros, Koen dePryck, and Katherine Hayles, and to the excellent popular treatments of chaos that have appeared in recent years. The point here is the overwhelming breadth and consistency of the emerging paradigm.

In choosing the term "chaos" to describe this new imaginative and intellectual arena, the discoverers of it pulled off something of a public-relations coup without perhaps fully intending to. They could have called it "antichaos," which would have been just as accurate a term, in fact a better one, as its implied double negative—"not not-order"—suggests something of its iterative depth. But "antichaos" would have sounded too much like law 'n' order to the avant-garde academicians, who would have dismissed it as yet another patriarchal Western mystification. Indeed, some theorists in the humanities have taken "chaos" to their bosom, as they once did quantum uncertainty, as a confirmation of their pro-random, pro-disorder bias.

Oddly enough, exactly the opposite thing happened in the nineteenth century. Progressive intellectuals and artists of the mid-century were entranced by the notion of determinism, psychic and social. Perhaps unkindly, we could say that the Newtonian penny had finally dropped (as the Heisenbergian one has today), and the implications of a mechanistic universe had coincided with certain cultural desires they seemed to substantiate. Intellectuals and artists wanted to be able to say that because they were in the grip of the great forces of Nature or History, their actions were above morality. So when the theory of evolution by natural selection came along, it was immediately interpreted in terms of its two least significant provisions. The first was that human beings might have inherited certain characteristics from their animal ancestors (though the theory's power was precisely that it showed how inheritance could *change* with time and adaptation). The second was that selection seemed to be a lawlike phenomenon, and though its causality was messier and less exact than the elegant determinism of the laws of planetary motion, it at least showed a way of extending that physical determinism into the realm of the psyche. Again the problem was that the theory's real thrust was not that nature was governed by deterministic laws, but rather that the operation of those laws, in combination with time, heredity, and chance mutation, could bring about results that are indistinguishable from originality, creativity, invention, and freedom. "Chaos" theory, then, like evolution, is the subject of a great misprison. Evolution was falsely taken to confirm determinism; and "chaos" is falsely taken to confirm the essential randomness of freedom.

In order to understand the deeply liberating point of chaos (or antichaos) theory, we will need to go into the differences between deterministic linear order and chaotic emergent order, and between mere randomness and creative chaos. Let us do so by considering an odd little thought experiment which I heard at a scientific conference. Suppose we were trying to arrange a sonnet of Shakespeare in the most thermodynamically ordered way, that is with the least entropy. We cannot, for the sake of argument, break up the words into letters or the letters into line segments. The first thing we would do, which is the only sort of thing a strict thermodynamicist could do, is order the words alphabetically: "a compare day I Shall summer's thee to?". As far as thermodynamics is concerned, such an arrangement would be more ordered than the arrangement, "Shall I compare thee to a summer's day?" as composed by Shakespeare. Here, in a capsule, is the difference between deterministic linear order and chaotic emergent order.

Although this did not come up at the conference, we could even test the thermodynamic order of the first arrangement by a further *Gedankenexperiment*. Suppose we coded the words in terms of gas molecules arranged in a row, the hottest ones corresponding to the beginning of the alphabet, the coldest ones to the end, and so on in alphabetical order. If left to themselves in a closed vessel the molecules would, because of the increase of entropy over time, rearrange themselves into random alphabetical order (the hot and cold would get evenly mixed). Just as in a steam engine, where the energy gradient between hot steam and cold steam, or hot steam and cold air, can be used to do work, one would be able to employ the movement of molecules, as the alphabetized "sonnet" rearranged itself, to perform some (very tiny) mechanical task. It would take somewhat more energy to put the molecules back into alphabetical order, because of the second law of thermodynamics.

As arranged in Sonnet 18 those words are already in more or less "random" alphabetical order. Yet most human beings would rightly assert that the sonnet order is infinitely more ordered than the thermodynamic, linear, alphabetical one. The information-theory definition of a system with high thermodynamic order (low entropy) is that it takes as few bits of information as possible to specify it, while it takes many bits to specify a high-entropy, low-order system. Indeed, it would take few bits to specify the alphabetical order, and many to specify the sonnet order: hundreds of books have been written about Shakespeare's sonnets, and they are not exhausted yet. For a reader of poetry this is not a sign of the poem's randomness but rather of its exquisite order. In other respects the poem does seem to exhibit the characteristics of order. If highly damaged by being rearranged, it could be almost perfectly reconstituted by a person who knew Shakespeare's other sonnets, and the rules of grammar, logic, and especially poetic meter; one would need only perhaps a fragment of the lost original, showing its meter and a rhyme, and this, together with a syllable-count of the whole, would be more than enough to reconstruct the sonnet. The sonnet can "do work": it has deeply influenced human culture, and has helped to transform the lives of many students and lovers. It is an active force in the world precisely because it does not have the low-entropy simplicity of the alphabetical order that might enable it to do mechanical work. Here, in the most primal sense, lies the distinction between "power" in the mechanical, political sense, and the mysterious creative influence of art.

Another way of describing this distinction is in terms of determinism and freedom. The old avant-garde paradigm could distinguish only two alternatives: deterministic order and random freedom. The extraordinary thing about many nonlinear self-organizing systems, like living organisms undergoing fetal development or sonnets in the process of composition, is that though in theory their next state might be exactly computed and thus predicted, there is not enough computing power in the physical universe to do so. The system thus essentially chooses, or even creates, its own next state, within the parameters of an infinitely rich attractor. This description is fully coterminous with the fullest possible definition of freedom. Thus there is deterministic order and free order; and the latter is the way out of the avant-garde bottle.

But though we have distinguished between the two kinds of order, it is equally necessary to distinguish between the two kinds of chaos. Otherwise we would be in the predicament of someone like Stanley Fish, the "reader-response" theorist, who has been forced by the "order–disorder" dualism into asserting that any random sequence of words, chosen perhaps by flipping the pages of a dictionary, would possess a richness of interpretive potential equal to that of the sonnet; and thus that the very idea of text is either meaningless or extensible to everything in the universe. If reader-response theorists understood information theory, it would be enough to show that their mistake is to confuse "white noise" with "flicker noise." White noise is made up of random amounts of energy at all frequencies. One could certainly imagine that one was listening to the sea when one heard acoustic white noise; there are even devices that make white noise to soothe people to sleep. But there is nothing there to understand or interpret. On the other hand, flicker noise, which does not at first sound very different, is the "sound" that a system makes that is ordered in itself and at the same time highly unstable and going through continuous internal adjustments by means of feedback. A good example is a pile of sand onto whose apex new grains of sand are being dropped one by one. There are many one-grain avalanches, fewer multi-grain avalanches, fewer still mass avalanches, and only the occasional collapse of a whole slope. The sequence of these avalanches, though still statistical and probabilistic rather than deterministic, obeys laws and forms an elegant fractal pattern when plotted on a graph. What one hears when one hears flicker noise is the combination of these events; and if one analyzed it carefully, one might be able to work out the size of the grains, the interval of their deposition, and so on. There is real meaning to be extracted. Our reader-response theorist refuses to extract it.

Flicker noise is not just the "sound" made by piles of sand. It is also what we get when we "listen" in a crude way to highly complex organic systems. For instance, suppose we take the temperature of an animal: that reading is flicker noise. The temperature is made up of a combination of fantastically organized and intricate metabolic processes; yet it is indistinguishable from the "same" temperature taken of a simple chemical reaction, or of a random mixture of unrelated processes, which would be white noise. The problem is that a thermometer is a very crude instrument. It is not enough to do what reader-response theorists would do, that is, to accept its crudity as accuracy, and to make up for it by imagining all kinds of exotic meanings for the animal's temperature that had no necessary connection with its organic metabolism. What makes it a crude instrument is precisely that it makes no allowance for the organized nature of what it is measuring. This is the problem also with interpretative theories of literature, the arts, or history, which discount the inner personal intentions and meanings of the author, whether the author authorizes a poem, a piece of music, a painting, or a historical act. By discounting those personal meanings, and perhaps substituting the crude statistical measures (the "temperature") of gender or race or class interest, we may avoid the bugbear of Authority, but we lose any understanding of what it is we are dealing with: we cannot distinguish a living organism from a stone, and are in grave danger of treating them the same.

Another example of flicker noise is what you would "hear" from a set of electrodes applied to someone's skull if the electrical signal were translated into sound. Just because one could imagine that the squeaks and booms and whistles resembled perhaps the song of humpback whales, this does not mean that the sound "meant" humpback whales, or that the person was not actually thinking something, or that one could never know what he or she was thinking, or that it was meaningless to seek for some absolute meaning, or that it is quite legitimate for us to interpret it as thoughts about humpback whales.

Let us return to the sonnet. Like the strands of DNA that specify a living animal or plant, it somehow has the power to express itself, repair itself, edit itself, and reproduce itself (in memory or print). It even feeds, in a curious sort of way, by focusing current linguistic energies through its hot matrix in such a way as to take on renewed relevance. It is antichaotic, not random; yet it is not a deterministic (for instance, alphabetical) order either. To deconstruct the sonnet is to break it down to a uniform consistency so that one can then take its "temperature" or hear its white noise; and one is then quite free to interpret that noise in gender or race terms, or however one wishes. It would be like boiling the DNA of a live animal or plant into a soup of simple organic molecules, and claiming one had thereby got down to the reality of the living organism. The tragedy is that in the course of its metabolism and reproduction a living creature will briefly "boil" very precisely specified parts of its own structure, for instance the weak hydrogen bonds that hold the DNA zipper together; it is always, in a controlled way, on a kind of continuous light boil. But there is a cruel literalism in extending the boiling process to the destruction of the whole delicate hierarchical structure. "How with this rage shall beauty hold a plea/Whose action is no stronger than a flower?"

One attempt by the avant-garde to deal with the problems raised by the order–disorder dualism has been to try to imagine network or interdependence structures that do not possess the damning characteristics of hierarchy and subordination. For instance the brain is sometimes cited as a sort of democratic network, a "heterarchy," in Douglas Hofstadter's phrase, where no particular neuron is in command. Natural ecosystems are seen as a web of interdependence; and there have been attempts in communes, consciousness-raising groups, and the like, to develop consensual "participatory democracies" or "unstructured" mutual support groups that eschew the evils of phallocentric domination. Such attempts are clearly on the right track, in that they recognize that mere randomness is not the only alternative to repressive linear order, and that there is a rule-governedness in the connections that make up the network. But this concept, because of its ideological roots in anti-authoritarian myth, cannot take the final imaginative step of exploring possible kinds of authority and hierarchy that might be justified and beneficial. As a result, its webs and networks and heterarchies remain pure of hierarchical taint only when they are kept in their initial condition, when they are contentless and memoryless, and when hierarchy is defined in the most limited and literal terms.

Let us look at some examples, so as to make this point clear. The description of the brain as a purely democratic network of neurons does not survive close study any better than it does a few years of experience. For a brief period in the development of the fetal and baby brain, the pure "network" description might look plausible. A mass of brain tissue is produced (through the *very* hierarchical process of cellular specialization and development), whose interconnections are without much differentiation, except that some are inhibitory and some excitatory. However, the process does not stop here: the experience of perception and memory rapidly facilitates some neuronal pathways at the expense of others. The whole class of "Hebb cells" emerges, upon which specific synaptic junctions are expanded and rendered more sensitive, and thus a highly complex but highly specific multidimensional geometry of preferred connections begins to emerge. This geometry is the substance of memory and association, the content and the recorded past of the brain. The connection patterns form circuits, which, when one part of them is sufficiently stimulated, will continue to fire iteratively around and around, until inhibitory messages from other parts of the brain damp down the reverberation. The electrical signal, made by the iterated sequential firing of a whole circuit, constitutes an antichaotic attractor which is the very form of memory and experience. Relatively limited and simple circuits, meanwhile, are "chunked" or subordinated to larger and more comprehensive circuits, and they in turn are contributors to larger ones still. The taste of a madeleine cake is an antichaotic attractor evoked by Hebb-cell circuitry; that attractor can fire off a larger one, of the taste of tea and Sunday morning; and that in turn is subordinated to one of the social and psychological rhythms of a whole childhood. A network can never be any more than a medium; any message has to be hierarchical.

Thus with content and a past comes a complex collection of hierarchies—a hierarchy of relative Hebbian facilitation, a hierarchy of circuits, a hierarchy of memories, and a hierarchy of relative abstraction, as we go from cells to synaptic pathways to circuits to attractor-signals to experiences in the mind. Note that *qua* neurons, no particular cell is boss or leader, and most cells take part, as crossroads, so to speak, in many pathways and circuits, some not very closely connected with each other. Thus some of the "democratic" myth is preserved, but only trivially. The system becomes a person's brain and mind only to the extent that it very richly and subtly hierarchizes itself by an antichaotic process of emergent nonlinear order. In childhood the less-used cells are demoted to the role of helpers, and in adolescence there is a massive pruning of the brain, in which most connections not maximally involved in such circuitry are dissolved: discriminatory processes which, in terms of the contrarian myths, would seem to have the most sinister implications.

The same kind of hierarchizing process takes place in a natural ecosystem. When a barren area, say Mount St. Helen's or Krakatoa after their eruptions, or a northern plain after the retreat of an icecap, is first colonized by seedlings and insects, a hierarchical relationship among the colonists may be hard to see (though it is still there). As the ecosystem settles down and goes through its process of succession toward climax, a clear food chain emerges, and it is easy to distinguish the low-level, low-energy producers from the more complex, refined, and high-energy herbivores and predators that depend on them but which also, by their reproductive and consumption cycles, govern and set the tone for the whole system. More important still, hierarchically nested subsystems emerge, so that there develops a real but abstract *systemic* hierarchy. The attractor of any nonlinear positive feedback system always has the hierarchical property of self-similarity. In other words, interdependence is not the opposite of hierarchy, but the precondition for the dynamic and nonlinear emergence of natural hierarchy. And natural hierarchy is creative, flexible, free, the very opposite of closed, rigid, repressive. The healthy human heart beats by means of a self-organizing, nonlinear though hierarchical feedback of heart–nerve firings; the sick and fibrillating heart shows a collapse into a linear and lockstep order; the dying heart has no order whatever. Thus instead of the avant-garde modernist and postmodernist model, in which the ordered is the unfree and the random is the free, we can substitute a different model, in which the random is the most unfree, linear order is somewhat freer, and nonlinear self-ordering or autonomy is freest of all.

Democracy itself could well be defined as a formalization of and efficient operating system for the natural evolving hierarchy that emerges from human interaction, when its development is not stunted by an egalitarian "network" ideology of Popular Will and total consensus. Democratic institutions, such as fixed terms of office, freedom of the press, separation of powers, and federalism, remove roadblocks to communication within the system and prevent any one hierarchical configuration from becoming rigid and tyrannical. The popular vote is a sort of crude numerical system to insure a canvass of all participants and thus genuine political feedback. Of course these institutions are usually unnecessary in very small communities, like hunter-gatherer bands, and could even be said to be poor and clumsy substitutes for the close discussion, informal leadership, trustful agreement, and quick decisions of such a group.

We could put this point in a more radical way by saying that all functioning traditional communities are already more or less democratic in an informal way. Very small communities may, without democratic institutions at all, be more efficient at being true democracies than democratic nations are, and a democratic legal constitution may only be a way of extending the principle to larger groups of people, rather as money is a formal means of extending the reciprocity of gift-exchange found in small communities to large economies. This description would take away some of the éclat of the modern democracies, but it would establish as the heart of democracy a deeper principle, of feedback and iterative mutual influence leading to the emergence of flexible, complex hierarchies legitimated by consent. Our present democratic institutions, though the best we could come up with so far, are not necessarily the most perfect way of insuring the antichaotic nonlinear political process that we want. New political ideas and new technology may lead to a closer approximation.

Sociologists like Emile Durkheim and Max Weber have charted, and by implication bemoaned, the decay of traditional community in the modern rational state and economy. It may be that there will be a further stage, in which the immediacy and comprehensiveness of modern communications, the move away from mass production to cybernetically controlled custom craftsmanship, and the increasing sensitivity and range of financial instruments, will usher in an age when many democratic institutions will wither away from lack of use and need, or at least fade into the background as a sort of emergency backup system. Thus one day modern state democracy may even be seen as a crude attempt by linear means to mimic the richness of nonlinear human organization, and as only a step toward a new dynamically hierarchical traditionalism. Vaclav Havel's notion of "civil society" and Amitai Etzioni's communitarian philosophy are encouraging signs of this emerging political configuration.

In the economic sphere, we can speculate that the generation of wealth is likewise the emergence of order out of highly nonlinear feedback systems of human activity and exchange. The problem with socialism is that it thwarts the communications between the elements of the system—prices, wages, demand, dividends, interest, and depreciation rates, and so forth—by interposing linear, abstract, top-down notions of social justice, themselves bounded by the imaginations of the socialist economist, by the current technology, and by the feasibility of contemporary hopes and desires. Thus the feedback is quenched, and the wealth remaining within the system begins to obey the laws governing thermodynamic order; it operates in a more and more deterministic fashion, ceases to be inventive, and simultaneously drains steadily away into waste vibration; and the result is inflation and the decay of the capital stock of the economy. The living market, by contrast, is creative and nondeterministic. Of course we are a long way from perfecting such a market. It would have to reflect cultural and ecological demands in a much broader fashion than it does at present, and it would need ways of translating necessary long-term investments, such as in education, arts, public welfare, and environmental restoration, into attractive short-term profit, without undue linear distortions.

One of Marx's errors was to envisage money in terms of ownership—a linear power relationship—when in fact it makes sense only in terms of debt and obligation, the moral foundations of exchange. The "possession" of a large amount of money ideally means nothing more than that many people are obligated or indebted to the "possessor." Even if the obligation is only in being allowed to postpone the cancellation of the obligation by a benefit in return (by the payment of interest), the obligation is real. Certainly money does not always work ideally as a measure of obligation, especially when my obligation to a "rich" person is indirect, and concealed by the fact that I am obligated to other people who are in turn obligated to that person. Even when the direct flow of obligation is obscured by this turning of corners, it must exist if the currency remains stable; if money did not accurately measure obligation, it would soon lose its objective value. But it is human nature to hate our creditors; it was largely for this reason that people hated the Jews between the wars, hated the United States after the Second World War, and hate the Japanese now. We are willing to imagine any evil on the part of someone to whom we are indebted, and to redefine and rationalize our debt according to any principle that would seem to relieve us of its burden.

Our hatred of our creditors has even deeper, perhaps religious, roots, suggested by the derivation of the word "creditor" itself. Our creditor is someone who believes in us, as well as being our benefactor. The more we see around us the remarkable gifts of Japanese labor, intelligence, and generosity, the angrier we get. Yet what of "ours" do "they" possess in compensation? Largely, only a *belief* in our good faith, our industriousness, our sense of obligation. That faith and obligation are symbolized and tabulated in the form of money; but what is that money? Pieces of paper with our promises written on them, or worse, intangible patterns of electromagnetic domains signifying the same thing, in computer memories. The guilt of the Japanese is their faith in us, a faith not unlike what one must have in one's God. That faith, whose pressure we feel, shames us, reminds us of our abjectness, our unworthiness. We would be rid of our believers. And perhaps the same sense of indebtedness for the faith in us that others demonstrate is at the root of anti-Semitism (for the Jews have given the world so much, and trusted it so innocently to repay) and of many other deep prejudices, such as those of the third world against the developed countries, and those of the developed countries against the third world. Each part of the world feels but represses its sense of debt; since the debt is repressed, neither is capable of translating, and thus cancelling out, those debts in terms of each other. The fact that these ancient and sacrificial feelings are now symbolized by money and financial instruments, and concealed by the math of economics and the smokescreens of Marxist ideology, does not remove the sting of them.

As in the realm of economic value, so in the realm of spiritual value, the idea of nonlinear systems generating emergent forms of order can prove very illuminating. When, in the move away from traditional societies to the modern state, we abandoned the old religious and essentialistic notions of the soul, of beauty, virtue, higher values, honor, truth, salvation, the divine, and so on, we suffered a genuine loss. Indeed, the theoretical justification for those notions, an eternal, omniscient, and omnipotent God, may have been philosophically and politically untenable. Perhaps now we can refound some of those beautiful notions upon a new–old basis. The strange attractor of a chaotic system can look very like an Ideal Form: though any instance of the outcome of such a system at work is only partial and apparently random, when we see all instances of it, we begin to make out a beautiful, if incomplete and fuzzy shape. If memories are stored as attractors of Hebb circuits, might not virtues, ethics, values, and even in a way spiritual beings be stored so too? And might there be larger systems still, including many brains and the interactions of all of nature, that would have attractors not unlike the gods of our old religions?

Thus the new nonlinear science tends on many levels to refute the existing order–disorder dualism of the avant-garde, and to break the connection between order and determinism. It lends unexpected support to many traditional ways of looking at the world, though it has replaced eternal essences with dynamic attractors.

Dissolving the Nature–Culture Dualism: A Natural Theology

The flight to the aleatory, fragmentary, deconstructed, and random in the arts was an extreme outgrowth of that tradition in the humanities which sought independence from a nineteenth-century natural-science view of the world as deterministic, ordered, and unfree. That tradition had originated in Kant, who accepted the Newtonian account of nature as the realm of necessity, while positing a cultural realm within which ethical freedom and beauty could exist, but only in isolation from natural motivations and constraints. As our own century wore on, other approaches to the paradoxes of nature and culture began to emerge. One of them was that it is human *culture* that is deadeningly ordered, and *nature* that is free and wild. Using another idea rooted in Kant—that the "thing in itself" was inaccessible, and all we could know would be our own categories of perception—the findings of natural science could be dismissed as the constructions of a technocratic power elite; nature itself might remain a mystery, unapproachable by the killing analysis of science. Another approach was more radical still: that nature is ordered and harmonious, and culture is free and destructive; that there exists a wise and modest ecological science informed by feminist and traditional ethnic perspectives, opposed to the disordered white male death-forces of chemistry, physics, and engineering; and that we human beings must accept restrictions on our freedom if nature is to survive. Out of these reversals of the traditional dualism came the radical environmental movement.

The villain of the radical utopian environmentalists was technology. Those who had arrived at the position out of a Rousseauvian nostalgia for a state of nature condemned technology as the instrument of our Fall. Those who came to it from traditional conservative origins saw technology as the breaker of old lines of authority. Those whose origins were in the Old Left disliked technology as the arena in which capitalism had triumphed over socialism. But if technology was our chief means of doing and knowing, then to save nature was to bind and blindfold human beings—surely a counsel of despair. If humanity were synonymous with technological progress—and archaeology showed such progress even in our most archaic stages of development—then the trouble with nature is nothing more nor less than human beings, and the sooner they are obliterated from the face of the earth, the better. Nuclear war did not seem so bad; it was only the threat of nuclear winter, and the ecological changes it would bring, that fully cemented the environmental and peace movements together. Some contemporary environmental radicals have welcomed AIDS as nature's way of redressing the ecological balance. The net effect of this line of thought was that we should despair of humanity and human activity.

I propose to analyse the environmental ethics that underwrite this despair, and to disentangle from the despair-complex the wholesome and hopeful elements of environmentalism. To do this it will be necessary to replace the current ecological philosophy with one which offers grounds for hope as well as an activist role for human beings in the protection and promotion of the beautiful natural world of which we are so remarkable a part. Let us begin by a close examination of the assumptions of contemporary radical environmentalism.

If asked to state the goal of the environmental movement, a participant in it would probably say something like: "to promote a sustainable relationship between human beings and nature." How could anyone possibly object to such a formulation? Yet hidden in it is a set of assumptions that may paradoxically lie at the root of our present environmental crisis. There is a close resemblance between this stated goal and a much older idea from the rationalistic theology of the modern West: that the goal of the moral life is to promote a sustainable relationship between human beings and God.

The environmentalist ethic has in effect replaced God with nature; and the God it replaced was the God of modern theism, the abstract, unchanging, emotionless, moralistic authority who dwells outside the universe and who, knowing all in advance, can never be surprised, or grow, or have a story. Very often the environmentalist's idea of nature retains many of these characteristics. As the phrase goes, "It's not nice to fool Mother Nature." Many contemporary environmentalists would probably accept without much question a set of assumptions that are essentially religious. They would include the following—what we might call the unspoken principles of the ecological religion:

- That the essential feature of Nature is homeostasis: that is, there is a natural balance that is restored when it is disturbed, and a natural harmony. Nature in this view has an ideal state, which is perfect and should not be tampered with.

- That happiness is doing the will of Nature. Human beings are evil and distorted creatures, filled with greed and the desire to dominate, an unnatural presence in the universe. However, if they are converted, then they will find true happiness in humble service to the ecology. (This feature of the environmental movement is much like the doctrine of original sin and salvation.)

- That happiness for human beings is essentially stasis, an unchanging and secure state in which the future is more or less predictable. Change, especially swift change, is evil.

- That human beings are different and separate from, and subordinate to, a transcendent Nature. Here the environmentalist religion ignores the central scientific principle of evolution, which treats human beings as a part of nature. However, environmentalism is quite happy to use scientific research if it seems to prove the point of human wickedness.

- That human beings are no better and no more important than any other species (thus the Christian doctrine of the equality of souls before God has been translated into a doctrine of the equality of species before Nature). In a sense, this principle contradicts the previous one, in which human beings are uniquely wicked among species, and separate from Nature. The contradiction can be partly resolved by saying that in a state of nature, human beings are just another animal species; where we went wrong, where we "fell," was in thinking ourselves better than the others. But the problem remains: why shouldn't it be natural for us to think ourselves better, and why shouldn't it be true?

- That an (unelected) community of environmentally conscious, morally refined, sober, devout, humble and self-denying ecological brahmins should interpret to the masses the will of Nature and direct them accordingly, chastising the merchant/industrial caste, humbling the warrior caste, and disciplining the farmer caste.

This creed stands or falls on whether Nature really is as its believers maintain—eternal, unchanging, and so on—and whether human beings are indeed as the theory says they are. As far as I can make out, there are four main problems with what I call the "Ecotheist" creed.

The first problem is that nature is not and has never been static and unchanging. It is easy to demonstrate that nature is a process of irreversible changes at every level of the microcosm and the macrocosm, both in the living world and in the world in general. Among living organisms, the number of species has pretty steadily increased, with occasional episodes of mass extinctions, from the origin of life about four billion years ago until now. One of those mass extinctions was at the Cretaceous/Tertiary boundary, when it is thought a giant meteorite hit the earth near the coast of Yucatan. This cataclysm, swifter and more devastating than any human effect on the environment, actually resulted in the rise of many more species, such as the mammals, and in the long run an enrichment of the ecosystem. It is not just the number of species that has increased over the lifetime of this planet; so also has the complexity, hierarchical organization, and neural development of the most highly organized species. Though many very primitive and simple species still exist, there is a much greater range of development among species than existed in the past. Thus the Ecotheist principle that nature is essentially homeostatic is false for living creatures.

It is false also for the inanimate parts of nature. In the universe at large, there has been a steady and irreversible increase in several crucial measures. They include its size (it has been expanding since the Big Bang), and its age. The thermodynamic entropy of the universe has increased: that is, energy has distributed itself into smaller and smaller packets, with less and less difference between them. The complexity, sensitivity, and degree of freedom of even inanimate objects has increased: the definition of time required to describe a photon (which preexisted all the more complex forms of matter) is much simpler than that required to describe an atom, a molecule, or a crystal, which successively appeared later. The amount of feedback or self-reference in the universe has increased irreversibly, as has the amount of information in the universe. The universe has cooled down irreversibly and will continue to do so. Even the *rate* of all these changes has been changing irreversibly; some of them also unpredictably.

Parts of nature do not, indeed, change very much; but they are the least alive parts, neutrinos for instance. Other parts of nature are governed by negative feedback loops which are cyclical and homeostatic, and if permitted to do so restore their balance when they are disturbed, like a thermostat regulating the temperature of a house. Other parts, however, are involved in positive feedback processes that are irreversible, catastrophic to their predecessors, and often wildly original and creative. If one puts a live microphone in front of the loudspeaker, any small sound can be magnified by positive feedback into an uncontrolled shriek. Nature does not avoid such situations: they can be found in the sudden crystallization of a freeze, in the wild multiplication of bacteria in a dead animal, in the recolonization of volcanic wastelands, and in the famous "butterfly effect," whereby the turbulence caused by a butterfly's wingbeat can, in the right humid circumstances, be amplified into a whirlwind, a tropical storm, and finally a hurricane.

Life especially is full of such processes; collectively they are called evolution. The air of the earth itself was the result of catastrophic changes brought about by the evolution of photosynthetic organisms, which gradually "poisoned" the early terrestrial atmosphere with oxygen so that most of the ancient prokaryotic inhabitants of the planet could no longer survive and had to give up their places to new, more adaptable eukaryotic organisms that were their descendants and our ancestors. The natural disasters which have punctuated the Earth's history, whether the result of gigantic volcanoes or meteor strikes, may well have speeded up the process of evolution. It is entirely possible that the increase in carbon dioxide in our atmosphere will cause an increase in plant metabolism and world precipitation, and lead to an age of unparalleled natural fertility and species proliferation, rather than to an age of ecological catastrophe. It is only the faulty assumption that any change is unnatural that makes us assume that the greenhouse effect will be bad for the planet.

Thus the idea of "sustainability" and general homeostasis is a profoundly unnatural goal. The universe does not, except in certain temporary periods and places, sustain or maintain: it changes, improves, complexifies. Sexual reproduction, to take a good example, consists of a sophisticated and powerful mechanism to ensure that the genetic inheritance of a species changes irreversibly: it is a system to subvert and disrupt sustainability and maintainability. Organisms that clone themselves, and play it safe, are opting for sustainability; but it is the more advanced sexually reproducing organisms, which allow their genetic codes to be reshuffled every generation, that have driven evolution. We human beings may still strive after the security of sustainability: but we should not invoke the authority of Nature to do so. The philosophical error of assuming that nature is essentially unchanging has led to actual damage to ecosystems managed by well-meaning believers in natural homeostasis. The ecological scientist Daniel Botkin cites many examples, including the reduction of huge fertile nature preserves in Africa to semideserts because environmentalist true believers could not face the necessity to cull the exploding elephant population. Another example is the way in which various different but equally erroneous notions of natural balance led to the recent destruction of large areas of the Yellowstone National Park, errors well documented in a recent collection of essays edited by John Baden. Wiser managers of prairie preserves in the Midwest have learned that a good prairie needs to be burned from time to time; fire, the destructive element, must be wielded by human beings if we would keep nature in the same state. A similar philosophical puzzle confronts the managers of Niagara Falls, who may need to turn the falls off for a time, while the natural undermining of the rocky scarp over which it flows is repaired with concrete!

There now exists a more sophisticated version of the environmentalist position, which abandons the usual praise of natural homeostasis and asserts that it is only in the wild, the wilderness areas, that Nature can find its true freedom to evolve and develop, in its naturally irreversible and unpredictable way. This argument reverses the usual complaint against human culture, that it changes things too fast, and asserts that human culture by taming and domesticating Nature robs it of its creative powers of metamorphosis. This is a serious and interesting argument, and clearly holds some truth that should be incorporated into the wiser environmentalism that is our goal. But the position shows a limited imagination. For is not the disturbing, horrifying, unpredictable, dangerous, and protean character of human culture and technology (like Max in Maurice Sendak's fable "Where the Wild Things Are") the wildest thing of all, the true wilderness that lies beyond the edge of the tamer, more serene and self-maintaining fields of the terrestrial ecology? Is not human culture, as compared to the rest of nature, like a sexually reproducing species as compared to a surrounding ecology of clones?

This reflection leads us to the second major objection to the Ecotheist creed. That is, that the distinction it draws between the human and the natural is patently false. We are descended in a direct evolutionary line from natural animal species, and are ourselves a natural species. Our nature, certainly optimistic, transformative, activist, and bent on propagating itself, is not unlike that of other species, only more so. We are what nature has always been trying to be, so to speak. Nor can it be objected that it is the *speed* at which we transform ourselves and the world around us that is unnatural. Higher animals evolve faster than more primitive organisms, just as they in turn do so faster than nonliving systems. If we take flexibility, complexity, hierarchical organization, and self-referentiality as the measure, we may define nature as acceleration itself. For us to slow down would, if we take nature *to date* as the model of what is natural, be a unnatural thing to do.

Not that I am necessarily advocating a continuous indiscriminate acceleration of our activities; but any moratorium we call cannot honestly be claimed to be in the name of nature. Nor am I denying the human fact of evil actions, both against other human beings and against the rest of nature. In the old religion which serves as the tacit model for some aspects of current environmentalism, that evil was explained by the Fall. But in that old religion there was also a wisdom which called the Fall a *felix culpa*, a happy fault. The good of knowledge, freedom, and the possibility of divine redemption came with the darker lapsarian consequences of death, guilt, and the propensity to sin. My claim is that nature itself, like ourselves, is fallen, is falling, and has always been falling, outward into the future from the initial explosion of the Big Bang; onward into more and more conscious, beautiful, tragic, complex, and conflicted forms of existence, away from the divine simplicities and stupor of the primal energy field.

Thus for good and ill we are in solidarity with the rest of nature; and thus though there may be a vaguely good moral intention to the injunction that humankind should live in harmony with nature, the idea is essentially incoherent. Perhaps one might take it as a slightly stretched metaphor, as one's doctor might advise one to live in harmony with one's kidney or liver, or that our brain should live in harmony with our body. But the brain *is* the body, the body *is* the brain. Muscle and internal organ cells are like neurons in their irritability, capacity to pass on information, susceptibility to habituation, and connection with the rest of the body. Neurons, though more refined and indispensable, evolved out of cell populations in the fetus originally indistinguishable from skin tissue. The same identity-in-difference obtains for human beings vis-à-vis the rest of nature.

The third objection is to species equality. One of the fundamental principles of nature is hierarchy: the food chain, the delegation of control down the nervous system, and the branched subordination of functions within a given living organism amply illustrate the principle. Though interdependence is indeed another basic principle of nature, it does not imply equality. The brain and the kidney are interdependent, but medical ethics would rightly insist that the kidney is subordinate to and less valuable than the brain. Any surgeon would rightly sacrifice a kidney to save a much smaller volume of brain tissue. It should not really be necessary to argue whether a human being or an AIDS virus is more valuable, but we are forced to such measures by the assertions of some of the more extreme Deep Ecologists. These latter question our right to consider ourselves more important and valuable than other species, and thus to affect their destiny. This point looks reasonable if we think about whales, bears, and other animals with whom it is easy to identify. But it leads to deep absurdities. Is a bear committing an ecological crime by scratching itself, and so killing several million of its own skin cells which have just as much right to exist as the bear itself? Why indeed should such theorists of universal species equality draw the line at living organisms? Are they not guilty of vitalist chauvinism, in not giving equal rights to crystals, clumps of amorphous matter, atoms, photons? To be consistent with the doctrine of equality, we should not consider energy any less valuable than matter. Since energy is often locked up in matter, should we not "liberate" the billions of photons tyranically imprisoned in the matter of the Earth, by blowing it up with nuclear bombs? The equality argument is plainly absurd.

The final objection to the Ecotheist creed is political. Any attempt by an ecological elite to impose brahminical control over the masses—over the merchant, warrior, and farmer castes—is doomed to failure. In Eastern Europe the Communist party was just such an enlightened and refined elite, and indeed, as we are finding, it did help to keep down such atavistic tendencies as ethnic hatred. But all over the world those masses have sacrificed themselves, suffered, and died, to escape or overthrow this new form of priestly control. Moreover, the best-intentioned brahminical bureaucracy can be ecologically disastrous. Even the very mild forms of state control over natural resources that we have instituted can, especially when energized by ideology and the urge toward bureaucratic survival, paradoxically produce serious ecological damage, as John Baden points out in the case of the Forest Service and the public rangelands. There are more miles of Forest Service roads (which determine the Service's budget) than interstate highways.

It is a utopian axiom that human beings are happiest when in harmony with an unchanging natural world. But it is surely naive to assume that human happiness can consist in stasis and obedience. Elementary psychology tells us that we are sensation-seeking animals, and that our brains work upon a principle of habituation and fatigue; if we encounter the same stimulus for a period of time (say, a ticking clock), we very quickly discount it and cease to notice it. It is our nature, and the nature of many higher animals, to seek out new stimuli. Stasis is thus sensory deprivation, which is a subtle and severe form of torture. Human happiness cannot reside in lack of change. It used to be thought that so-called primitive tribal societies lived in an unchanging and harmonious state of peace, without history; but a wiser anthropology has shown us that this view is in error. Such societies do change spontaneously every generation, in their rituals, beliefs, fashions, even in their kinship system. My father, the anthropologist Victor Turner, could not at first understand why the Ndembu people of Central Africa would laugh when he asked about their clan system. This kinship system had been recorded by an earlier anthropologist, Charlie White, forty years before, as being the key to Ndembu society. It turned out that the Ndembu had changed to a different kinship system twenty years before, and the clan was as obsolete as a Victorian shovel hat. Why had they changed? Boredom.

So to sum up, the formula "a sustainable relationship between human beings and Nature" is profoundly misleading. Nature does not sustain, but changes cumulatively, sometimes preserving earlier states of itself while inventing new ones, and integrating old and new together in a more reflexive and self-observing way than before. There is no "between" the human and the natural, unless there can be a special relationship, not between one thing and another, but between the most characteristic and quintessential part of a whole, and the whole of which it is the privileged part, privileged because it is the most developed product of its own evolutionary process. Human is to natural as brain is to body. Human beings are not equal to, but superior to, other species. The complete injunction to the sustainable relationship as formulated is politically impossible to enforce and often counterproductive when an attempt is made to enforce it.

Nevertheless the formula was an attempt in good faith to find a story to tell ourselves about postmodernity that could provide a new sense of purpose. We have indeed seen that this position is flawed. It is thus incumbent on us to provide a better story; the story I will tell about Gaia will be the first of several new myths, which together will provide the emergent shape of a new constellation of hope.

There is a residual wisdom in the call for the sustainable relationship between humans and nature. It might be worth our while to try to reformulate and rescue this goal, by providing for it a sounder philosophical (and theological) basis. If contemporary environmentalism is a new religion based upon a faulty idea of nature, how would it differ if we corrected its errors? What would a religion faithful to natural science look like? It may seem odd to cut our theology to fit our environmental ethics, but let us, in a playful spirit, do so anyway. Perhaps afterwards we can see whether the result makes sense philosophically and morally, and discover if it has any significant continuity with the best of our religious traditions.

James Lovelock's Gaia Hypothesis, which argues plausibly that in some sense the planet Earth is a sort of super-organism, perhaps like a giant polyp or colonial animal or coral reef, maintaining its own atmosphere, climate, and chemical environment, has supplied its more religious followers with a personal name for a new deity: Gaia. Let us begin by following the Gaia Hypothesis in its theological implication that the divine is present within the world, not detached from it. This is not necessarily to adopt a pantheist position, that is, that the world *is* God. If, by analogy, we assert that the mind and soul are present in a brain and body rather than detachable from them, we are not committed to believing that the mind and soul are only the brain and body. Thus the first axiom of a natural theology would be: THE DIVINE IS IN NATURE.

If, then, the divine, and let us call her "Gaia," is *in* nature, how might we discover the nature of the divine? Surely by examining and listening to nature itself, just as we find out about a man's or woman's personality by examining what they physically do and listening to what they physically say. That is, we should pay attention to the process, the *story*, of nature, if we wish to know its divine soul. Nature, as we have already seen, includes us as its acme and quintessence; so we must look especially at ourselves, the most characteristic part of Gaia's natural body. The way we find out, the process of knowing, the attempt to come to know the story of things, is called science. Thus our second axiom might be: WE KNOW GAIA BY MEANS OF THE SCIENTIFIC UNDERSTANDING OF NATURE AND OURSELVES.

A story is an irreversible process of events that are unpredictable beforehand but apparently inevitable and obvious once they have happened. If you are reading a good novel, the pleasure is partly that the next twist in the story cannot be predicted—which is why you want to see how it came out, whether the butler did it, for instance. Of course, afterwards there must be a good explanation; we should be able to say

"Why didn't I see it? The answer was obvious." Obvious afterwards, but not before. The very possibility of story implies that time is essentially asymmetrical, that truth can be a different thing prospectively than retrospectively. There are fixed truths, like the laws of gravitation and thermodynamics, or we would have no points of reference by which to know. But the newly emergent truths include most of what we consider valuable, good, and beautiful: all the exquisite forms of matter, life, and mind, that have evolved over the history of the universe. If nature has *no* story, then we can conclude that the divine being is indeed fixed and eternal, forever unsurprised and undisturbed. If nature has a story (or many stories) as it most manifestly and emphatically has, then we must conclude that the divine being has one too. Thus the third axiom of our natural theology would be: GAIA CHANGES; GAIA HAS A STORY.

If we examine nature and ourselves we discover that there are underlying unchanging unities beneath the variety of things—the mathematical forms, the constants of physics—but also that nature is an evolutionary drama, a competitive/cooperative dialogue among its parts, species, levels, and principles. Thus if nature is the body of the the divine, we may infer a fourth axiom: GAIA IS BOTH ONE AND MANY. She is one in her most remote, abstract, timeless, impersonal, simpleminded, and passive aspects, and many in her most immediate, concrete, changing, personal, intelligent, and active aspects. In deference to our own monotheistic tradition I refer to the divine as one, but it should be understood that the polytheistic and pluralist description of the divine as "the gods" is also intellectually attractive.

The transformations of this natural god of change are not exclusively random, reversible, and meaningless. As we have seen, the evolution of the universe is progressive, irrevocable, and dramatically meaningful. There is a one-way process of increasing feedback, reflexivity, self-organization, and freedom as the world evolves. Elementary particles have polarity but no shape. Atoms, more complex and self-referential than particles, have simple geometrical shapes that are symmetrical in many dimensions and asymmetrical only in the difference between center and periphery. With molecules (which could not exist until the universe had cooled enough to permit them) we see the first fully asymmetrical shapes and the birth of individuality. Molecules have complex feedback systems, many degrees of freedom, and the capacity to organize in periodic structures such as crystals. Living organisms are yet more asymmetrical, free, and capable of organization, and they contain a recording of their own structure in the DNA language. Mind continues this story into the most complex forms of consciousness, self-determination, and communication. Thus the fifth axiom: THE STORY OF GAIA IS ONE OF INCREASING INDIVIDUALITY, MEANING, AND FREEDOM. Progress is not a human invention, but a divine one.

If the universe is Gaia's body, then we—and by "we" I mean all the intelligent species in the universe—are the most sensitive, most aware, most self-organizing of its parts. Though we are not the whole, we are that which increasingly has some knowledge of and control over the whole. The most sensitive and aware and controlling parts of a living body are its nervous system. Thus the sixth axiom: WE ARE THE NERVOUS SYSTEM OF GAIA.

This nervous system is still very rudimentary and has penetrated and innervated only a tiny portion of the universe to date. It is like the nervous system of an unborn child. We stand at the first trembling moment of the history of the universe, the flash of a dawn which is a mere twelve billion years old, the dawn of a ten-trillion-year day. The universe is still only in its gestation; it not yet fully developed. It is partly up to us to complete that development, to increase the awareness and control we have over the rest of the universe, to extend the nerves of science and art into the inanimate and insentient parts of the world. Thus a seventh axiom: GAIA IS STILL ONLY A FETUS. Nature has not died, as some recent commentators have complained. It is only now awakening, and we are its eyes, its ears, and its tongue. From this follows an eighth axiom: WE SERVE GAIA BY HELPING HER TOWARD GREATER SELF-AWARENESS.

As organisms evolve, they develop more and more complex chemical, electrical, and mechanical systems, known as bodies, in order to control and be controlled by their environment, to act, and to sense. All bodies are prostheses; the matter of which they are made is not at first part of the living organism itself, but pressed artificially into service by that organism. For instance, the carbon atoms that my body uses to construct its protein and enzyme factories are exactly the same as they were before I commandeered them by eating them in my asparagus. Likewise, the coat of tiny sticks and bits of gravel that a caddis worm constructs for itself is part of its body, though in itself not strictly alive. The body of a termite colony includes its nest, that marvelously air-conditioned residence containing nurseries, storehouses, factories, and farms. The nest of the male blue satin bowerbird is not even used as a nest at all, but as a communication device to persuade a female bowerbird to mate, a piece of advertising. Yet in a strong sense that nest is part of its body. Plants and animals use probes, crutches, shelters, tools, vehicles, weapons, and other prostheses that do not need to be directly connected to their flesh or nerves, but which are essential parts of their bodies. All living organisms use tools at the atomic and molecular level, even the crudest microorganisms. The more advanced an organism is, the larger and more organized in themselves are the outside structures that it is able to use and transform into its synthetic body.

Artificial systems of investigation, control, and communication, as these are, have a name: technology. The body of a living organism is its technology; the technology of an organism is its body. Our life is, after all, only the pattern of information spelled out in our genes, a pattern which survives any given atom in our bodies, except for the ones we have not yet metabolized at our death. Our own technology is an extension of our bodies; but our bodies are nothing more than such cumulative extensions. Biological evolution, and arguably even pre-biological evolution, are in this sense precisely the increase in the complexity and power of technology. Nature is technology, then. Thus if nature is the body of Gaia, then we may formulate a ninth surprising axiom: GAIA IS THE PROCESS OF INCREASING TECHNOLOGY.

If our moral function is to serve Gaia, then it is to help Gaia change from a fetus into a fully developed being, to realize her future growth and self-awareness. The way to do this is to continue to innervate the universe by knowledge and control, and thus to extend our own bodies, the region of our own technology, throughout the universe. Thus the tenth axiom: TO SERVE GAIA IS TO INCREASE THE SCOPE, POWER, BEAUTY AND DEPTH OF TECHNOLOGY.

Our logic has brought us therefore to an astonishing and perhaps shocking conclusion, utterly at odds with the prevailing mood of our culture. How can we redeem this statement, and make it fit what we feel about our role in the world? The answer must be that we need a thorough reevaluation of what technology is and what we mean when we use the term. We know there is such a thing as bad technology; but the theological implications we have discovered make it essential that we define what is good technology, because without good technology, we cannot adequately serve God, if God is conceived of as being within nature. It will no longer be sufficient for us to attempt to get away from or to dissolve our technology; to do so, if it were even possible, would be to deny our divine duty and to commit a sin against the holy spirit. However, our investigation of what is good technology may have the virtue of clarifying what is bad technology, bad service of God, and thus constitute a powerful if gentle critique of society. The specifications for good technology that we discover may not be so different from the specifications of good art.

Thus if we dissolve the environmentalist dualism between the human and the natural, as we have already dissolved the dualism between order and disorder, we will find that we need no longer abhor the very means of our liberation—that is, our technology. And at the same time new grounds for a responsible and supportive criticism of technology unexpectedly appear. But if human beings really are a part of nature, then we must possess a nature. "Human nature" has been dismissed by the avant-garde as an authoritarian mystification designed to keep us all in line. To this problem we now turn.

Dissolving the Human–Animal Dualism: Moral Animals

When we encounter the word "nature" we think of trees and meadows and mountains and flowers, with distant wildlife, perhaps; the view is essentially green, and not like us at all. But there are parts of nature that are very like us indeed, uncomfortably so, because they remind us that we, too, might have a nature of our own. They are the animals. They breathe, perceive, move voluntarily, have limbs and a body plan we can recognize from introspection, and seem to think and feel in ways not unlike ours. If we have a nature, as we have seen, our whole fanatically maintained superstructure of social constructionist theory begins to crumble.

At present two utterly opposed conceptions of the nature of nonhuman animals are on a collision course. The irony is that they both arose out of the same liberal avant-garde "anti-establishment" ideology: some of us followed one of the tracks, some of us the other. The majority, unable for reasons of psychological comfort to see contradiction unless it is pointed out, somehow contrived to believe both, with different parts of the mind. One conception maintains that animals are automata. The other insists that they are "persons" with the same rights as ourselves (or even with superior rights)—but that they are the victims of human domination and cruelty. Both views maintain with intemperate vehemence that we cannot share animals' inner experience. Yet the common sense of millions of pet owners, farmers, scientific naturalists, animal trainers, and ordinary observers of nature seems to suggest that we can know very well and empathize with the thoughts and feelings of many of the higher animals at least, but that other animals are lesser beings than humans. This ordinary common sense denies both positions—that animals are automata, and that animals are born, as humans are, with rights. Both of these positions lead to despair, as I shall show.

The first proposition—that animals are automata—evolved from the great value placed on freedom, in the sense of being able to do what you want. The university was, according to this position, the institution best designed to foster freedom from social, economic, and sexual restraints. The raison d'être of the university is that people can be changed by educating them. Society would not pay for the university if this were not the case. The universities therefore taught that human behavior is learned rather than inherited. Behaviorism was the technical system that explained animal behavior and human psychology; sociology interpreted this account in terms of inescapable social and economic determinants of human behavior; and the Sapir-Whorf hypothesis that language determines how we see things, offered support in linguistics. Thus reality is a construct of sociolinguistic conditioning. If so, then nature is either completely incoherent and susceptible to cultural and political construction, or is in itself, *an sich*, unknowable, and we might as well accept the most politically correct language game to describe nature, since the truth is inaccessible. This would mean that the animals, which are part of nature, cannot be epistemologically determining our reality (or else our freedom would be impinged upon). They must either be passive and unintelligible, though susceptible to human technical and linguistic manipulation, or they must be automata, subject to mechanical determinism or to the cultural logic of linguistic structures (unlike human beings, whose freedom must be random and whimsical). The oppressive power structure has restricted us in the past by natural law, asserting that biology is destiny; we are not animals, but persons. Thus animals, like fetuses, cannot be persons, but must be automata.

There is an emotional component in the automaton theory of animals. In order to be independent adults, controlling our own bodies, we had to escape the authority, the mental habits, the smells and attachments and little loyalties and sentimentalities of home. Part of that home-complex was the family cat or dog, and the role it played as servant, loved inferior, intimate connection between family members, a link with nature and the world of necessity, and a reminder of our own nature as animals. Part of our liberation from home and family—and from our shameful origin in the act of sex between our parents, in the dear familiar smells of the bedroom—was the rejection of any sentimental tendency to anthropomorphize our domestic animals. So we revised our views. The moral motivations we had seen in our pets when we were children were replaced by half-digested notions of instinct, or by a belief in a world of smell, inaccessible to us, that determined their behavior; or else we refused to have pets at all, on the grounds that pethood was as demeaning to them as our own childhood was to us. We became embarrassed by our childhood books in which the animals talked. We named our animals "Kafka" or "Nixon"—names whose point was part of a closed human hermeneutic circle, and whose joke was partly that a name was of course meaningless to an animal anyway. Animals were automata, just part of a nature that is constructed by human will.

It should have come as no surprise, however—when we had so alienated ourselves from our family, from the other higher animals, from the smells and physicality and reminder of our own animal being, from the bonds of kinship and community that are mediated by domestic animals, and from the warmth and softness and relaxation they seem to promote—that our experience of society should have been one of alienation, hardness, coldness, and inhumanity. As dutiful educated thinkers we called for a rebirth of human community, a better relationship with nature, a reconnection with Being and an unmediated authenticity, when these goals were, so to speak, staring us in the face. But they come with certain bonds and strings and bloody sacrifices and moral constraints and undignified reminders of our own nature and contingency, which put them out of the question.

But we must bring them back into the question again, I believe. For if we persist in regarding animals as automata, we will collude in that artificial alienation from the rest of nature which is responsible both for our past crimes against the environment and for our present hysterical and counterproductive efforts to put them right. Both come from an absence of easy empathy with the rest of the world; and that empathy is normally mediated largely through our acquaintance with domestic and other higher animals.

The second line of argument about the nature of animals prevalent among the avant-garde is somewhat simpler. Again freedom is the great value; freedom means doing what you want. Liberation means liberation from social oppression. It is not enough to liberate the racially oppressed, if sexual or sexual-preference oppression remains. Every oppressed group must be liberated—old people, women, children—and we must be skeptical of every claim to superiority. In fact all claims to distinctions of value are suspect, part of the superstructure of hierarchical hegemony. Animals, too, have traditionally been considered inferior, just like women and nonwhites, but they have just as much claim to have rights as we; perhaps more, because they have not been corrupted by society, technology, and oppressive economic systems. Indeed, they are the ultimate victims of such systems, and true freedom will only happen when there are no longer any victims. The power structure always claimed that animals were not persons. The opposite must be true: they must be persons, with rights. If it is argued that they do not care about their rights, since they seem to accept their servitude, the clincher is: how do you know? How can we tell whether an animal is or is not feeling injustice? It used to be thought that racial others didn't feel pain, and that women couldn't make moral decisions. Who do we think we are, believing that we understand animals well enough to know how they feel? How can one person presume to understand the experience of another? After all, we are rightly angry when men try to appropriate the experience of women, which is uniquely theirs, and when whites appropriate the experience and unique culture of other races. Similarly, we should not arrogate to ourselves the right to know the feelings of animals. Animals are people; it is we, with our oppressive social systems, that are the automata.

When we treat animals as automata, we alienate ourselves from nature; but on the other hand, if we persist in seeing animals as victims, there is no way that we will ever be able to cease our "horrible crimes" against them. Even if we eat no more meat and free our pets, the only result would be a sharp decline in the numbers and well-being of those domestic species. We would still, by our very presence, be murdering millions of our fellow animals every day, not to speak of plants and bacteria. The mites I kill when I wash my face (one mite species lives only in human eyelashes) are animals too. If we abandon, as this line of reasoning requires us to, the idea of hierarchy that distinguishes human beings from other animals, we also abandon the principle that morally distinguishes between mites (and even malaria protozoa and herpes viruses) and harp seals, vervet monkeys, and cats and dogs.

Both lines of thought, then, the automaton and the victim, lead to despair; and there is a further cognitive despair implicit in the contradiction itself. The subtext of much of the behavior and opinion of the radical vegetarians and animal-rights activists is a dull, nagging rage against our consciousness, our powers of action and knowledge, our very humanity itself. Though these groups are still fairly small in number, the influence of their ideas is pervasive within the avant-garde. How may we find our way toward a more hopeful relationship with our fellow animals, and thus with our own animal nature?

One of the most original works of philosophy to have appeared in the last few years is Vicki Hearne's *Adam's Task*. Vicki Hearne is a professional animal trainer, a poet, and a philosopher, and her book has the wonderful ring of unexpected truth. Taken with an older book, Konrad Lorenz's *King Solomon's Ring*, and with the superb recent work that has been done by primate ethologists, sociobiologists, and the like, Hearne's book opens up what I take to be a great vista of hope for the twenty-first century. It suggests the renewal of a close relationship with the rest of nature. It reconciles the immemorial wisdom of the human race as animal husbandmen and breeders with new concepts and knowledge in biology; and, as I wish to show, it can lead to altogether new kinds of experiences and cultural developments. Hearne accepts on sophisticated philosophical grounds the everyday description of animals as subjective selves capable of limited but real moral decisions. This despised commonsense description of animals, though it is as yet unarticulated and without theoretical elaboration is, I believe, not only more or less correct, but full of the most delightful and unexpected hopes for the human future. G. K. Chesterton liked to say that popular misconceptions are usually right; and when the populace has intimate experience of a subject, as it does on some of the higher animals, this aphorism, so galling to academic experts, often holds.

The therapeutic use of animal pets in treating mental illness, cardiovascular disease, senility, and other human complaints is not, I believe, an isolated curiosity but a highly significant indicator. Friendship—I use the word without qualification—friendship with an animal can lower blood pressure, restore sensory and motor deficits in the aged, calm the autistic, and break the paralysis of the catatonic. It can help restore a human being's connection with the world, and has been used successfully in the rehabilitation of juvenile delinquents and the criminally insane. Anyone who owns a pet, especially a higher mammal, knows a kind of luminous goodness that can shine out of them. The goodness that shines out of a human being is greater, perhaps, but we often do not see it, and animal goodness can sensitize us to it in our own species. Domestic animals often have an astonishing sensitivity to human feelings, a tactful wisdom about our own psychic feedback systems that can gently admonish us from a self-destructive mood spiral or bad habit, and head us off from depression.

Vicki Hearne begins to show us why. What she maintains is that the fundamental component of communication between humans and other animals is moral—a moral agreement between the parties, a common recognition of moral ideals, and a mutual recognition as subjects. In this realm a well-trained dog, horse, or cat, which has been in a close relationship with its owner for a long period, is just as lucidly conscious as is a human being. Hearne points out tellingly that personhood is not primarily a matter of intelligence, whatever that is; the category of intelligence itself becomes less and less interesting. Our modernist pride in cleverness has blinded us to qualities of vision and insight, to which intelligence is merely the servant. As Hearne recounts, digger wasps are better than both dogs and human beings at retrieving hidden food, which makes them more intelligent in that particular respect. I recall an anecdote by a fruit fly scientist about a team of colleagues who had bred generation after generation of fruit flies for their intelligence at finding their way through a maze. Eventually it seemed they had created a super-race of fruit flies, which could beat any other group of flies through the maze in a fraction of their time. But then someone suggested they change the maze. The genius fruit flies all ran straight into the first unfamiliar corner. They were very intelligent, but only at that particular maze. The apes who have been taught American Sign Language are probably more "intelligent" than dogs, but they are not morally reliable, and so the communication between us and them is of an entirely lower kind. Hearne shows that with a truly noble dog or horse, or with almost any well-treated cat, the animal is quite capable, on some subject at which it is expert—tracking, jumping, even charm—of an authority that human beings can recognize and ought to defer to and obey. Such animals sometimes possess *more* moral clarity, and even subtlety, than a human being.

My family possessed a mixed Sheltie bitch called Lady, a bright and gentle dog who always had a quality of light and gaiety about her. Her only flaw was that she was incontinent and had to be kept outside. My interpretation of her incontinence was a subtle version of the automaton theory of animal psychology, with a dash of victim theory thrown in. I believed that when she was a puppy her previous owners had beaten her, and that she had used the canine submission gesture, of falling on her back and urinating, to try to avoid punishment. Because this gesture had been ineffective, she had become fixated in this respect at an infantile stage of behavior, and the stress of human company brought out this automatic propitiation reflex. For her, urinating in the house was a kind of comfort. This was my rather elaborate theory; but it was quite wrong. As time went by she would urinate every few minutes, and finally, though she was completely uncomplaining, it became clear she must be in pain. The vet found a huge tumor sitting on top of her bladder, inoperable by this time, and she was put to sleep.

The moral implications of this story (many of Hearne's are much better, but this one is my own) are very complex. First of all, I did have a real and personal relationship with Lady; if I had regarded her as just a biological machine, I might never have constructed a pseudo-Freudian theory about her behavior, and would have taken her to the mechanic, so to speak, to have the malfunction fixed. So my misunderstanding was not as crass as it might have been. In a way it was worse: I was treating her as a *psychic* automaton, and there was in my attitude to her a certain affectionate contempt, that as an animal she could not rise above her fixation. In some unspoken way I believe now that Lady was aware of this unjust and condescending opinion I had of her, and was wounded by it, though it did not diminish her love for me. Not that Lady knew Freud—but as we are already beginning to find, some animals have an extraordinary emotional intelligence, and emotions can be almost as complex and articulative of the world as propositions are. If I had believed my occasional intimation, that Lady was a moral and noble dog whose demonstrated loyalty and sense of rightness were unimpeachable, I might have worried more about her incontinence. She would ignore food, even when she was hungry, if there was a chance to play with one of her owners. But I dismissed such intimations as sentimental anthropomorphizing.

The irony is that my Freudian, automatizing theory was more really anthropomorphic, and more really sentimental, than the attribution of noble motivations would have been. I do not accept psychological weaknesses in myself as excuses for my own immoral behavior, though I do accept them in other human beings, as being preferable to moral condemnation. Perhaps I am wrong in this, and perhaps Lady has taught me something very deep about myself and about the nature of morality. It is now clear to me in retrospect, and a thousand nonverbal cues that I missed because of prejudice prove it to me, that Lady suffered the most terrible moral embarrassment about urinating in the house, and strained desperately against the painful pressure in her bladder in order to avoid doing so; and what made it worse was that my response was to dismiss her as a moral subject and make allowances for her as a dumb brute.

The skeptic might respond to such a story by asking how do we know that the moral explanation is the correct one? How do I know that I am not, out of guilt and the distress of loss, projecting human categories onto another species? The answer is that from a strictly scientific point of view we can only believe those hypotheses that best explain and predict the phenomena. Believing the psychic automatism theory, I failed to diagnose her tumor; if I had believed the moral autonomy theory, I would have correctly caught the problem while it was still operable. Of course if I had thought of her simply as a machine, I might also have caught it. But if I had really felt that way about her, I would either not have acquired a pet in the first place, or would have replaced her with a functioning unit (she was, after all, a mongrel, and not valuable) rather than pay for an expensive operation. Then again, had I done so I would have been a less healthy human being, if the medical reports on the therapeutic effects of pets are to be believed.

In any case, it is not clear whether it is the moral interpretation, or the psychic or mechanical automatism theories, that constitute the "human categories" which it is inappropriate to extend beyond our species. And this is the really exciting aspect of Hearne's ideas. Suppose that moral values are already, in an inarticulate form to be sure, inherent in nature even before we came along? Konrad Lorenz's studies of wolves and jackdaws would certainly suggest that this is the case. And suppose, even more radically in a sense, that though human moral values in their fully articulated state are not present in the rest of nature, nature is *ready* for them, that they really apply to nature in a way which is not arbitrary, and nature grows to accommodate them?

Here we encounter a problem that should give us pause: the articulated values that do apply to certain higher animals are of a particular kind, which is one of the reasons why modern consciousness has fled the intimacy of domestic animals and adopted the victim or automaton strategy. Animal morality, or the kind of human morality that applies to animals, has an old-fashioned, aristocratic, anecdotal, heroic, narrative feel to it; it subscribes to old ideas like service, sacrifice, personal responsibility, honor, loyalty, faithfulness, free will, transgression, sin, forgiveness, expiation, and above all, virtue. Hearne describes dogs that are like Spenserian heroes out of *The Faerie Queene*, and horses that are like Homeric visionaries. The wicked or depraved dogs and horses she tells of are evil and corrupt in ways that remind us of the absoluteness of Virtue by contrast. I do not believe that she is making it up: it is the way people think who deal intimately with animals, and I believe they ought to know. I have seen Africans and Chinese train their animals, and there is no difference. Indeed, when we train animals we seem to come closer to a common human morality; almost as when we make music, or metered poetry, all human beings find a shared deep structure.

These values are not the sociologically correct, "compassionate," "democratic," "liberated," "caring" values of the modern avant-garde. They teach the existence of proper authority and obedience to it; they exalt discipline and assert that inner discipline can grow from outer discipline; they insist on flawless courage and total honesty; they believe in the grandeur of love between unequals; they judge behavior according to admired ideals; they make few allowances for psychological weakness or social injustice; they are not ironic about respect and respectability, but require them as a necessary condition of existence; they are not attracted to the flowers of evil; they enjoin a total devotion to service; they know nothing of cultural relativism and situation ethics. If a dog or horse is a faithful retainer, a yeoman or thane or samurai who serves his master in the chase, in travel, and in battle, a cat is more like a loved court artist or singer or eunuch or jester, perhaps even a geisha, whose very charm lies in a certain unpredictability and independence.

Of course it can be rightly objected that the military and aristocratic virtues, when untempered by a healthy disrespect and skepticism, have sometimes made whole populations of obedient citizens into the tools of some masterful and evil dictator. Doglike devotion has its limitations. The point here is not to try to return to an imagined feudal paradise. Rather, it is to remind us that we do share with our animal friends certain values, better represented by the times of knighthood than today, and that without a judicious admixture of those values our lives can become dried out, trivial, and shoddy. We still find some of those virtues in the military, on the sports field, in the martial arts dojo; so they are not lost. It may be that they are a missing ingredient in our child-rearing practices, our governmental bureaucracy, our primary education system, and our universities. There has been a renewed interest in these virtues among some of the centrist artists.

If animals are persons to some extent, as this argument might imply, do we not become murderers and cannibals in our relations with them, just as surely as in the animal-as-victim scenario? Here we must discover a truly subtle moral move, one which, strangely enough, is also part of normal human common sense. What common sense maintains all over the world is that animals are, yes, persons to some extent, but inferior persons which, in a series of subtle gradations, it is more or less proper to kill and eat. The lines are drawn in different places; we have our sacred cows, our totem animals, our taboos on horsemeat or dogmeat or pork, our rituals of thanks or propitiation after the hunt or the slaughter. But the principle is that there is a hierarchy of permissible killings and eatings. The issue is not that all killing and eating is wrong, though some less wrong than others; rather that killing and eating is a sort of transaction, or exchange, or shameful act of sacrifice, and that there are rules of appropriateness, even a sort of economics, in how and when it is done. The casual eating of human flesh is abhorred in almost all human cultures;

but in some, cannibalism is permissible in the context of a great feast, a sacrifice to the gods, a divine victory, a funeral or an initiation, or when done by the emperor, the son of the sun, in his palace in the capital, wearing his regal garments. For many of us cannibalism is acceptable in extreme cases of need and survival. In most human cultures higher mammals are customarily eaten only in the context of feasts and celebrations; lower animals like fish and fowl in more homely repasts, and mollusks, arthropods, yeasts, and animal reproductive matter—milk, eggs, cheese—in baser collations. The pure mystic or the hermit eats only rice or roots and berries.

Perhaps we could argue that the wealth and technological sophistication of the modern world is such that we have come to ignore these gradations, and thus that there is a core of good-hearted sense in the anger and revulsion of vegetarians and radical environmentalists. When we have become sated with the convenience of eating steak and Chilean strawberries whenever we want, we may move back to a more graceful and truly organic way of eating. We may perhaps confine ourselves to eating the flesh of higher mammals—pork, beef—only when the grand and tragicomic poetry of holy days and celebrations and reunions justifies the sacrifice of a sentient being. Likewise, we may come to use only food that is in season (except on special festive occasions), growing some of what we eat, and matching our cuisine to the cultural connotations of the occasion—Christmas, Chinese New Year, Fasching, the celebration of Italian or French art, the performance of West African music. Thus we acknowledge the sacrifice of all other times to this time, the sacrifice of all other places to this place, and so hallow and celebrate the here and now. Already those of more wealth and leisure are moving in this direction. Such practices are likely also to be very good for our bodies, and our bodies are, as Blake said, that part of the soul that is perceptible to the senses five.

The point is, though, that the ideological vegetarian or radical environmentalist is just as careless of the delicate hierarchy of nature as is the thoughtless eater of everyday steak. To put it brutally, there *is* a calculus that can justify the sacrifice of a sentient being, and perhaps a graduation dinner or a funeral or a Thanksgiving is only properly celebrated by some such sacrifice. We already kill every day and in a thousand ways in order to live at all; the intentional slaughter and eating of a food animal is a healthy reminder of our holy impurity, of the great debt we owe the rest of the world for our existence, and our inescapable responsibility to live so nobly and so productively and so finely as to justify all those deaths. In fact to avoid the eating of meat altogether, unless the avoidance is for health reasons or as part of a religious ritual that already acknowledges our debt, is morally questionable, for it denies the special value of human beings, it deceives us that we can live a pure life, and it shirks the duties for which our carnivorousness is the payment. Human dignity requires blood, just as human love requires aggression. Without that dignity human life is nothing, and genocide and slavery are matters of indifference.

In other words, the eating of meat is not, as its critics maintain, necessarily an arrogant assertion of human superiority. Done in the proper spirit it is a humble acknowledgement of our roots in the rest of the physical universe, an admission of our fundamental impurity and debt, a celebration of the value of what we have sacrificed, and a promise to make the world better, more real, and more beautiful by our presence. Even hunting can be justified on these grounds, though it would seem to me that only the achievement of true art, as in fly-fishing, for instance, or the sacramental celebration of religious value, as in the Eskimo whale-hunt, or the pursuit of scientific knowledge, can justify the practice today when advanced technology makes food readily available. The argument that is usually made, that hunting is evil because the animal does not know what is going on, can be seen in this context as a version of the automaton/victim evasion. All wild species live in a world in which they prey on, and are preyed upon by, other species. They have bought into the system of eating and death as much as we have, and the true arrogance consists in thinking that they cannot in their own way know this fact. They are as prepared to suffer, as to do. All life is cannibalistic, with the exception of the most primitive plants and microorganisms; and if we abandon the artificial barrier between complex chemistry and organic metabolism, they are cannibals too. Let us accept and celebrate this condition, rather than blind ourselves to it.

There are far larger implications to the argument than a justification for eating meat. As we have seen, one of the key arguments of avant-garde cosmology is that reality is constructed by the language used to describe it. The philosophy and science of the last four hundred years have shown that to a certain extent human beings do indeed construct reality through language. The avant-garde found this idea so tempting that it made it an absolute, and ignored the possibility that the rest of reality was, at the same time, constructing us. In some spheres, such as the invention of the rules of a new game (or even in the choice of whether to observe a single photon as if it were a wave or a particle), human construction is dominant or even absolute; but in other circumstances, such as when a social constructionist jumps off the top of a tall building, his human construction is entirely outvoted by the mass of the planet and of his own body, and he must submit to rules not made by human beings and fall down, not up. Animals are part of the physical world and share its power to help construct such processes as gravitational attraction or chemical combination. But they also seem to share in our own capacity as subjects to invent rules for ourselves. If animals have a limited but real personhood, they are subjects, and as such play a major part in the construction of reality: less than the human part, but greater than the part played by plants, or inanimate matter.

A Moral Universe: The Branching Tree of Time

If we have a nature and are part of nature, what is the role of morality in such a universe? Suppose the universe were so constructed as to make morality as meaningful as it can possibly be. Suppose, to be more specific, moral action were efficacious and really changed the future. Moral action could not, for instance, be a mere test or charade to demonstrate our worthiness for salvation in a world which is already being taken care of by divine providence and does not require our efforts, as some Christian theology suggests. Nor could it be simply the predetermined result of an irresistible divine grace, as other Christian moralists aver, or of genetic predisposition or sociocultural conditioning, as biological determinists and social constructionists believe. Our actions would have to have at least a strong dash of pure free will in them, which would imply that another wholly plausible universe might come into being if we chose the opposite action from the one we actually took; and likewise, there should be no divine "safety net" of providential compensation to render nugatory the evil effects of our actions if we chose wrong. To be fair, also, there would have to be no evil demiurge to turn our good actions to ill either.

Certainly if the future is laid out like a single track before us, morality is something of a mockery. The universe must be open-ended to make human goodness mean anything. Such a universe might at first glance be a welcome one to those bold and energetic moral adventurers who welcome the opportunity to make a difference. But when we consider the weakness, foolishness, ignorance, shortsightedness, self-deception, wickedness, and sheer evolutionary recidivism of even the best of us, the picture does not look too bright. We need all the help we can get; providence, if it existed, might barely level the odds against us.

In fact morality can be meaningless in another sense too: if there is nothing to tell us what is right or wrong before we go ahead and do it, we really aren't free at all, since we have not had a chance to see how things turn out. James Hans makes this point powerfully, following Milan Kundera's insight in *The Unbearable Lightness of Being*: that one chance is no chances. We cannot rehearse our lives beforehand, and therefore are not really responsible for them. The danger of having only one chance is that, in the absence of a signal from the future to tell us whether we will have done the right thing or not, we are at liberty to imagine any justifying outcome of our actions that our self-interest or will to power or vanity suggests. True freedom, paradoxically, requires us to have a guide or adviser in our actions. After all, nobody in ancient Greece or ancient China or the old slave states of Africa and pre-Columbian America could have imagined that the then eminently moral condition of slavery might some day be considered evil, or that unlimited sexual permissiveness, "free love," might some day be considered good. Huck Finn has to defy his conscience when he decides not to turn in the runaway slave, Jim, to his lawful owners. Perhaps in the future our assumption that children belong to their parents will be thought of as an abomination as evil as slavery; perhaps, on the other hand, we may one day come to believe in a religion in which Pain, as in David Lindsay's theology, is the highest good and the sign of the divine. What if I, now, were to act as if these changes were coming? Would I be a visionary or a monster? This is the problem with Nietzsche's notion of the transvaluation of values. Dostoyevsky's Raskolnikov believes that great actions can retroactively change the morality by which they are judged; there were Nazis who claimed, and no doubt believed, that the elimination of European Jewry was indeed horrible by contemporary standards but that it would be justified one day in retrospect.

In order for us to be morally free we must have wise guides who can advise us: but the very presence of those wise guides seems to compromise our freedom, since if we do the wrong thing they will surely be able to put it right. The future has to be open in order for us to be able to affect it; yet if there is no assurance of some kind of justice, no ratification of our noblest choices, no friendly welcome and recognition in that rarefied air at the very edge of all we have been, where we must make our most important decisions, then we might well make the wrong choice, believing it to be right.

One way of putting this problem is in terms of a pair of ideas that originated in Talmudic studies: the prophetic and the apocalyptic. In some form this apparently irreconcilable dichotomy exists in all religious and secular ethical traditions. Should we work for a better future or save our souls? Redeem the World or reject it? Love the things of time as God does or cleanse oneself of the temporal? Hope for posterity or the afterlife? Should we be active or contemplative? Is this life the only arena of spiritual action or only a preparation for another? Should we, as Yeats puts it, seek out perfection of the work or of the life? The issue is present in the Analects of Confucius, in the *Bhagavadgita*, in the Bible, and in the Koran. Among secular atheists it can be heard loud and clear in the contradictions between the Marxists, who believe in praxis and work for the future, and the existentialists and their descendants, who believe in the total immersion in immediate experience, authenticated by the imminence of death.

The question boils down to whether we look horizontally forward to the future as the justification for our actions, or whether we look vertically, so to speak, up to eternity or down into the depth of immediate experience, as the source of validation. If we look to the future we subject ourselves to a contingency of outcome that makes any action seem irresponsible. If we look to the eternities of heaven or existential experience we seem to abdicate our responsibility, giving it over to some all-wise Father or, in the case of the existentialists, put an utterly unwarranted trust in the wisdom of the senses and feelings, and of phenomena in general. The result of this impasse has been a kind of moral paralysis in the face of the horrifying experiments of this century, an attempt to do everything by majority vote, a proliferation of unenforceable rights, a resort to obsessive legalism, and a loss of the chief quality in human beings that gives them dignity: their sense of creative agency.

How might this problem be resolved? Or better, can it be reframed into a fertile paradox or perhaps a recursive and generative concept of its own? Suppose there were some way in which the future could influence and inform its past, including our present: we would then be able to get a look at the consequences of our actions, perhaps not in any detail, but with enough of a moral and esthetic "feel" so that our most imponderable choices would have some guidance. We would, of course, be free to cooperate with that guidance or to reject it, as with some of the ingenious and rather neglected theories of Christian grace. But our actions would not be totally unrehearsed. Thus the visitations that so many have experienced and reported, that we seek feebly to explain by psychological theorizing—the angels or muses or kamis or shamanic spirits or genii, the presences in Yeats's poem that passion, piety, or affection knows—might be our descendants, our future. They would come to us in our distress of spirit and gently advise us which way to go. Nor would we be the passive recipients of their wisdom, the helpless participants in a great plan over which we have no control. For their very existence would be contingent on our actions; they would need us as much or more than we need them. They would be able only to suggest whereas we, by our voluntary noncompliance with their wishes, could compel.

This view of things might also make sense of the frequent reports of "near-death experiences." Suppose that when we have stepped out of our bodies and passed through the dark tunnel, that light and those loving presences are indeed the light of the future and the faces of our descendants. Imagine that in a million years our descendants have mastered the art of perfect reconstruction of past events (a sort of ecological restoration on a submolecular scale) and that they have become capable of resurrecting in perfect detail the bodies of the dead. Imagine that, just as the consciousness of a sleeper leaps over from the body that retires to bed to the slightly different body that wakes up in the morning, our consciousness should be able to leap over from our dying body to the reconstructed one awaiting us in the future. Our descendants, with their exquisite sense of ethics, would feel obliged, if there is any possibility of "natural" revival, to offer the dying person the choice of whether to go on or return. This interpretation would explain the awkward fact (for religious commentators) that the near-dead sometimes encounter at that threshold not only the beloved dead but also people who are still alive. By the time they are to be resurrected, all of this generation would of course be dead, and by then perhaps "already" resurrected, or at least those that would have opted to be. Likewise, it would give a new meaning to the peculiar iconography of the spiritual world, in which *putti* and cherubs are painted as little babies, Christ, the "son of man," is an infant at the breast, and the Buddha is sculpted as a big fat happy child. They are our divine children, or anticipations of them.

If we were to adopt this theory of time we would have collapsed the future and eternity into each other. Or rather, we would have recognized as the future what the great religions have been talking about all this time as eternity, "illo tempore," Olympus, Heaven, the spirit world. In this theory, the prophetic and the apocalyptic are reconciled. Thus to work for the future *is* to save one's soul, because to work for the future is to aid in the construction of the very heaven that can reach back into the unenlightened past to advise us. Similarly, by rejecting the world as it is, we can redeem it as it will be: we need not hate the world, since it is the place we shall transform into our future spiritual home. Again, this view of time makes perfect sense of the uncomfortably paired injunctions to love the things of time and to renounce the temporal. Our posterity would be our afterlife, activity would be contemplation, as the *Gita* says it is, perfection of the work perfection of the life. This life would be both preparation and the real thing. There would be plenty of room in this doctrine to accommodate Christian resurrection and Jewish covenant and Hindu reincarnation and Islamic paradise; and if we allowed the spirits of places and animals a role in this economy, for animism and totemism too.

The way would be open for a new and radical conception of spiritual depth. For if the present causes the future, but the future also influences the past, a nonlinear feedback loop has been closed: the present which causes the future is the present as influenced by that very future; the future that influences the present is a future caused by a present which has been influenced by the very future it causes. Every moment is the resultant, then, of an infinitely deep recursion between its future and its present. Perhaps our experiences of déjà vu, and more importantly our "moments in and out of time," our epiphanies, our sense, in Blake's terms, of holding infinity in the palm of your hand and eternity in an hour, derive from that underlying depth of temporal iteration. Perhaps our spiritual disciplines, of Zen and Yoga and meditation and contemplation, are but practical ways of pushing through the obviousness and the veil of the first iteration and exploring the riches beneath. Certainly the mandala, which meditators are enjoined to contemplate, and which may even be a sort of picture or diagram of contemplative consciousness, is suggestively concentric, iterated, and fractal in its design.

The idea of temporal iteration, by the same token, empowers us in some measure over the past: by our creative awareness we cause otherwise insignificant events in the past to spring into being as precursors, heralds, and embryos of present realities. We are indeed caused by our past, but we have, according to our theory, had a hand in guiding that past toward us. Our new conceptions reach back into the past and tickle their necessary antecedents into reality. Once, when Henri Bergson was asked what the next great work of literature would be, he replied that if he knew, he would be writing it. A work of art before its composition is totally unpredictable, but once it has been created, it then suddenly seems, and indeed really is, foreshadowed and inevitable. Bergson went on to develop this notion into a theory of creative evolution, in which the creative acts of the present call into existence, *qua* possibilities, a whole pattern of previously unrelated incidents from the past. And before Bergson, no less a thinker than Aristotle himself imagined a final cause for every event, a deeper meaning drawing it into existence; and his insight takes on a new, and less merely metaphorical, meaning in this light.

There is a major problem with this whole idea so far. If the future can influence the past, the future already exists in some sense, and thus the implication is that it is laid out before us, willy-nilly, and we are not free to change it. So conceived, the future tyrannizes us with its retroactive inevitability, in rather the same fashion as does the theistic idea of eternity with its omniscient and omnipotent God. However gentle and uncompelling the promptings of the unborn, their very existence, with the implication that we are fated to bring them into being just so, is compulsion enough. Our free will itself, according to this objection, would be just a charade, for whatever we choose will bring us, like Oedipus fleeing his terrible auguries, to exactly the same spot, the meeting of the three ways, which is really a meeting of only two, or only one. If the three "legs" of time—past, present, and future—are totally symmetrical with each other (or stapled together, which is how Oedipus got his name), there is no way of telling them apart, no way of answering the Sphinx's ghastly recursive riddle. If I am my own father and my own son, every path I take will lead me back to the dark place whence I came.

Turning this objection around to look at our relations with the past, it is we who become the tyrant, the Big Brother: we are justified in any rewriting of the past we wish, according to our political objectives. Extreme "revisionings" can lead to a hideous kind of temporal colonialism, in which the integrity of past cultures is brutally violated to please our contemporary appetites for justification or revenge. Of course, to the defenders of those past cultures there is a gloomy satisfaction in this view of things, for the future can be just as ruthless with us as we are with our own past; our mistreatment of our ancestors will be visited with interest on ourselves by our descendants. How foolish contemporary environmental or ethnic or sexual ideologues will look, helpless under the pitiless gaze of the future, having had no compassion themselves for the mistakes of their past! This nasty, Oedipal, dog-eat-dog conception of time does not have much room for grace, for a gentle guide in our decisions.

Let us see if we can modify our idea, that the future can advise the past in some subtle way, so as to deal with these objections. Suppose there were not one future, but many, depending on how we—and all other agencies past and present within our event horizon—act and have acted. There would not be one present, but multiple presents, deriving from alternative choices taken by our predecessors. This is the "branching time" or "parallel universes" theory, and it has much to recommend it, especially if we include some form of the weak backwards influence we have already suggested. The physicist Hugh Everett III indeed proposed that the many-universes theory, in which every quantum event was a new branching of time, was the only intelligible solution to the problem of quantum indeterminacy. In this recension the quiet voice that speaks to us out of the future is not one, but many. Every set of ethically reconcilable futures would have its own voice, its own suasion to do the thing that will bring it into full being. The quietness of those voices is now explained by the relative tenuousness of their probability: the most unlikely futures speak so softly we cannot hear them at all, those with the best odds of happening speak most clearly. Each future speaks most anxiously when its own existence is in question; and sometimes, as with Faust, a spirit hovers by each ear, one good, one evil. When we act we silence some of those voices forever, and this is the dark, murderous tragedy of action. By the same token an act of creative goodness will make the angels sing indeed. There is much sense in clapping if you believe in fairies, for perhaps they do indeed depend on our endorsement, these distant children of ours, their heads packed with magical software, their shoulders fledged with genetically grown wings.

As modified, our idea now provides the clearest possible asymmetry between the past and the future; without that distinction we are trapped in an incestuous and Oedipal marriage of the two. Our past is one, though deeply iterated; but our futures are many, and our present role is to create them. As we do so we are beckoned and advised by them, in the form of conscience, intuition, the inner voice, the promptings of our joy. The evil futures speak to us too, but we should be able to learn to diagnose them as evil, as we judge a person by his or her words and attitudes; at least we will not be acting in a void, without warning of the consequences. Time is a tree, and the present is always a branchpoint. As anyone knows who prunes a tree, the most promising branch thickens and is fed by the twigs and leaves of its future. The earlier produces the later by causality; the later draws the earlier by competitive influence.

This revision of the idea of time also has the profoundest consequences for how we imagine the cosmos. By analogy, early brain science assumed that all the higher-level functions of the mind—consciousness, creativity, humor, morality—were simply the passive results of lower-level processes in the various sections of the brain, in the cells, in the molecules, in the atoms, in the particles of which the brain is made up. Only "bottom-up" causality of this kind was allowed. Contemporary brain science, however, has been pushed by the very rigor and exactness of its early reductionism into observations and experiments that clearly show a "top-down" kind of causality at work as well. *As well*, not *instead*: this is an important caveat. Some "new age" theorists, and in a different way some social constructionists in the humanities and social sciences, would be quite happy to throw out "bottom-up" causality altogether, replacing one linear view of the mind with another. It is the combination of the two that is fascinating; it closes a feedback loop and makes of the brain a wild and unpredictable place, where positive feedbacks among the self-modifying synaptic circuits can grow themselves harmonically into unprecedented patterns. The Hebb cells, those master-neurons whose synaptic geometry is clearly altered by the repeated firings of thought, sensation, and memory, testify to the power of mind over matter.

It is becoming increasingly clear that the genes do not so much specify, like a blueprint, the exact shape of the organism, as set in motion a set of feedbacks among an ensemble of proteins that result, amazingly, in a coherent living creature. The process is drawn to its conclusion by a strange attractor that is often powerful enough to override quite serious genetic errors and environmental deficits. If, say, the intricate mechanism of a hawk's eye had to be exactly specified by the genes, any mutation or early lack of nutrients, however small, could throw the whole thing out of alignment and it would be useless. On the contrary, the process is robust because it is recalibrated all the time by its final cause, its strange attractor, which is the mature eye in the mature bird. The adult organism is as much the partial fulfilling of this strange attractor as the realization of a preordained plan. In this sense the completed life form strangely determines the genes that generate it. Here again we encounter a two-way causality.

What we have done with the cosmos and its time environment in our thought experiment is not unlike what the brain scientists did with their conception of the brain and the developmental biologists did with fetal growth, as their sciences evolved. The future of the universe is its higher-level processing, its thoughts, desires, imaginings—"the prophetic soul/Of the wide world dreaming on things to come," as Shakespeare puts it. The past is its mechanism, its organs, cells, and dead material constituents. The past causes the future, as brain causes mind; but in turn the future reaches back and transforms its own elements and antecedents, as we do through introspection or decision or self-exhortation; the mind, which is the whole, changing the chemistry and physics of the brain, its parts. Here our idea converges suggestively with that odd natural theology we proposed earlier in this chapter, in which we humans are the neurons of a divine embryo, gradually wiring up, through our scientific instruments and artistic insight, the brain of God. In other words, the demands of freedom and the demands of a coherent environmental metaphysics issue in the same answer, the same peculiar nonlinear relation of past and future.

However attractive this idea, can it be true? There are two sorts of objections to it, one logical, the other empirical. The logical one is this: if we *define* the past as that which cannot be changed and as all that has ever existed, and the future as that which cannot be known and does not exist, then the theory is in trouble, because it seems to violate those definitions. There is good reason to define past and future in that way. Only thus, we might argue, can the future be kept as a realm in which new creations can take place and free actions be performed. Only thus can some notion of a truth and a nature that can surprise us out of our solipsism, that can resist our wishful thinking with the cold refreshing shock of reality, be kept inviolate, for if the past is malleable to our desires, it loses its historical independence and power to deny our expectations.

How might we respond to this objection? First, we must query whether we need so absolute a distinction between past and future to preserve those values that the definition enshrines. In other words, could not the openness of the future be preserved in just as strong a way by an assertion of its infinite multiplicity, the relative tenuousness of its various probabilistic tracks, and its complete sensitivity to our decisions, as by the flat assertion of the future's nonexistence? Could not a blanket ignorance of the future be revised without loss into an ignorance of which future is going to succeed, combined with an intuitive prompting and a creative quickening in the direction of that prompting? Again, to influence, to persuade, to entice the past is not necessarily to cause it, or to rob it of its power to surprise and shock us. Indeed, in human terms it is precisely those people over whom we have the most influence, our close relatives and friends and spouses, who are most prone to astonish us, to change us, to shock us, to give us the feeling of coming up hard against reality. It is specifically in the past's partial resistance to our persuasions that we encounter its independence and its historical facticity. If we could not even contact it to attempt to interrogate or persuade it, it would lose its opportunity to deny us. Likewise, our distant descendants, in our theory, are no doubt knocked sideways sometimes by our resistance to, or by the oddness of our compliance with, their suggestions. This may be one powerful reason why they would bother with us at all, above and beyond ensuring that they do actually come to be. Time is still perhaps sufficiently asymmetrical to serve its intellectual purposes in its revised version.

It is now a truism that complex nonlinear feedback systems can be by definition unpredictable, even if they are deterministic, because the amount of information-processing capacity required to predict them is greater than the complexity of the whole universe itself, and therefore any computation of the next event would take more time than the event itself. It is precisely this characteristic of the universe that justifies us in calling it "free." This description itself contains a paradox: how does the next event itself know how to happen? If there is not enough computing power in the universe to tell where the process of crystallization will begin in a super-saturated solution, and what the shape of the resulting crystals will be; if the next little whirlpool in the river is by definition unpredictable; if the weather next March can never be exactly determined— how can these events themselves decide how to occur? What tells them to collapse their wave function in just such and such a fashion? How do they know just how and when to bifurcate into a new state? Newton revolutionized physics by insisting that all actions had to be directly mediated by physical forces. The equivalent requirement in the information age is that all physical events should be computable by the systems that produce them. In this theory the question is answered by saying that it is their future, or rather, that one of their futures that has the strongest pull and attraction, that is the trigger, the minute touch that resolves a metastable, far-from equilibrium state into one of its possible outcomes.

At this point we have already begun to answer the empirical objection to our idea, which is that there is nothing in experimental and observational science that would suggest, let alone justify, the idea that the future and the present can influence their past. And here we may begin to comply with the second half of Thoreau's injunction, that we should first build our castles in the air, and then put the foundations under them. This chapter might, if we followed the traditional bottom-up practice of science and scholarship, have started here. I have chosen instead the top-down method, stating the conclusion before the premises and the evidence, in order to demonstrate how the future of an argument can influence its past. Sometimes if we know where we want to go, it is easier to get there.

Certainly if we choose this method, we have to be especially on guard against wishful thinking, tampering with the evidence, and the assumption of what we want to prove. That is why I have tried to give the counter-arguments in their strongest form. On the other hand to write a book is a moral action, and if we can prove that a moral action requires a particular sort of universe, and a particular geometry of time, then the very act of writing already confirms that that universe and geometry is the case; and now additional empirical evidence would both illustrate and act as an experimental check on the hypothesis, in case our logic was faulty. Contrariwise, if one believed in a different kind of universe, one in which moral action was without significance, it would certainly be in bad faith to write a book at all, and so one might never get a chance to deploy the evidence that one was wrong. In other words, all books tacitly assume by their existence what this book makes explicit.

What is the empirical argument for our thesis? Of course the term "empirical" is going to have to be stretched a little in what follows; but it is not entirely out of place. The Cosmological Anthropic Principle of the physicist John Archibald Wheeler, in its strong form, might offer one promising direction. (Other ways of doing this might instead be based on Penrose's idea that intelligence is inherent in quanta, or on Hawking's nonlinear geometry of time, or on Fredkin's notions of a computational reality. All these theories share an emergent theme in theoretical physics, which is that the old linear view of time will not suffice.) Wheeler argues from the now established fact that in quantum physics the precise nature of a subatomic event is undetermined until it is observed. Its "precise nature" can be defined as how it affects the rest of the universe, for instance, as a wave or as a particle; or, in particle-pair formation when two opposite particles are generated, which particle carries which charge or polarity. Since Wheeler first developed his idea, he has recognized that a human observer as such is not necessary, and that any organism capable of unambiguous response, even an atom or molecule, would do if it were sensitive to the kind of event taking place. In other words, the history of the universe as it is is partly as yet undetermined, partly the settled consensus of its own constituents, each of which in turn is confirmed in such definite identity as it possesses by the "vote" of the rest. As Melville said, this is a joint-stock universe. This consensus is by necessity retrospective and retroactive, since every event of observation must, delayed by the speed-limit of light, postdate the event it observes.

If this is the case, our own observations of the Big Bang, the original singularity that began the universe, must be partly determining its precise nature. This argument carries special weight because in the first few fractions of a second the universe was smaller than an atom and thus entirely within the horizons that define quantum physics as opposed to classical physics. In other words, everything that happened at that unimaginably brief epoch of universal history was subject for its very identity to later interpretations of it, since no contemporary observer existed that could validate its exact constants, fundamental ratios, and basic quantitative values. The point is that only one set of constants, ratios, and values— only one value for Planck's Constant, the Electron Volt Constant, the speed of light, the gravitational constant, even perhaps Pi and the value of the Golden Section ratio—could bring about any conceivable efficacious observers of it.

One way of dealing with the problem of how an event that cannot be predicted knows how to happen in the way it actually does is to posit a branching universe, as we have done, in which all possible outcomes actually come about, but in which the one we are on is cut off from all the others. Wheeler's theory offers a way of pruning this unmanageable foliage of bifurcating timelines, and consolidating them into one world, but a world with fuzzy edges, great depth, and buried unrealized possibilities. The pruning is achieved by the fact that only those outcomes that will continually generate reliable observers will come about. In the case of the Big Bang, perhaps only one outcome was possible, and all the others remain only as an irreducible noise in any system. Later decisions might leave their alternatives floating about as a sort of ghostly accompaniment haunting the fringes of measurement. As I interpret it, Wheeler's universe implies that all the timelines are indeed faintly present to each other in the form of a low-probability penumbra to actuality, and are thus not separated from one another.

For our immediate purpose, which is the investigation of a morally viable world, the interesting implication of Wheeler's theory is that if we by observing it can partly determine the origin of the universe, then by extension we must also be partly determining, at least on the quantum level, all events that have come since, and our descendants will be performing the same offices for us. It is now becoming quite clear that the firings of the neurons of the brain are triggered by changes as minute as quantum events. We can describe the brain as at least partly a mechanism for amplifying quantum events into the macrocosm, for killing or sparing Schroedinger's famous cat, so to speak. Tiny changes across quantum thresholds are not always damped out, as is usual in stable matter, but can cascade up into major transformations. Thus the human brain is one place that is especially sensitive and susceptible to the wave-function-collapsing influence of future observers of it. Perhaps, further, we might speculate that evolutionary selection designed the human brain especially for this function, since it is clear that any species that could listen to the advice of its descendants would be at a superb adaptive advantage.

So hunch, intuition, prophecy, visions, premonitions, and all those other mysterious human gifts, and even the lesser but impressive capacities of other higher animals in this respect, might have a factual basis. Those angelic visitations to which we are so prone may not be mere fabrications. Future Frenchmen and Frenchwomen may well have spoken to Saint Joan, if only in order to keep their own elegant tongue alive and independent of English. Did poor Montezuma dream that Cortés was a god, because the future of Latin America was so beautiful that its inhabitants were prepared to take that tragic way to stay his destroying arm? If there is any substance to this extension of the Anthropic Principle, and to the idea that the future can communicate with the past, it seems likely that our remote descendants might indeed be able to reach back to us in the ways that we have stipulated as necessary to a meaningful and free universe. They would, after all, be the beneficiaries of many centuries of scientific and technological progress, enhanced by cybernetic and biological prostheses, having command over more and more fundamental aspects of the physical universe, and able perhaps to alter the fabric of local and global space-time.

The revised cosmology sketched in this chapter renders much contemporary avant-garde thought simply irrelevant to the arts, either because it is wrong or because it is less interesting than the new worldviews that are becoming possible. It remains for us to explore the cultural implications of the new cosmology.

Chapter 4

Cultural Implications of the New Cosmology

Guidelines to the Solution of Cultural Problems

The cosmology of a culture profoundly affects what it can or cannot do. Consider how Taoism in China, for example, encouraged technological innovation while somewhat discouraging a mathematically based science. Or how Renaissance cosmological ideas spurred exploration, industry, and new financial instruments. Or how Mayan calendrical expertise made possible kinds of institutional memory that in turn organized city states and empires. In the previous chapter I discussed how our own culture is beginning a cosmological revolution; what practical guidelines arise from the new cosmology, that can help us repair the cultural damage created by our old myths and generate new myths, more hopeful, more internally consistent, and with a better basis in fact?

As we have seen, power is not the only, or even the most important, factor in social events. The theory of power depends on a cosmology of one-way linear cause and effect. Very few events in the universe can be accurately described in this way—indeed, the whole art of scientific experiment is needed to isolate straight cause–effect processes. In human affairs, oppressors are causes and victims are the recipients of effects. However, the overwhelming majority of real events, especially in the human sphere, are nonlinear and cannot be reduced to a dualistic oppressor–victim or cause–effect model. Moreover, the more deterministic and one-way a system is, the more subject it is to thermodynamic decay. Thus any would-be oppressor is condemned to the realm of entropy: the greater the power, the swifter it seeps away. It took Stalinist communism only seventy years to dissipate; Hitler's national socialism less than twenty. The most important implication of this observation is that if tradition is defined as human institutions which have lasted a long time, and if longevity is not thermodynamically consistent with oppression (the exercise of one-way power relations), then the older a tradition, the less likely it is to be oppressive, and the more likely it is to have enjoyed the consensus of the broad mass of its participants. This principle—the first of our guidelines for the solution of social problems—is not new; contemporary social theorists have not yet caught up with the simple insight of Confucius.

A second guideline is that to the extent that human arrangements are an outgrowth of natural evolutionary possibilities and potentials, they will be successful. Since it is nature's way to generate emergent forms and processes, this fact does not constitute a limitation on our social arrangements: rather it becomes an opportunity for them, one which, if neglected, will likely lead to decay and collapse. Thus if a political and legal system is predicated upon a struggle for power between the sexes and between racial groups, and neglects the actual opportunity nature presents for loving cooperation and cross-fertilization, we can expect that system to ossify and die.

A third guideline is that freedom is constituted not by the ability to "have one's own way," but by the actual process of creative work and evolutionary emergence. Freedom is what happens when, given the choice between A and B, we invent C. Thus political freedom, which is usually taken to mean freedom of choice, is secondary to true freedom, which is the freedom to create. If people need freedom of choice in order to select the needed materials, physical or spiritual, for the making of their work, then political freedom is important. But if those materials are already at hand, or materials are not needed, then political freedom is meaningless and may even be a nuisance, like having too many soap powder brands on the supermarket shelf, too many e-mail messages, or too appetizing a dessert tray. Self-discipline is far more important to true freedom than the choice of material goods or even life-styles. Likewise, access to a living tradition of creative work (connection, that is, with our evolutionary past) is far more important to true freedom than any ideology of revolution, because a living tradition empowers the imagination, whereas revolution diminishes the available tools of creativity. The fact is that in the long run the only really free people are the ones who have developed their gifts to the point where their contributions to others are indispensable. Thus relationships in which one person's welfare is heavily dependent upon another's, such as parenthood and all other forms of service, are not, as the avant-garde has thoughtlessly assumed, the medium of oppression but an opportunity for freedom. Finally, creation can consist not just in the addition of new entities to the world, but also in a beautiful refinement or simplification of what already exists.

A fourth guideline takes the form of a revision of the vexed question of equality. The issue is not hierarchy versus equality. Legitimated self-adjusting hierarchy assures a measure of practical equality. Rigid linear hierarchy under the guise of theoretical equality destroys equality. Equality of persons is achieved through complexity of relationships and multiple interdependence within the community. These in turn are brought about by a rich medium of functional and evaluative hierarchy in the realm of work organization, ideas, art, ethics, and science. A theater or a laboratory, whose activities may be highly stratified in their service of the ultimate goal of truth or beauty, generates a remarkable camaraderie because of the many indispensable work niches that are opened up by the hierarchy itself. Props, lighting, costume, are subordinate to mise-en-scène, mise-en-scène subordinate to action, and action subordinate to the total artistic meaning of the play; but actors, director, designer, costumer, and lighting techies share a wonderful easy creative equality as a result.

A fifth guideline is that spiritual values are real. The lack of them kills a culture, by destroying its economy, and stunts its individuals. The presence of them can easily override and eventually reverse economic disadvantage. They are the strange attractors that draw out of a chaotic yet interacting human system emergent forms of order.

Closely related to this guideline is its corollary, a sixth: that economic matters are not the bottom line. The economic value of goods depends on how much they are desired, and desirability depends on other values, such as aesthetic, moral, or veridical ones; these are generated by the creativity of human beings and of the rest of nature.

A seventh guideline is that the human world is not a tiny insignificant speck in the universe. Measured in terms of space this planet is indeed smaller relatively than a grain of dust, and measured in terms of time our tenure upon it but an eyeblink. But measured in terms of unified complexity, interconnection, significant event, emergent properties, and evolutionary history, our momentary place bulks huge in the cosmos. A single human brain possesses more potential brain states than there are particles in the physical universe. More *happens* in a year in one of our forests than has happened on Mars for the past million centuries. It would take more bytes of information to describe Belgium than it would to describe an entire galaxy (given that there are no other "belgiums," or living worlds, within it). Thus any ideology which is based on the "tiny insignificant speck" worldview (such as that we might as well give up the enterprise of civilization and devote ourselves to exciting as many of our membranes as possible before we die) is founded on a false premise.

Using these guidelines, then, let us examine two major avant-garde movements, feminism and multiculturalism. Though there is much to applaud in the moderate versions of these movements, the tenets of radical feminism and radical multiculturalism are in fact not so much a description of the problem, as its main source. Equipped with a more sophisticated cosmology we may now be in a position to construct better cultural myths that will help us rather than hinder us in our shared goals of better art, more integrated, human, and classical in the best sense.

The Feminist Myth of Patriarchy

After a few heady years of revolutionary righteousness and manifest destiny in the seventies and early eighties, feminism began to find itself trapped in a web of contradictions. These contradictions become particularly acute when a rapprochement between feminism and environmentalism is attempted. On the face of it, "eco-feminism," the marriage of radical environmentalism and radical feminism, looks like a natural. Both have a satisfyingly contrarian flavor, both seem designed to annoy the imagined world of cold (male, capitalist, scientific) efficiency, both have a warm, pacifist, and emotional tone, both have an egalitarian basis (equality between sexes, equality between species). Yet bringing them together intellectually has proven very difficult. It has even been necessary to invoke the biggest, and unfortunately most two-edged and unwieldy, weapon of all, which is the idea that rational consistency and logical coherence are themselves the bugbears of an oppressive masculinist and species-centered hegemony, that instead, the truth is what good people want it to be. But how do we tell who are the good people? If power is the only social reality and social good, then as Plato's Thrasymachus argues in the *Republic*, the powerful must be the good!

One of the most important historical strains in feminism is the insistence on individual human rights, an insistence which paradoxically goes back to the seventeenth-century bourgeois-capitalist invention of democracy as a way of making the world safe for trade, profit, and no-strings-attached employment practices. Individual liberty took on a grander and nobler aspect in the nineteenth century (consider Beethoven's *Fidelio*, or the lives of the romantic poets) and became a metaphysical imperative in the existentialism of the twentieth. Although liberation was originally conceived as mandated by Nature, as in Rousseau's system, the very notion of human nature itself eventually became targeted as an oppressive mystification designed by the powerful and wicked to oppress the good and weak. Some existentialists (Sartre, for instance, in *La Nausée*) saw nature as the final cloying seduction that would lure us away from the lonely and precedentless path of the authentic free subject. In the politics of the twentieth century this strain of thought is realized in two important ways: as the emphatic rejection of racism, and, eventually, as the feminist denial of the proposition that anatomy (or biology) is destiny.

But here's the rub. Radical feminist environmentalism is deeply exercised over whether human beings are part of nature or not. If human beings are not part of nature, and if our own peculiar capacities give us power over nature, and if that is the right and proper state for us, then human sovereignty over nature, including the destruction of it when it thwarts our freedom, becomes justifiable. If human beings are part of nature, then everything we do must be natural and there can be no natural basis for complaint about our destructive activities. Our destructiveness would be no different from that of a giant meteor, or a volcano, or a swarm of locusts. The only solution is to say that in our present ("fallen," technological) state we are alienated from nature, but that our true and proper state, toward which we should strive, would be to exist as just another species in a harmonious ecology. For us to be just another species cannot mean anything but that biology, that is, anatomy, should be destiny. The problem is compounded by yet another strain in the contrarian ideology of the last two hundred years: the notion that Western Man (I use the masculine noun intentionally) has become alienated from his body, from nature itself as it is immediately present to him in his feelings, impulses, and desires. The roots of this idea are also very distinguished: we can list Rousseau again, the Romantics, Freud, D. H. Lawrence, and the whole modernist performance tradition from Isadora Duncan to Jerzy Grotowski. A large wing of feminism has adopted the position that women's ethics and aesthetics are superior to men's precisely because women are closer to the body and to nature: hence the French feminist idea of "writing through the body" and the fashion among some American women poets of writing poems about the taste of one's own menstrual blood.

If we are to be just another species, and if we are to live through our bodies, and if we are to accept rather than oppose the restrictions that nature imposes upon us, then we cannot at the same time assert that biology is not destiny. We cannot simultaneously claim that our brains are better (and different) because of our biology, and that biology makes no difference to the quality of our brains. We cannot simultaneously assert that we ought to be docile members of a human and natural community, and that we are radically free individuals. Within the feminist community deep political strains and splits are opening up along the lines of these logical inconsistencies. Anyone who has observed intra-feminist politics can vouch for the astonishing virulence, bitterness, and underhandedness of its factional struggles. The "mommy track" controversy, which directly pitted the idea of special female reproductive virtues against the idea of the irrelevance of biological difference, together with its agonizing subtext of the ticking of the biological clock, is a case in point.

Other struggles involve the proper attitude toward men. If men are simply the same as women, then how can the imbalance of power between them (an imbalance which is the *sine qua non* of feminist belief) be explained? Sheer historical coincidence? If women are the same as men, then surely they would be just as capable of tyranny as the other sex, and thus it would be unfair to blame men for doing what women would have done if they had had the chance. If the advantage of being socioculturally enfranchised is that one can cultivate superior moral and intellectual virtues, then men must be better than women. If sociocultural enfranchisement is, on the other hand, corrupting to those virtues, then women would be wrong to desire it. But if men are by nature morally inferior to women, more power-seeking and tyrannical, the feminist position begins to look dangerously like a sexist one, attributing moral and intellectual differences to biological causes. If childbearing does not put people at a disadvantage in other spheres of activity, then it cannot explain the imbalance of power; but if it does put people at a disadvantage, then it should come as no surprise, and should not be construed as an indictment of society, if childbearers are not as active in other spheres of life. Professional athletes do not win many Nobel prizes; one finds few leading mathematicians among the ranks of the *cordon bleu*. Indeed, when fair-minded feminists consider the list of great human achievements—penicillin, the plays of Shakespeare, the art of the fugue, calculus—they cannot deny that these were gigantic gifts to the human race, often created at enormous sacrifice and in the face of bitter opposition and incomprehension. It seems fantastic, insane, to attack their givers for their privileged position. Think of poor Blake, or Mozart, or Van Gogh, or Hopkins, or Kafka, and the struggle of their brief lives to give their art to a hostile public; the idea of their having some special social advantage because of being male is morally obscene. Many women in the feminist movement, who love their fathers, brothers, husbands, or especially their sons, have all along denied the premise that male achievements were simply the symptoms of privilege. It makes more sense not to attack the givers of these great gifts, but instead to recognize the work of mothers as being entirely commensurate with them.

Finally there is a deep feminist ambivalence about the very nature of the goods that they feel they have been unjustly denied. Those goods are not so much the kind that are consumed; indeed, one of the complaints against society is that women have been made into passive consumers, spenders, recipients rather than makers and doers. It is the more intangible kind of goods, consisting of the opportunities to act and create, and the debt of obligation others owe one for acting and creating, that has been refused to women. But those very opportunities themselves must have been made by men, since men have arrogated to themselves the role of making. Thus the goods women want have the taint of having been made by men.

This problem is an agonizing one, and various mutually contradictory solutions have been proposed. One is that women have been prevented from creative activity by men. But part of the heroic story of male creativity has always been the artist's or scientist's or philosopher's long struggle for recognition, the bitter resistance to class, ethnic, religious, and personal oppression; could not women have won the same contest? Perhaps the male model of Oedipal rebellion is the wrong one; but how could one differentiate between those male insurgents and the contemporary struggles of liberated women? Is it not an abject borrowing of male methods?

Another solution is that women have all along been just as successfully creative as men. The problem with this idea is that it denies the premise that men have effectively reserved the creative roles for themselves. The argument then shifts to the proposition that women's creative activity has not been properly recognized. But there are only two sexes of people who could recognize such achievements: men and women. If men are as tyrannical and corrupt as the history of sexual oppression suggests, then recognition by men would itself be an undesirable boon, signifying that the achievement itself met the corrupt criteria of the enemy. Or suppose men were not as evil as this, but were basically fair-minded, if perhaps blinded by their own political history as oppressors. Was not the spectacle of women begging for their attention and praise a rather ignoble one? Should they not earn it instead of nag for it? If recognition by other women is the only desirable thing that has been lacking, women have only themselves to blame for their obscurity. And is not the desire for fame, for the everlasting name, for the monument and commemoration and place in history—is not this desire itself a male fantasy, a silly kind of pissing on fireplugs, an assertion of hierarchical male values, that women should rightly reject?

The great myth of the patriarchy embodies many of the contradictions and anxieties of radical feminism in a narrative of the origin and moral drama of the human race. That myth has many versions, some of which contradict each other, and many different historical time scales, but we can summarize it thus.

Originally a matriarchy ruled human society. In this golden age the female values were uppermost: human equality, nonviolence, sharing, love, caring, an organic and personal relationship with Mother Nature (Gaia), a consensual system of decision making, and a wholesome and natural system of spiritual and bodily health. Sexual taboos were unknown and unnecessary; conflicts were resolved through communal negotiation and sharing; prejudice, war, hierarchy, money, private property, objective science, and alienating systems of logic and quantification and technology were unknown. There was no sexual division of labor. Society was centered on the home, which was a holy place, and on nurturing child care. The dead were revered; fear of death was impossible because the selfish individualism that makes us afraid of losing our personal consciousness was never allowed to arise. Wise matriarchs, representing the goddesses of a bountiful earth, gave advice, oracles, guidance, and gentle correction. The central symbol of creativity, artistic and otherwise, was the womb, and the female arts of weaving, singing, and storytelling were extensions of the mysterious work of the womb.

Into this arcadian age of happiness entered a new and terrible force. Male lusts for property, the exclusive sexual possession of women, individual self-display, and dominance could no longer be restrained. A patriarchy struggled with and eventually usurped the matriarchal rule. Women were subjugated and became the property of males, serving them as slaves. Private property was introduced, with all the anxiety, alienation, injustice, and vanity that go along with it. Male aggressions erupted into bloody and violent wars. Elaborate social hierarchies were established. A cold, alienating system of logic and empirical reason replaced the older, more organic and intuitive wisdom. Sex was poisoned by the introduction of sexual taboos, and by the exclusive possession of the female and her reproductive capacities by the male. Terrified of death, limited to a narrow definition of the self that included mind and consciousness but excluded the unconscious, spiritual, and communal elements of personal being, human beings clung to a miserable existence. A public world of marketplaces, courts, armies, temple priesthoods, and impersonal institutions replaced the home as the center of human life. Laws, codes, and punishments replaced sharing and consensus as ways of resolving disputes. Science arose as a way of repressing, dominating, and exploiting Nature, and we became increasingly separated from the web of natural life. The cold, sadistic gaze of impersonal reason replaced warm intuitive feeling as the way to understand the world. The symbol of creativity became the phallus, and the act of creation was imaged as rape.

It was only in the West that the patriarchy fully triumphed. Other cultures, gentler and less exploitative, preserved remnants of the old wisdom. Even in the West a sisterhood of wise women—artists, visionaries, midwives, and intellectuals—carried on the traditions in secret. They were oppressed and labeled as witches when they were discovered. Their heroic resistance to the patriarchy has recently won for them the franchise, but there is no way that the patriarchy will ever give up its real power. Modernity, with its alienation, rationalism, and anomie, represents the triumph of the patriarchy. Colonialism and capitalism are destroying the traditional cultures, and many women have gone over to the enemy. Western technology is now on the verge of creating an ecological crisis, and the Earth itself will protest against its long rape by some natural catastrophe.

This myth has all the delights of paranoia, combined with the full satisfaction of our very human desires for purity, scapegoats, self-justification, and a morally noble explanation for one's own imagined or real personal failures. Some of its propositions also contain a grain of truth.

What are its disadvantages? The most obvious one is that taken as a whole the myth is not supported by the historical, mythological, archeological, ethological, anthropological, and sociological evidence. As far as any reputable ancient history is concerned, there never was an exclusively matriarchal golden age. In mythology, Apollo indeed replaced the chthonic goddesses at Delphi, but he was also replacing the cult of Poseidon, and his voice was the priestess, who wielded enormous political power among the Hellenes. His sister Artemis gained cult power through the whole period, and Athena replaced Ares as the leading war-deity. Later, in Rome, goddesses of nature, love, domesticity, and fertility made big comebacks, while Jupiter languished; and even in Christianity it was the cult of the Virgin Mother that built the cathedrals. Old gods and goddesses are superseded by new gods and goddesses; it will not do to select for study only the goddesses who are replaced and the gods who are elevated.

Archaeology tells a story of male hunters and female gatherers who are succeeded by male farmers and female weavers, but does not support the myth. Ethology—especially the work of Jane Goodall—shows unquestionably that our primate cousins, and thus probably our primate ancestors, were violent, possessive both sexually and territorially, highly hierarchical in social organization, and even more prone to wars, child abuse, and rape than we are. Anthropology gives us many examples of healthy matriarchal systems (as many of them in the West as elsewhere), but always in societies which also contain a powerful patriarchal or male-dominated system as well. These last distinctions are very important, for there is no reason why a matriarchy cannot happily coexist with a patriarchy; and not all male-dominated systems are necessarily patriarchal. Moreover societies with strong matriarchal power structures do not seem to be any less violent, hierarchical, or ecologically exploitative than societies without them.

Sociology would point out that the three main characteristics attributed by the myth to the patriarchy: its primitive and violent brutality, its stultifying conservatism and moral stuffiness, and its cold, legalistic, scientific rationality, detached from the warm reality of the body, could not possibly coexist. The myth's alienating science and technology, for instance, would require a revolution against conservative attitudes and an environment protected against violent brutality. Feminists who contend that new technology and ideas are breaking up the old pattern of women's subjection are in direct contradiction to the feminist "golden age" theory. If the patriarchs are both rational and stuffy, they certainly will not have the spirit and energy to be brutal and violent. And if the myth resorts to elaborate theories of conspiracy, in which the patriarchy masks its violence behind legalism and science, the element of stuffiness and stupid conservatism is lost, and the enemy seems more brilliantly cunning and diabolically collusive than the worst dreams of the paranoid. If the myth chooses only one of the three patriarchal characteristics, it falls apart, or at least can only cover a limited period of history and loses its larger moral implications. To tell the truth, the myth is so flexible as to be easily stretched to cover whatever it is that its adherents currently dislike about the imagined enemy: but by the same token it tells an incoherent story and is therefore almost untestable by the sciences.

But since the integrity of these very sciences by which we arrived at the new cosmology is itself called into question by the myth of the patriarchy, as male justifications for the status quo, I shall argue for the replacement of this myth by a better one on other grounds than on the clear evidence. (If the evidence is tainted, it can therefore be used neither by the challengers of the myth nor by its defenders; indeed, what untainted evidence could we use to decide which parts of the evidence were tainted, and which were not?) I intend to show that the feminist counter-myth I propose is in much better accord with the evidence, even evidence cited by the adherents of the old myth. But the grounds for my argument will instead be the internal self-contradictions of the old myth, and its manifest conclusion in despair; and the greater imaginative richness, consistency, and hopefulness of the new.

A New Feminist Myth

The new myth recognizes the coexistence of different sources of authority in society, so that matriarchy can coexist with patriarchy. It is aware, as the myth of the golden age is not, that the repressive and hidebound patriarchy described by the myth could not possibly create the revolutionary social, intellectual, and technological changes which have resulted, for good or ill, in modernity. The new myth distinguishes between patriarchy and another, newer form of social organization that we might call "juventocracy"—the rule of unattached young men and (increasingly) women. The new myth acknowledges values in the modern "Western" political, intellectual, scientific, religious, and artistic tradition that no true feminist would wish to sacrifice to the myth of the patriarchy. It includes an enormously important historical change, the overthrow of the patriarchy, which is totally ignored in the previous myth. It avoids a sexist attribution to the male of a special criminality, and also avoids a debilitating and sexist attribution to the female of a special purity. Further, it avoids the dualistic Cartesian separations between nature and culture, nature and humanity, nature and nurture which are implied by those sexist attributions. It is not anti-intellectual, as the other myth tends to be, and thus it does not undermine as it does the achievements of the great female intellectuals together with the great male ones. It is not Luddite, and therefore does not rely for its credibility on an ideal world population some five billion smaller than our present one. To a fair-minded and educated feminist of either sex it offers a way out of the procrustean dilemma presented by the myth of the patriarchy, that in order to be a loyal feminist one must accept an account of human history that is improbable, self-contradictory, sexist, simplistic, and unsupported by the evidence. Finally, the new myth presents a reinterpretation of contemporary sexual politics which is diagnostic of its difficulties, sympathetic, and full of hope for the future.

Like any other narrative of history, the feminist myth I propose here is partial in scope and subject to exceptions of all kinds. However, it is, I believe, less inherently contradictory and more productive of friendly effort for the future than the former myth, and makes possible exciting insights into coherent connections among large masses of historical evidence. These insights might prove to be rich material for a new centrist art of storytelling. "Once upon a time," then . . .

In traditional societies ranging from the hunter-gatherer stage to the agrarian empire, the human world divided itself into two moieties, the male and the female, with two somewhat different cultures, often two different dialects, and two different forms of authority, the patriarchy and the matriarchy. Together they carved up reality: in early cultures between the male region of hunting and the female region of gathering; in later cultures, between production and reproduction, and between the public (the village, marketplace and city) and the private (the household). For millennia there was a rough parity between these two spheres, with some fluctuations as technological and political changes slowly spread.

The household was the core of a traditional society's economic, artistic, intellectual, and spiritual life. Though the male patriarch had always been its titular and administrative head and the leader of its protectors, it was the women of the household who held the real power of decision and the conduct of its life and creative activity. Like a university, which is in some ways a survival of the ancient household structure, and which is judged not by the efficiency of its administration but by the creative activity of its faculty, a household's vitality and direction lay in its women. The extended family and the widespread use of servants and slaves provided a constant oral community within which the female culture could flourish, arranging marriages, telling stories ("old wives' tales"), training and indoctrinating the children in their first five or so formative years, creating the web of gossip that constitutes a community, performing the central religious rituals that were the spiritual and ideological heart of society, making clothes and fabrics and preparing food.

The major economic activities were carried on in the home. On the periphery would be the menfolk, the farmers, hunters, craftsmen, warriors, and traders, who constituted the household's outer shell and conducted its tenuous and infrequent relations with other communities and the outside world. In a world in which everybody belonged to someone, the peasant to the chieftain, the chieftain to the king or emperor or paramount chief, the king to the gods, and in which ownership denoted an intimate, reciprocal, and emotional attachment, women indeed "belonged" to the household and thus nominally to the household's head. But he too "belonged"; and it would be inaccurate to equate ownership in this sense with modern property ownership. It would be much closer to the sense of the genitive when we speak of our children as being "ours," or when a dean refers to "her" faculty. Women were no more slaves or property than children or university faculty are. This model is roughly true of most traditional societies, both past and present.

Within the traditional male value system very few men desired those goods valued by the female culture, and within the female value system equally few women would desire male-valued goods. Exceptional temperaments like Tiresias or Virgil's warrior-maiden Camilla might cross the sexual boundaries from time to time, and if they did it with panache they might thereby win a kind of wondering praise. Greek tragedy and comedy often treat of such characters, and they are usually accorded great sympathy even when they commit questionable actions.

Given the state of medicine and technology, early societies could scarcely be arranged in any other way. No reliable form of contraception existed (fertility was controlled when necessary by infant exposure) and disease and famine usually required the maximum birthrate to compensate for the shortness of life expectancy and to replenish the population. Male upper-body strength, size, and aggression made a significant difference in a world largely without machines, as did female physical dexterity, sensitiveness, and flexibility. There was no substitute for breastfeeding. A protected environment for children and for expectant and nursing women was essential. It was only in the nineteenth century, and only in very advanced economies, that technology began to alter this state of things. Safe feeding-bottles and pasteurized milk may have contributed more than any other invention to the end of sexual specialization. From a modern point of view that old system was very wasteful of human intellectual and imaginative talents, which I assume are on balance equal between the sexes: males would have little opportunity to develop natural aptitudes suitable to the female culture, and in women some talents suited to the masculine life would likewise be wasted.

There is no evidence that women in significant numbers refused to accept the division of labor, or despised the female culture, or yearned to join the male culture and were prevented from doing so. In women's writings there are some protests about the state of things; but women writers were self-selected by their choice of a traditionally male medium of expression. In like fashion one might expect Western practitioners of traditional Chinese ink-painting to be defensive and uncomfortably aware of their status as interlopers in a foreign discipline. The women's *oral* tradition tends to criticize men for not keeping their side of the bargain (just as the male tradition scolds women for not keeping theirs) but it rarely attacks the terms of the contract itself. It might be argued that there was much more female discontent than shows up in the record. There is a multitude of evidence of unsuccessful religious, ethnic, dynastic, and economic rebellion from ancient documents and monuments, and from contemporary anthropological accounts, evidence which by its very presence would counter any claim that gender protest could have been erased from the record. Only with the emergence of the modern world does such protest begin to appear, and even there only in a minority of the population. Those few women who did choose a "male" role were often regarded by both sexes as patterns of excellence—for instance Sappho, Diotima (as philosopher), Queen Berenice of Alexandria, Lady Murasaki, Eleanor of Aquitaine, Margery Kemp, Juliana of Norwich, Saint Teresa of Avila, Saint Joan, Christine de Pizan, Marie de Champagne, Elizabeth of Urbino, and Elizabeth Tudor, among others.

The world thus divided between the patriarchy and the matriarchy presented a profound problem to the young males of the group, especially those of exceptional personal strength, intelligence, and talent. They were not unlike the young males of the baboon or chimpanzee troop, who must either accept the domination of the high-ranking senior males or settle for a position of marginality on the outside of the troop, deprived of reproductive opportunities. It was from this group that a new force emerged, which I call the "juventocracy." This force would, after many centuries, unseat the patriarchy. A part of the old male culture, released by the gradual growth of new technologies and increased leisure, and finding its desire to play a significant and creative role in society blocked both by the old patriarchy and by the monopoly held by the matriarchy over the household and the dynasty, broke away and created its own new value system. More mobile and innovative than the traditional matriarchy/patriarchy, it began to develop arts, technologies, activities, and ideologies of its own (many of them recorded in epic poetry). Its archetype was the hero, and its central idea was transformation. In modern terms we would say that it emphasized evolution rather than ecology. Through a series of dialectical metamorphoses, prompted by a sort of Oedipal impulse to honor, emulate, and supersede the past, it eventually brought forth an extraordinary series of institutions: cities, writing, precise and enduring records of the past, new communications technologies, money, individualism, democracy, accounting, art as an ideological rather than just a decorative and celebratory activity, logic, bureaucracy, science, power-assisted production technology, and political liberty.

This development can be seen in the West as passing through three phases. First was the age of the heroes, which may have begun with and been associated with the invention of writing and historical records. Next came the age of legitimation, roughly coinciding with the rise of the state, in which the young usurpers, attempting to justify their rule, devised the legal and cultural systems that underlie modern society. Last came the age of technology, in which the juventocracy came to duplicate and replace many of the functions of the old matriarchy.

Many myths and stories recount the rebellion of the heroic juventocracy against the rule of the patriarchs. Of course the whole matter is fraught with guilt and shame, and haunted by questions about the legitimacy of the hero's rule, once he has taken over the leadership of the city. The earliest known epic, *Gilgamesh*, attests to this anxiety. One common pattern, by which painful parricidal feelings can be exorcised, is to have the old king's younger brother actually perform the act of regicide and usurpation. When the king's son kills the usurping uncle, he is at one and the same time legitimately overthrowing a member of the patriarchal generation, and reasserting a lost legitimacy by avenging the death of the father. Examples of this pattern include the stories of Aeson, Pelias, and Jason; Agamemnon, Aegisthus, and Orestes; and Hamlet the elder, Claudius, and Hamlet the younger. But the young hero cannot be so easily divided into the wicked usurper and dutiful avenging son; part of Hamlet's moral agony is that he sees himself in Claudius and Claudius in himself. Sophocles' Oedipus is indeed both fratricidal "younger brother" and grieving son, both parricide and just avenger, both usurper and true heir.

In this heroic overthrow of the patriarchy the young male hero looks for an ally in his sister or lover (sometimes she is, by mythological implication, both). Jason enlists Medea, Orestes Electra, and Hamlet Ophelia. In other words, the young male rebels originally hoped for a corresponding rebellion by the young women against the patriarchy. Here the myth predicts painful difficulties: the patriarchy was in the long run the best protector of the rights, freedoms, and powers of the matriarchy, and the matriarchy, which reproduced the very life of the tribe, could not be sacrificed. Thus the young female ally of the hero finds herself in terrible predicaments: abandoned by her unreliable lover, and forced into infanticide, like Medea; guilty of matricide, like Electra; or, if unwilling to leave the protection of the patriarchy, spurned by the hero, like Ophelia.

This new juventocratic system was from the beginning in direct competition with the old patriarchy and fought it vigorously; it tended to leave the old matriarchy alone, because the task of reproducing the society was too important to be tampered with. Hamlet is enjoined by his father's ghost not to harm Gertrude; Orestes is pursued by Furies for his mother's murder. Remembering with some bitterness, however, the struggle to free itself from the conservatism of the matriarchy (symbolized by such myths as the hero's battle against engulfing female monsters), the new culture tended to take a rather condescending and even mocking attitude toward the matriarchy, even as it took over from the dying patriarchy the task of maintaining and protecting it. However, it was never as good at this task as its predecessor; and eventually it would break the contract with the matriarchy that it had inherited.

Anxiety about the legitimacy of the new heroic regime, and the divisiveness that was the result of the destruction of paternal authority, led to the creation by the juventocrats of a more elaborate legal system that would maintain order and legitimate the new rulers. At first the *tyrannos* who replaced the king would find ways to claim the old king's authority for his own, and the patriarchy would be apparently restored; but with each new rebellion the credibility of orderly succession would be lost. The personal charisma of fatherhood itself began to fade, and though there were many attempts (such as the doctrine of the divine right of kings) to replace it, history was running the other way. The young heroes were forced to develop democratic and consensual forms of government, governments of laws not men. The *Oresteia* concludes with such a transfer of authority from family and personal authority to legality and the vote. *Antigone* is the story of a woman who conservatively resists the new legality; her insistence on proper burial for her brother, as the anthropologist Robin Fox has brilliantly pointed out, reasserts a much more ancient tribal law. Of course the irony and tragedy is that her dead brother is, many layers deep, one of the new usurping juventocrats. Much later, during another period of expansion for the juventocracy, Shakespeare would work through the whole long tragedy in his two historical tetralogies, *Henry VI–Richard III*, and *Richard II–Henry V*. Prince Hal must find a new way to restore the legitimacy lost when his own father, Henry IV, usurped the throne of Richard II. He does it partly by making his surrogate father Falstaff into a sort of sacrificial victim.

We can see the struggle between the new democratic/heroic culture and the old patriarchy very clearly in such central political documents as Locke's *Two Treatises of Government*, which forms the basis of Anglo-Saxon democracy and thus of most national constitutions. The first treatise is devoted exclusively to a bitter and comprehensive attack against the patriarchy as enunciated by Robert Filmer, that is, against the rule of fathers. That attack was not merely a rhetorical one. It finds its concrete expression in the executions of Charles I of England, Louis XVI of France, and Czar Nicholas of Russia. But having overthrown the patriarch, one must either be totally amoral in the pursuit of unifying political power (Machiavelli), or establish a social contract (Locke and Rousseau). Or one can rely on the supposed natural virtues of the uncultivated noble savage, which replaced the older image of human nature as the product of an inherited natural sociality, enshrined in and cultivated by the patriarchy/matriarchy. But as in *King Lear*, the goddess Nature who stands up for bastards seems to sanction the most horrible atrocities; uncultivated man is more savage than noble. The nobility of those technologically "primitive" people that the European explorers discovered was, so the anthropologists found, not the result of an imagined wild free natural innocence, but of the intactness of their patriarchal/matriarchal social structures. And Rousseau abandoned his own family in typical Faustian style.

The patriarchy, then, has since become a rather feeble political force in the West, surfacing occasionally in the form of local political patronage, western ranch structure, good-old-boy networks, and the Mafia; but it, and the ideals of loyalty, honor, tribalism, and chivalry it enshrined, have been much eclipsed. Feminists who attack the patriarchy surely have the wrong target; their betrayer was the new democratic individualist modernity. Matriarchy and patriarchy are mutually supportive, whereas individualist modernism must despite itself erode the matriarchal foundations. The modern crisis is that the old patriarchy is no longer able to protect either itself or the matriarchy from the modern world.

For even though its interest lay in preserving the ancient matriarchal system, the new modernism could not help diverting the matriarchal sources of economic, psychological, cultural, and spiritual nourishment. The rule of the juventocracy, sanctioning as it did the replacement of old ways of doing things in every generation, was enormously innovative not only in political philosophy but also in science, art, and technology. New textile machinery replaced the household weavers; writing and history replaced the oral tradition; democracy and bureaucracy replaced the old matriarchal consensual hierarchy; labor-saving devices and industrially prepared foods took away some of the household's raison d'être, schools and universities took over the role of educating the young, and industry soaked up the labor market, thereby depriving the household of its vitalizing retinue of servants and companions. The center was decentered as more and more of the household functions were distributed through a grid of impersonal social institutions. The tasks that remained seemed more and more repetitive, trivial, and boring, and began to attract the scorn of feminists. The arranged marriage, which involved the whole family, was replaced by modern ideas of romance. Personal freedom and mobility grew by leaps and bounds, especially for the young, first for men and later for women. The population shot up as a result of better hygiene and more food, inflating societies to the point that even the most powerful traditional houses, like those of the Bourbons and Hapsburgs, or more recently the Marcoses in the Philippines, the Brezhnevs in Russia, and the Somozas in Nicaragua, were unable to respond adroitly to the increased flow of information.

In visual art, music, philosophy, and science a two-phase process was at work: first, a rejection of patriarchal ideas, and then an undermining and betrayal of the matriarchal element that remained. The traditional visual icon was replaced in the Renaissance by perspective and realism, as the patriarchal system of natural emblematic significance was overthrown. This was the first phase. Then, in the late nineteenth century, came the second phase: the modernist rejection of realism itself, of any kind of derivation of the image from nature, a rejection that marked the symbolic death of the matriarchy. Likewise in music, the patriarchal polyphony was replaced during the Renaissance by the *nuove musiche*, in which the word was to be the master of the music: the juventocratic logos would now dominate the paternal pattern or harmony (this latter word cognate, by the way, with *arms, aristocrat, order,* and *ritual*). In the late nineteenth century we see the second phase, in which traditional melody and tonality were in turn undermined and questioned; the new music was "not for old women." In philosophy, likewise, as the patriarchs lost their power, logos replaced the patriarchal nomos as the ruler of cosmos, and mind was separated from and elevated above matter. Then in the nineteenth century, epistemology triumphed and the *mater*—matter itself—was first reduced to passivity, and then to a state of poststructuralist absence. In science the early patriarchal/matriarchal world, which was alive, sacramental, and indissoluble, and in which anatomy was destiny, was first replaced by the dead, dissectable, manipulable, and materialistic universe of Francis Bacon and Doctor Faustus, and then by the relativistic/quantum universe in which matter has disappeared altogether.

It is surely significant that in visual art both the iconic and the representation of nature are returning, that in serious music harmony, melody, and tonality are making a comeback, that in philosophy there are those who dare to call themselves realists and who even posit a cosmos as the region of broadest ethical concern, and that in science the theories of the likes of Whitehead, Prigogine, and Wheeler seem to indicate that the universe is alive and whole after all. Perhaps the story isn't over, and perhaps a new–old kind of hope, heralded by the centrist movement, is emerging.

By the nineteenth century the rebellion of the juventocracy had entered a new phase. Having outgrown the need for paternal legitimation, the young men who made up the new modernity began to reject the ancient contract with the matriarchy that promised women permanent protection and bonded economic service by men in return for a relative certainty that a male's children were his own. Contraception separated sex from reproduction and from the rest of human life. Society seemed so crowded that the dominant ethnic groups no longer saw the need to replenish their numbers, and ignored the demographic trends which foretold a total ethnic transformation of their societies, and a passing over of the power to determine the composition of future societies into other hands. The result was "sexual liberation," which was the death knell of the old matriarchy.

Mozart's *Don Giovanni* marks an important phase in this process. The young hero is not content with overthrowing the old man, but has broken the ancient contract with the matriarchy and has used his male sexual force to attack the sanctity of marriage and family. (Goethe's Faust likewise goes beyond the Renaissance Faust in betraying and destroying Gretchen, the woman who would be his wife.) It is of the utmost significance that Don Ottavio (Octavius was, of course, the "legitimizing" successor to the murdered patriarch Caesar) is himself incapable of dealing with Giovanni and protecting his Donna Anna from the powerful young sexual predator. It takes a patriarch, the Commendatore, who must be brought back from the dead to do so, to restrain the sexual depredations of the young hero; the juventocracy is helpless to protect the reproductive system of society. We find much the same line of mythic thought in Richardson's *Clarissa*.

A similar pattern of betrayal of the woman by the sexually liberated male is played out in the great nineteenth-century novels: *Madame Bovary*, *Anna Karenina*, and *Tess of the D'Urbervilles*. Note that in these works the young woman colludes in her own betrayal; she is torn between identifying with her magnificent rebellious betrayer, returning to the maternal system out of which she has come and which she must herself betray if she is to be liberated, and seeking out the kind and authoritative father whom she will not find because her lover has got rid of him. Mozart and Da Ponte draw her character in Donna Elvira. In *Wuthering Heights* Cathy becomes, like Electra, the accomplice of her brother-lover, the rebel Heathcliff. In *Pride and Prejudice*, on the other hand, the male betrayer, Wickham, is finally seen by Elizabeth in his true colors, and she must come painfully to terms with the wisdom of the matriarchy even though her own mother has betrayed and dissipated it. In order to recover that wisdom she must transform Darcy, the young nonconformist, into a true and gentle patriarch who will be a fit partner for her own prospective renewed matriarchy. In *Middlemarch* Dorothea rebels against her husband Casaubon who is inadequate both as patriarch and as lover; and in choosing the charming and boyish Ladislaw for her lover she assumes for herself not only a matriarchal role, but also a patriarchal one.

The current feminist movement is in fact a reaction against the effects of sexual liberation, a reaction which has borrowed some of the rebellious rhetoric of its opponent. If the males broke the old contract, why should not the females do so too? But if they do, what role is provided for them in the spiritual and social economy? What will replace the traditional system of the matriarchy, so deeply human, creative, and fulfilling? In desperation and anxiety some feminists abandoned the old matriarchal value system and culture, and sought to appropriate traditionally male roles and values instead. They imitated what they thought were the male virtues of aggression and the desire for dominance. It is naturally insupportable to adopt the values of the enemy, and thus tacitly admit defeat by him; therefore the only recourse was to claim that those values were female values all along, which had been prevented from realization by male tyranny. Worse still, freedom seemed to demand the betrayal of the culture of the mothers; but to admit this to oneself was too anguishing. Feminist rebellion resembled that of the young male heroes so closely that it was very hard to see that it was these very brothers and lovers who were their enemy, or at least the occupiers of the ground they coveted. It makes a kind of sense, then, to divert the attack, turning it against a patriarchy that does not really exist except in the imagination. In this light one can deeply sympathize with feminism, and admire the development of its ideology as a courageous and intellectually agile struggle for psychic survival.

But once the generation of transition has passed, and women no longer feel unconsciously that they had no part in creating the values by which they must live, the feminist anxiety and unconscious rage at defeat may well abate. It is entirely within the principles of the new game of modernity that women should participate in it equally with men. The technological/capitalist/democratic system does not in itself care what sex one is; it does not even care very much whether or not one is a human being or a robot, as long as the job gets done. Within the democratic and capitalist-trading ethics of the new dispensation, the fact that to a large extent men invented the game does not make it their exclusive possession. Indeed, like the Westernized economy of Japan, the women may end up playing the game better than their teachers.

It may be psychologically necessary for some women to claim that they were oppressed throughout those many centuries. It seems much more plausible, however, that within the women's world those male values and activities were regarded as boring boy-noise, less interesting than the vital activities of arranging marriages, childrearing, running a household, tending the ancestral spirits, weaving beautiful textiles, perfecting the ancient art of cooking, and maintaining personal relationships. Those activities are now on the way to being like hunting, riding, sailing, and gardening: archaic forms of work that have become pleasures reserved to a wealthy and leisured class. Perhaps it is more comfortable for the rest of us not to miss them too much, even to tell ourselves that they are the burdens of oppression. Then the problem is how to avoid demeaning the traditional values of the matriarchy, of service, love, and wholeness.

One of the advantages of the new feminist myth is that it may tend to diminish the causes for hatred between men and women. Within the context of the old myth of the patriarchy it is easy enough to collect an infuriating list of traditional misogynistic and ill-tempered male diatribes against women, and turn them into a sexual *casus belli*. But when we realize that for most of history there were three rather distinct cultures, a patriarchy, a juventocracy, and a matriarchy, the case becomes more understandable as another example of natural human xenophobia, not very different from what we can see between ethnic groups even today. The fact that the women's culture was largely an oral one makes it a little harder to collect an equivalent set of female complaints about and criticisms of men. Still, it is quite clear that Geoffrey Chaucer was good-naturedly tapping into a rich and vital oral tradition of female misanthropy in his portrait and tale of the Wife of Bath; and the same tradition crops up frequently in fabliaux, in topical drama from all periods, in anthropologists' accounts of traditional and emerging societies, and in women's letters, oral history, and the like. The fact that the sexes have often found it hard to get along with each other is neither new nor remarkable; and it is not surprising that they should relieve their feelings by verbal abuse.

It is clear that in some male individuals, perhaps enough to constitute a minority tradition, misogyny became systematized into sexism, a belief that women are innately inferior to men. Though there have always been wiser heads to contradict them, both male and female, and though it is possible that within the women's tradition there existed serious and systematic beliefs in the inferiority of men, masculinist sexism does stand as a hideous blot in the human record. Some avant-garde critics have interpreted the whole human tradition of art, literature, and science as expressions of patriarchal sexism. The new myth, however, does not require the wholesale rejection of the great human masterpieces of imagination and intellect. And it does not require the distortion of literary history to fit a mold of pro-male, anti-female propaganda. For there are surely far more male villains in fiction, poetry, drama, and narrative sculpture and painting than female villains. While male villains can plumb the depths of inhuman evil, female villains are almost always treated with subtlety and sympathy. Dido nearly steals the show; Cleopatra certainly does and transvalues all the Roman values. We surely find ourselves applauding Medea and Clytemnestra despite our disapproval of their violent crimes, and it is hard to imagine that the Athenian audience would have felt differently. There are perhaps at least as many heroines in literature, of various kinds, as heroes. Penelope, Alcestis, Electra, Antigone, Beatrice, Rosalind, Viola, Portia, Milton's Eve, Tess Durbeyfield, and so on are glorious archetypes of full human being; and one cannot look at the sculptures of the Greek goddesses and medieval Virgins without a shiver of recognition of the divine human essence.

Furthermore, it is not at all clear that women are represented in the arts in any more stereotypical ways than men. One could certainly categorize male characters in as limited and as unhelpful a way as the virgin-mother-whore-slave pattern that some have professed to see in male portrayals of women: hero-father-fool-slave, for instance, and then one could likewise trim the rich and complex artistic creations one finds to fit this trivial procrustean bed. For every passive female character there is an equally passive Richard II or Bishop Proudie or Pip; for every male adventurer there is a magnificent Judith or St. Joan or Dorothea or Isobel Archer; for every female failure, Emma Bovary, Anna Karenina, Tess of the D'Urbervilles, there is a male Werther, Antony, or Lear.

If women have often been portrayed in the domestic context, this may have more to do with the demands of realistic representation than with oppressive ideology. I have already suggested that the domestic scene has not until recently been considered an inferior one, but rather a state of the highest honor. In fact we might well marvel at how many past fictive heroines have been depicted in quite atypical situations, engaging in typically male activities and adventures; as if the male authors yearned to have enthusiastic female comrades but were rebuffed in their implied invitations by women who would rather stay sensibly at home. Every whole man understands the great sigh of joy with which Othello greets Desdemona as she descends from her storm-tossed ship: "Ah, my fair warrior!" It is the prospect and hope of such equal comradeship that makes the tragedy more terrible. Some of the "misogyny" attributed to male writing is surely a misreading of a misguided male appeal to the intelligent young woman to throw off the shackles of the matriarchy, an appeal which is disappointed when the lady turns out to have more sense than to do so!

The same can perhaps be said for those studies based on the old myth, which claim that for art and literature to represent, even to gaze at, is an essentially dominating and tyrannical male act. Such radical feminist criticism either itself represents something, in which case it stands accused of its own indictment and its publication is an act of bad faith, or it does not represent anything, in which case, making no assertion, it does not need to be corrected. And the Gaze seems to be even more offensive when it is *not* directed at oneself, and one does not get the attention one deserves, than when it is so directed. Such double binds are the figments of despair; what we need is hope. More dangerous in the long term, because it may affect one of our few avenues of unwelcome, unexpected, and therefore salvific knowledge, is the notion of "male science," which again relies on the myth of the patriarchy. In refutation of old-myth-based claims that the male mind is linear, it should be pointed out that while indeed the glories of linear algebra and mathematical logic were first revealed by men, so also were the even more beautiful contemporary fields of nonlinear algebra, fractals, dissipative systems, multivalued quantum logic, catastrophe theory, and chaos. Another target of old-myth critique is the linearity of male narratives, especially the "grand narratives" that give meaning and direction to human activity. Here one might point out that women were the traditional tellers of old wives' tales and fairy tales. Recent studies of narrative, moreover, demonstrate that there is nothing quite as nonlinear as a good story, with its strong temporal asymmetry, its fanlike branching of alternative futures, and surprising collapses of the field of possibilities into new gestalts. Stories, like great music, are not predictable until they are over, and often not even then. Male "dualism" is another favorite target; males, it is claimed by the patriarchal myth, tend to separate mind and matter, spirit and body, culture and nature. Here it should be pointed out that men were also the originators of the great monist systems, like the mystical philosophy of the Upanishads, Darwinian evolution, and Whiteheadian process philosophy.

In the patriarchal myth, the dominant oppressive culture dualistically equates men with culture, women with nature. Such an interpretation ignores pertinent facts like the clear reversal of this schema in nineteenth-century America, when it was the men who were seen as close to nature, and the women (nearly twice as many of whom graduated from American high schools in the period than did men) who were associated with culture. A glance at almost any old Western movie will confirm this observation. It is the men who are like animals, who live in the wild, who solve things by bodily action and are no good at writin' and speechifyin'; the women who are the schoolmarms, the pianists, the embodiments of civilization, negotiation, custom, and reason. Indeed one might make a case for such a reversal throughout the nineteenth century, starting with Joseph Conrad, for whom women, like Kurtz's Intended, are a shining light of spirit and culture in a savage and bestial male world. Going further back it might be noted that the divine powers representing the mind are usually female: Athena, Santa Sophia, Urania, the Shekinah. In conclusion, it is surely the adherents of the old myth who in current debates on sociobiology and human evolution insist dualistically on the utter separation of sex and gender, biology and personal rights.

There is no question but that the old matriarchal/patriarchal system did severely limit the potentials of both men and women, and waste talents which could not fit into the stereotypical gender roles. Nor is there any question but that the liberating effect of the rise of the modern world was first experienced by the young males who, for the most part, created that modern world; and it is only recently, both because of socioeconomic forces and because women began to demand it, that women have begun to experience the same liberation. Though institutions of great value—the extended family, the old brotherhoods and sisterhoods of male lodges and female sewing circles—have been lost, perhaps forever, we must assert that the individual liberty that we gained in return is far beyond them in value. As the struggle for equal rights is not yet over, we must not relax our efforts in that direction. But it is not accurate to portray that struggle as the effort of an oppressed sex to throw off the tyranny of an oppressor sex. Nor would it be wise in the long run to do so. Some, perhaps many, of the classical values and institutions of the old matriarchy and patriarchy may be salvageable, reshaped and detached from the restrictive elements that limited human achievement. Moreover the struggle is one in which both sexes have an interest, and will not be achieved if one sex is excluded or alienated by being the target of hatred and prejudice.

Nor should the struggle be glibly described as the throwing off of an evil and tyrannical old system designed to foster the interests of a few. Given the technological limitations, the old patriarchy/matriarchy was a remarkably fair arrangement for making sure that everyone in society got some chance for fulfillment, even if the necessities of survival dictated that one did not get much choice as to the kind of fulfillment one would be offered. It was a very human and personal system, and we can still learn from it. If we forget it or suppress it or distort its history to suit our politics, we will paradoxically cut ourselves off from one source of creative social change in the future. Modernism is not the last word in human achievement, and new generations will want to create cultural environments of their own. Past wisdom is often a great storehouse of evolutionary potential for a society (witness how the Renaissance used apparently outdated classical ideas and values), and the postmodern world will need all the wisdom it can get.

By the same token it would be unjust and counterproductive to attack the very process of modernization, the technological, scientific, and political change which brought to us the remarkable new opportunity we have for a kind of social arrangement that allows such wide choices for both sexes. If it was indeed men who initiated and until its final phases drove that change, this is a reason for gratitude to the male sex, not for resentment. Resentment would be appropriate only if after a reasonable period of readjustment male modernity had refused to share what it had discovered, once it was asked. But this cannot yet be said to be the case. At present we are in a new age of heroes, or rather, of heroines, who are doing what their brothers began to do three thousand years ago. The means for this liberation—the laborsaving and reproductive technology that makes babies less of a burden—is now available; that technology is the gift of their brothers, but it will not and should not determine what they do with it or how the heroines will transform the technology once they take command of it. But the emergence of the heroines is not enough. I believe that the new myth predicts and recommends a *revival* of the patriarchy, in its best sense—as the conserving wisdom of the old men, of that husbandry and concern for the past and the future that characterizes, for instance, the best aspects of the environmental movement. And as *Don Giovanni* shows, the young men do not yet have the wisdom and insight and compassion to restrain themselves and each other from heroic sexual exploitation. There needs to be an antique, honorable counterweight that will transform their sexual aggressivity into gentle and humble knightliness.

Furthermore, the full richness of human experience will not be properly represented in our culture without a healing and restoration of the matriarchy as well. The household is rightly the center of human life. Most children need a stable and loving home environment in order to achieve their potential. The greatest arts are, I believe, not those which cause a stir on museum walls or extend some "shocking" modern or postmodern critical theory into yet another posture or attitude, but those arts which intensify ordinary human existence and fill it with meaning, that make a home into a place that recalls all our beautiful and tragic past, and point to futures that are as human as they are strange and adventurous. New technologies of communication and data processing are making the home once more a viable economic entity, where men and women can lead full and public lives. Now we need truer myths of our past, that will enable women and men to live together without rancor and prejudice.

The Myth of the Oppressive West

The myth of the oppressive patriarchy deceives its followers by promising a story of moral regeneration and underdog crusade, but instead delivering a set of logical, moral, and psychological double binds which can cripple its adherents. Still more paralyzing and self-destructive in the long run is the avant-garde myth of "Western hegemonic dominance." These myths, with their traps, excuses, contradictions, and double binds, are as much the enemy of unfulfilled human potential as any brutal sexist or arrogant racist. Sexists and racists can be opposed with firmness, imagination, compassion, hope, and a cheerful mind. But the aggrieved myths that catch and concentrate and praise the free-floating hatred and the shamed shame that are the leeches of our human condition, and fasten them on their followers, do not allow the exercise of the creative human virtues. They penetrate the mind and heart and suck out their imaginative nourishment; or to change the metaphor, they turn mind and heart against themselves and kill the seeds of hope.

What is the myth of Western hegemonic dominance? Essentially it proposes that a single social and racial group—white Europeans—developed an alienating, hierarchical, and dualistic mode of thought which, by sacrificing the human values of bodily experience, relatedness, and harmony with nature, gave them a kind of Faustian control over society and nature. Other human cultures lived in peace and mutual tolerance with their neighbors, welcoming their cultural differences, but the Western conquerors were racist by nature, and oblivious to the cultural riches they were destroying. The victims could have raised the economic and technological demon to defend themselves, but did not wish to, because of their greater wisdom, which warned them against the perils of ecological destruction, social discrimination, commodity fetishism and economic oppression.

The new Western tribe of cold, grasping, and arrogant white males, closely identified with the oppressive patriarchy as described in the previous section, spread out over the world and reduced the other cultures to colonial subjection and slavery. The process continues unabated, as the West moves into a new phase of "late-capitalist" economic colonialism; its most subtle twist is to use "Western values," which are in fact hypocritical systems of control and mystification, to maintain its dominance. Among those so-called values are rationality, empirical objectivity, democratic due process, the control of the body and emotions by reason, delayed gratification, and such abstract, essentialistic ideals as goodness, truth, and beauty. The central tenet of Western ideology is that there is only one overarching truth; this totalizing idea denies the diversity and relativity of cultural values, and the great ideals of diversity and pluralism.

According to this myth, the traditions of Western art, literature, science, and philosophy are riddled with hidden justifications for oppression, and thus politically poisonous, except for some works, which were either composed by persons of non-Western ancestry or influenced by non-Western sources. Western mathematical, physical, and chemical sciences reduce the living world to a passive and inanimate colonial victim, to be exploited and raped by technology for the sake of power. Western biological science, especially the theory of evolution, in asserting that human beings are subject to biological constraints and possess a human nature, is fundamentally racist and should be controlled or abolished. The continued teaching of the Western artistic and literary canon in schools and universities is a racist ploy to suppress other cultures whose achievements are as great or greater. The purpose and net result of all these Western techniques has been to keep the masses of people in the third world, and their brothers and sisters, the minority populations in the West itself, in a state of poverty, misery, and powerlessness.

This myth, despite its compelling story, apparently clear scapegoat, and occasional correspondence with fact, is deeply self-contradictory and in essence a counsel of despair. It can only harm the very victims it pretends to elevate and justify. Let us examine its factual errors and inconsistencies, so that by correcting them we can construct a truer myth, one less harmful in its effects.

The first factual error is that the West is uniquely patriarchal in its organization and worldview. The opposite would be much closer to the truth. If the West is unique, one of the ways it is so is that even before the twentieth century brought worldwide cultural communication, the West had largely *overthrown* the patriarchy of authoritarian fathers and substituted a legalized and individualized government of men appointed without regard to their family status. It had then begun the journey toward the emancipation of women; and by the time worldwide communication came about, the West was more advanced toward gender blindness in its institutions than any non-Western society.

Nor is the West unique in its ethnocentrism, xenophobia, and racism. All three are culturally universal, though they tend to diminish among the elite and better educated groups in any society. Indeed, one of the problems of democracy is that it empowers the broad masses of people, who because of their poorer education are much less likely to be tolerant of differences than the elites tend to be. The recent appearance of bitter ethnic conflicts among the newly enfranchised peoples of Eastern Europe once the educated communist elite was overthrown is a good example; another is the eruption of tribal genocide in Africa once the colonial elites had given way to populist native rule. Racial and ethnic prejudice is a normal feature of every society, from Serbia to Brazil, from China to Honduras, from Lebanon to Australia, from Sri Lanka to Azerbaijan. It is only in those countries in which there is a serious attempt to wipe out racism, mostly, that is, in the West, that racism is considered anything other than common sense.

Indeed, prejudice and stereotyping could be seen as the essential mechanism of all human (and perhaps all mammal, vertebrate, even animal) perception and information-processing. Our visual and acoustic pattern-recognition systems work by comparing new stimuli with earlier ones and categorizing them with what they resemble from previous experience (i.e., prejudice), and by iterating and emphasizing small quantitative differences until they appear to be major differences of kind (i.e., stereotyping). This is the "default option" of any intelligent system of knowledge and memory, and it takes great discipline and vigilance to override it. The European traditions of classical study, objective scientific experiment, the Grand Tour, and the like, were deliberate efforts to override this default option, to overcome the Baconian idols of the tribe, the cave, the marketplace, and the theater, and to give the educated person the capacity to look at something clearly, without prejudice. Paradoxically, though, the very ideal of unprejudiced scientific objectivity is condemned by the detractors of the West as a cold and inhuman perversion. Paradoxically again, it may have been this very capacity, this unnatural ability to overcome prejudice, that was the key to European success in world conquest; such minds could adapt to the unfamiliar, see how it worked, and act accordingly. The story of the Aboriginal tribesmen who were able to recognize and perceive Captain Cook's rowboats but could not notice his ship because it was so huge and unfamiliar, is a disquieting index of the limits of human awareness, limits that Western science was designed to overcome. It is indeed one of the tragedies of history that despite these disciplines, many educated Europeans and Americans fell for the horrible and intellectually lazy superstition of racism, descending to the level of the human norm, to the racist mental habits of the very people whom they despised for their lack of rigorous objective self-criticism.

Another factual error in the myth of the West is that the West was unique in instituting slavery. To the contrary, many human societies have practiced some form or other of slavery. It seems to be almost a cultural norm in those stages of human cultural development from the early agrarian empire, through the city state, feudalism, and mercantile colonialism up to the ascendancy of the national urban industrial middle class, when it begins to die out. It is found throughout the ancient and classical Mediterranean, most of the high civilizations of South and Southeast Asia, among the precolonial African kingdoms, and in the pre-Columbian American empires. It was still practiced within living memory in some parts of the Islamic world.

But here a distinction must be made. Slavery as commonly practiced, for instance in the old Greek and Roman empires and in China, did not necessarily involve racism. Freed slaves could and did rapidly integrate into the general population; indeed, the population of contemporary Europe is descended in part from slaves belonging to Greek and Roman masters. The final form of slavery, as practiced by mercantile colonialism, was peculiarly virulent, involving large differences in technological development between the enslavers and the enslaved, early industrial forms of exploitation of labor, and especially racism, compounded by obvious differences in skin color, which acted as a marker to prevent easy social assimilation into the general population. It is in the struggle against this form of slavery and its after-effects that a large part of the social conscience of Europe and America has been formed. In this light the myth of the West, which attributes a special evil to the white race, can be seen as merely the obverse of the ideology of the mercantile racists, and is as damaging to the cause of human justice as its original. It promotes a loyalty among the once oppressed to the psychological mindset of oppression, and perpetuates the cultural damage done by race slavery.

The West is not unique in the practice of conquest and imperialism. The imperialistic exploits of Islam and the Han Chinese, the expansionism of the great Mesoamerican and Andean empires, the epic conquests of the old African kingdoms and the odyssey of the ancient agrarian peoples of Taiwan who swept through the East Indies on their way to Polynesia and Madagascar, are now under study by historians, archaeologists, and linguists. One of the greatest waves of conquest was that of the Bantu peoples of west Africa, who drove east and south, enslaving or exterminating the indigenous Pigmy and Khoisan peoples that they encountered, to meet the Boers in the seventeenth century as they trekked north from the Cape of Good Hope. There are no human beings anywhere who live where their ancestors always lived; we are all the children of interlopers, conquerors, enslavers, aliens, as well as of their victims. There is also no cultural purity anywhere in the world, no set of simple and unadulterated folkways, no authentic wellspring of human innocence.

One of the principles of the myth of the oppressive West is that the West is unique in suppressing and controlling the body and its emotions, and in conceptually dividing the body from the mind, soul, or spirit. Every known culture, however, has traditions, institutions, and training designed to control the body and to suppress some of its autonomous functions. For instance, all societies have an incest taboo, almost all have some kind of formal training for the skills of hunting or dancing or martial arts, most have some form of ordeal, such as circumcision, to mark the coming of adulthood, and many, such as the Indians, the Tibetans, the Chinese, and the Japanese, have long traditions of extreme asceticism designed to bring all functions of the body and the emotions under the control of the spirit. It might be in the interest of those who have little stomach for such disciplines to claim them to be the tools of hegemonic Western control; but wherever such critics went, they would find the same thing.

An important element in the myth is that the oppressive West is unique in imposing a barrier between human beings and the natural world. On the contrary, the fundamental human distinctions between nature and culture and between the "natural" elements in the human makeup and the "supernatural" ones, are culturally universal. Different societies, and different moieties and historical periods within societies, draw the line differently between body and soul (are the emotions physical or spiritual? Is there a sharp dualism or a subtle hierarchy?), but almost all draw the line. The "Westerners" Jesus, Plato, Lucretius, Augustine, Descartes, Hume, Berkeley, Blake, Hegel, and D. H. Lawrence all had wildly different views of the matter; but the distinction is not unique to the West. Indeed, just the opposite might be argued: that the West is the only culture to have seriously questioned the distinction between the human and the natural, the body and the soul. Western evolutionary theory shows the continuity of the human with the natural;

Western biopsychology interprets mental, emotional, and spiritual events as real, effective higher-order activities of a physical body. There are dualists and monists in every great human cultural tradition; in the West monism has been given some of its best intellectual arguments, by thinkers from Heraclitus and Parmenides to Whitehead and de Chardin, from Democritus and Lucretius to Darwin and Wheeler, from Emerson and Swedenborg to Freud and Marx.

Another error implicit in the myth of the West is that human beings are born as blank slates and are inscribed and determined by culture (which, depending on the severity and purity of the myth-exegetes, is determined by social conditions, which are in turn determined by economics and the struggle for power). Most of the scientific evidence—from neurochemistry, neuropsychology, sociobiology, twin studies, physical anthropology, and genetics—indicates that to the extent that either is a determinant of human behavior, the "nature/nurture" or "heredity/environment" ratio is something like 70/30 or even 80/20. That is, a child's genetic inheritance will be two to four times more important statistically in determining how successful he or she will be in society than his or her upbringing. However, and this is an important distinction, the success of the *social group* into which a child is born is highly dependent upon its general level of culture, education, and technology. Thus a gifted child born into a stunted or self-limiting community—an Amish village, an urban youth gang, a colonial plantation—will normally succeed only in the terms of that community; it would take an exceptional individual to reject that community, a rejection which might well feel like a betrayal.

A more subtle error is the assumption that the myth makes, that to assert the greater importance of genetic heredity over social construction in the determining of the individual is tantamount to racism. The inference does not in fact follow at all. For instance, the dependence of the individual's potential upon his or her genetic inheritance could be perfectly consistent with the following nonracist positions: that the races have statistically different distributions of talents, but the distributions are of equal value; that the races have exactly the same distribution of talents, though within a given race there is great variation in individual abilities; that the races are extremely recent and transient phenomena in the history of the human species, and their differences are completely superficial; and that the "races" do not in any serious genetic sense exist at all, since there has been so much interbreeding within the general human population that differences in skin color and so on are statistical variations within a single actively communicating gene pool.

It should be noted that a community filled with clever and talented people with excellent genes might well make a false technological turn or poor cultural choice, or through bad geographical or meteorological luck find itself trapped in a cultural pattern that employed the potentials of its members to relatively fruitless ends; and the result might well look very like an "inferior race." The disadvantages of such a community might well make it vulnerable to another society which had had better luck in its choices and circumstances, and which would, until a better scientific understanding of genetics came along, rather naturally assume that its own individuals, rather than its institutions, were innately superior to those of its rival. The weaker society would then be faced with the agonizing choice of giving up its own counterproductive cultural practices and adopting some of its enemy's, ceasing to exist as a society, or continuing to justify the reasonable but uninformed racial prejudices of its oppressor. The point is that it should be possible to make a critique of a culture, while maintaining the primacy of nature over nurture in the makeup of the individual, without necessarily taking a racist position.

The most fundamental contradictions in the myth of the West arise from the question: is there one set of coherent, correct, and genuine values, or many, or none? The first alternative, that there is only one, is ruled out by the tenets of pluralism, diversity, and cultural relativity; but in the morass of contradictions that the myth generates, it keeps coming back as a tantalizing but treacherous guide. Suppose we take the second alternative: that there are several different correct and genuine value systems, without an overarching value system to translate and adjudicate among them. In the absence of a higher value system, how could we say that they are correct and genuine, or incorrect and false? Western values, for instance: if they are false, against what standard? In what terms can pluralism and diversity themselves be defended, if they are only the values of one group and have no higher standing? Why should it be wrong for one value system to swallow up the others? Particularly irksome is that the ideas of equality, pluralism, and relativity were pioneered by the West. The West has always been intensely curious about and attracted to other cultures, a trait which is not universally shared. Most of what the world knows about other cultures was discovered by Western anthropologists, who were often fiercely committed to the culture they were studying and deeply skeptical about their own; anthropology was a Western invention.

If there is no overarching "human nature," but only a plurality of culturally determined concepts of the human, how can there be human rights? If one ethical system believes in clitoridectomy or slavery, and another does not, how do we decide which is right? If there is a plurality of true value systems, there must be values other than the economic and the political; if true happiness can consist in the life of virtue or mystical experience, divorced from materialistic concerns, then those who lead such a life would surely be only too glad to leave the miseries of wealth and power to the West. But if the West is on an equal footing in a contest with all other cultures, then it has humiliatingly and totally "won." If other cultures did not perceive it as a contest, then they need not complain that they have lost, since they were noncompetitors. If Western values—that virtue is its own reward, that we should prefer personal and interpersonal goods to materialistic ones, that we should practice thrift and delay gratification, and so on—are simply hypocritical mystifications to deceive the oppressed, then without an overarching set of ethical rules, we would be quite free to praise these subterfuges in the struggle for success. Would it even be an absolute virtue to practice what we preach, since there are no absolute virtues? If the values of the West are those of denial of the body and the emotions, then who could envy them a wealth they cannot enjoy? But if, on the other hand, the West is hedonistic, lazy, and wasteful, how can it have achieved its economic success?

Western values may be hierarchical, dualistic, or alienating, as the myth claims; but they cannot be all three. Hierarchy, which implies a branched structure of inclusion and connection, a wholeness whose top-down control is balanced by bottom-up feedback, is, as we have seen, the least alienating of all systems. (Of course the only effective kind of hierarchy, human or biological, is one which is legitimated by consent, regulated by due process, and flexible in its accommodation of differences; ineffective hierarchies can offer neither threat nor benefit to their neighbors.) Hierarchy is a way of multiplying levels of inclusion and control, so as to avoid complete lack of structure and connection on the one hand, and a barren, uncommunicating dualism on the other. Without the idea of hierarchy, we must either think of the human body as a mere valueless piece of matter, or as an illusion of the soul or spirit, or as a partner in a dualistic combination of soul and body that can neither sense nor act, because the natures of soul and body are so different. The West has pioneered the attempt to find substitutes for hierarchy in human organization, but to no avail; the best we can do, it seems, is to legitimate, loosen, strengthen, and complexify it by democracy, federalism, and the separation of powers. "Network" systems of organization, which some have proposed as an alternative, turn out to be either hierarchies in disguise, or else little hivelike totalitarianisms which sacrifice diversity and freedom to consensus and political correctness.

If there is a plurality of different true value systems, then there is a plurality of goods defined as such by those value systems, and thus no competition, and no possibility for injustice, since the good of one would not involve the loss of the good of another. To the extent that there can be injustice in the allocation of goods, the contestants must share a value system. The kicker of a field goal should not feel aggrieved that his achievement does not count toward his earned-run average. The idea of justice and the accusation of injustice depend upon the overwhelming of diversity, the resolution of pluralism into unity, the replacement of relativism by shared absolutes.

The third alternative in our analysis of values in the myth of the west—that there is no such thing as correct values—offers even less comfort, though it is the last resort of thinkers like Foucault, who have the intelligence to perceive the traps of the first two. Without values, power is the only constraint upon desire. If this is the case, the moral complaints of the "loser" cultures are without substance, though they might be a useful and effective strategy for persuading sentimental members of the "winner" culture to abandon their own interests and yield themselves up for plucking by their erstwhile victims. It might seem that such a world would be pleasant for the strong and horrible for the weak; but I believe it would in fact be even more horrible for the strong, who in their greater insight, clarity, and leisure would perceive without self-deception and distraction the horror of a valueless world.

However we take the myth of the West, then, we are faced at every turn with despair. It is indeed despair for the West, as morally irredeemable; what reparation would be possible for its imputed crimes, if they are unique? Any moral accounting of the story as told by the myth should lead to all Westerners committing suicide in part payment for their crimes. But it is despair also for the "third world" and the "minorities," as losers either in the game of values or in the game of power. If the West is as bad, as powerful, as cleverly conspiratorial, secret, and self-aware, as the myth proposes, then there is no way that it will give up its power, and no way to force it to do so. Indeed, the only intelligent recourse would be to give up the struggle and learn to enjoy the doubtful pleasures of the oppressed: the satisfaction of physical desires, the oppression of those even weaker than oneself, the relinquishing of any attempt at objectivity, the sense of complete irresponsibility for one's own condition, the loss of anxiety about the past and future, and the feeling of solidarity with others who have likewise given in.

This despair is concretely exemplified in the condition of the "underclass" in some economically advanced countries with large "ethnic minorities." Within the myth of the West, any personal individual success tends to undermine the proposition that the racist majority, by oppressing the ethnic minority, renders the individual member of it incapable of positive action (since it is culture and society that determine the individual's achievements, not that individual's genetic inheritance). Thus personal achievement by a minority individual is by its very nature a betrayal of the myth that is the "loyalty oath" of the oppressed group and an affront to other members of the group who have not succeeded in rising above the general condition of economic misery, poor education, drug addiction, teenage pregnancy, and unemployment.

There are indeed oppressed groups, which, if group identity translated easily into individual identity, should receive massive reparations sufficient to enrich every member. But another paradox of despair emerges here: if oppression does lead to personal damage, and if personal damage makes an individual less capable of contributing to society, and if one's personal deserving is measured by the extent of one's contributions to society, the greater the social reparations one deserved, the lesser the personal ones. According to the anthropologists, it is in the nature of human beings to desire fair exchanges, a fair balance between what one gives and what one receives. The double bind of the myth is that the more one deserves as a member of a group, the less one deserves as an individual; the more one were given in compensation as an "ethnic minority," the less one would find oneself, as a *person*, in a satisfactory and respectable condition of fair exchange with one's neighbors. The political need to assert the determinism of cultural, social, political, and economic factors over biogenetic or personal spiritual ones essentially makes individuals helpless and shamed, and empowers only the "caring professions" and political leaders that are paid to look after them.

One final act of despair has been to deny the very reality of the person, the self, the individual, to assert that the self is only a social construct. If we do so, we also abandon the only unit in which it makes sense to talk about right and wrong action, ethics, morality, and obligation. If I do not have a real self or person, then I cannot have any personal moral responsibility. Perhaps the social group to which "I" belong has such a responsibility, as the author of the social construct of the self, but that cannot translate into any obligation on "myself" to do anything about it, since there is no myself to be obligated. If society wants you to behave differently, it had better change you; you cannot change yourself. And so we return to the ideological reeducation camps, and so on.

To sum up, then, perhaps the worst and deepest feature of the myth of the oppressive West is that it ends up doing exactly the opposite of what it was designed to do, rendering impossible any improvement in the world's glaring social and economic inequalities, dissolving the sources of moral authority that might mandate such improvement, paralyzing the victims of injustice, and exonerating those who have happily escaped it from any obligation to help; because, being socially determined, they cannot be expected to take an individual initiative to do so without the aid of forced social reeducation. Like the myth of the patriarchy, the myth of the oppressive West is good only for one thing: to serve as a justification for personal failure, an argument against hope, and a rationalization for despair. As large areas of the globe descend into ethnic conflict, and racial separatism becomes fashionable in America itself, the myth of the West becomes increasingly recognizable as just another version of the ancient hatred story—of heathen Turks or imperialist Greeks, of idolatrous Sinhalese or fanatical Tamils, of grasping Armenians or ruthless Azerbaijanis, of loveless whites or violent blacks, of lazy Arabs or expansionist Zionists. The fact that this essentially racist myth is being propagated by the very people who claim the mantle of desegregation and civil rights makes its widespread acceptance still more tragic.

What are we to do when one of the chief intellectual and imaginative instruments of the movement toward racial equality and human enfranchisement, the myth of the oppressive West, turns out to be not only false and self-contradictory, but deeply damaging to the cause it was designed to serve? The answer, I believe, is to seek out a different myth, that better enshrines the truth, and that will serve as a fruitful guide to positive action. To do this, though, will require a radical rethinking of many of our most deeply held assumptions, and a redefinition of many of our fundamental terms. The very words "race," "ethnic," "nature," and especially "West" may need to be transformed or even abolished in their present meaning. We must radically redefine the "nature–nurture" debate and the "nature–culture" distinction. We must rechart the story of human history upon a projection that no longer distorts it out of true recognition. We must find the courage and the intellectual subtlety to be able to reassert some unfashionably absolute ideas, such as truth, goodness, and beauty, though on a new footing that will contain and neutralize the philosophical objections that led to their rejection. We must dare to stare once again into the horrifying, beautiful, and challenging implications of our evolutionary descent from our animal ancestors. And we must discover in the heart of what seem to be humanity's darkest and most terrible traits—our xenophobia and aggressiveness—the roots of some of our finest and most beautiful moral capacities.

Clearly the old myth, of mechanistic essentialistic oppressive dualistic white males ravaging an unoffending world, will not stand up. What can we replace it with? What *is* the "West"?

The answer is that it does not exist in the sense of being a single culture, even a dominant single culture. If we see it as "a" culture, we might well be inclined to identify it with some particular race or ethnic tradition, and be rightly disturbed if it unfairly dominates some other culture (whatever that means) just as worthy of consideration. Instead, let us trace the emergence of what is often called the West but is in fact a composite culture, composed of hundreds or perhaps even thousands of highly different human cultures from all over the world, a multiculture which is rapidly becoming world human culture, and which is enormously fertile of new diversity within itself.

The great theme of human prehistory, that is, the period before writing, monuments, and records began to connect the generations by other means than memory, is divergence, diaspora, separation. According to genetic archaeology, the technique of tracing back mitochondrial DNA lineages, the human race is most likely descended from a single small population, residing, probably, in Africa. Since that time the huge migrations of hunter-gatherer groups, and then later the invasions and diffusions of farming peoples all over the world and their genetic isolation in new habitats, produced enough genetic diversity to form distinguishable races, and the budding and branching of several major language groups.

Since the beginning of recorded history, however, the pattern has changed. The same technology that produced records and communications also produced agricultural, metallurgical, political, and military institutions that led in turn to empires, huge amalgamations and assimilations of peoples and languages, trade and interbreeding. The theme now becomes unification; not the disappearance of cultural differences, but the denser and denser superimposition of them within the minds and lives of individuals, and the emergence of larger concepts, of logic, science, money, law, and art that could contain the diversity and make sense of it. During this time, like tiny flaws or "seeds" in a liquid undergoing crystallization, certain cultural nodes formed, around which the emerging unity of world culture began to take shape. Those nodes included the pyramid empires of Africa, Southwest Asia, and Central and South America, and the great riverine irrigation civilizations of India and China. As time went by, some of these growing centers of convergence merged in turn.

Let us trace the development of what was perhaps the largest and most important tributary of this huge human river: the one that began in Mesopotamia. Seven major phases can be distinguished.

The first is the Mesopotamian phase, which connected a great swathe of Middle Eastern peoples, from the mountains of present-day Iran and Turkey to the forests of Lebanon. Trade links formed with the ancient Indian civilizations, with Egypt, and with the farmers and herders of Europe and the Mediterranean. Through Egypt came influences and traders from Nubia and the east coast of Africa. The story of Abraham's migration from Mesopotamia is but one episode in the great cultural and genetic mixing that was going on throughout the Fertile Crescent.

The second phase can be called the Greek phase. Through the Phoenicians and the Hittites, the Greeks absorbed masses of cultural material from Mesopotamia and further east. Egypt and especially Crete contributed their own influences. The invasion of Dorians from the north brought new currents into this human river of ideas and genes. And then the explosion of the Greek colonial empire began to unite the cultures of the whole Mediterranean and the Black Sea, connecting Etruscans, Persians, Indians, and many other peoples from Asia, Africa, and Europe.

The Roman Empire, like the Greek, is often thought of as "Western" and homogeneous, but in many ways it was a thoroughly mongrel culture. Its main currents were Italic, Greek, Celtic, Jewish, and Egyptian, but again dozens of other peoples, from Picts and Germans in the north and Dacians and Parthians in the east to the peoples of North Africa in the south and of the Hispanic peninsula in the west all contributed their ideas, arts, rituals, religions, and technology. The Romans traded with the Indians, the Chinese, the East Africans, and the peoples of Scandinavia, Russia, and Siberia.

The Muslim civilization in turn inherited much of the cultural riches of Greece, Jerusalem, and Rome, via Alexandria and Byzantium, and added to them powerful and original influences from Africa and the Orient. As it spread, it deepened the links with India and China, and added new influences from as far away as Indonesia. Its many flowerings in Arabia, in Cordoba, in North Africa, in Turkey, and in the Indus valley, integrated the old learning with new developments in logic, poetry, mathematics, medicine, and metaphysics.

The next phase might be called the European. During the Dark Ages, waves of new cultural influences, and new genetic strains, poured in from Asia and northeastern Europe: Goths and Wends and Tatars, Magyar and Finnish shamanists from the Altai, Slavs, and Teutons. Through Sicily and Spain and Hungary the heritage of Muslim civilization began to infuse the emerging culture of medieval Christendom. The old civilizations of Greece and Rome were rediscovered; and in due time the influences coalesced into that incandescent period of creative integration and imagination, the Renaissance. Now all those accumulated intellectual disciplines, whose roots spread out over much of Africa and Asia, were focused into that remarkable human achievement we call science, the union of mathematics with controlled observation and experiment, which marks a fresh phase in the evolutionary history of the universe. The integration of these ideas was unique; though most human groups had already contributed to it, the "butterfly effect" by which it came together could only happen in one place, where the accumulation was densest and the pressure highest.

The next phase, the colonial period, was the time of the metastasizing of this remarkable and ancient human "disease," the radiation of this new cultural species across the whole planet. Though the techniques of the European conquerors felt to their victims like the special strangeness of an alien culture, this was a tragic illusion; science and technology were not merely a European invention or possession, but, as I have shown, the direct creation of most of the human species, and indirectly the proper achievement of humanity as a whole. Colonial peoples such as those of India and Africa were sometimes unaware that they had contributed some of the key ideas that their colonial oppressors now used against them. Now at last the relatively isolated cultures of the Americas, of sub-Saharan Africa, and of Oceania began to pour their own contributions into the great stream of the human plenum.

At present we are rightly appalled by the atrocities of the colonizers. But it is only the fact that they took place in the full glare of historical record and advanced communication, that they were conducted with greater technological efficiency, and that they were essentially the last wave of human integration, that distinguishes them from the bloody genocides of the past; genocides that are part of the dark inheritance of every surviving nation or tribe, without exception. The great virtue of this emerging world civilization, falsely called the West, was that it was passionately interested in other cultures, and could so profoundly imagine the world of the other that the other was no longer the Other. Orientalism, despite the sneers of the likes of Edward Said, was a movement of extraordinary imaginative generosity: we see it issue forth in the exquisite Japanese visual sensibility of Mary Cassatt and Aubrey Beardsley, in the Chinese musicality of Gustav Mahler, and in Yeats's Noh plays. The Benin bronzes transformed European sculpture. Anthropology was invented, at its best the first systematic attempt by any culture to see another culture as it sees itself. In the stories of Rudyard Kipling, that are rightly considered by Indians to be masterpieces of Indian literature, in Melville's *Typee* and *Omoo*, in Gauguin's painted Tahiti, in the African influences of Picasso's *Demoiselles d'Avignon*, in the great translations of non-European literatures, in *Black Orpheus*, in Frank Lloyd Wright's

Maya architecture, in Frida Kahlo and *The Plumed Serpent* and Joseph Conrad and Joseph Needham and above all in jazz, the emerging world culture ecstatically took to itself the inner life of the Other.

The last phase might be called that of the information age. This period can be compared to the "shaking down" and integration of ideas, cultures, and racial strains that took place in medieval Christendom, wherein the old tribes of Europe lost part of their political identity but gained the heritage of all their neighbors; a period that flowered in the Renaissance. We have much more to integrate, and there is an even stronger reactionary tendency toward tribalism and Balkanization, in fear of the terrible light and pressure of full humanity. That reaction presently goes under the banner of "diversity" and "pluralism" in America; it is not deeply different from the bloody conservatism of the Serbs and Croats, of the Azerbaijanis and Armenians, of Israeli fundamentalists and Palestinian extremists.

One paradigmatic expression of the new world integration is Peter Brook's *Mahabharata*, whose cast contains members of almost every major ethnic group. But we can find it also in many contemporary phenomena: "World Music," the international financial markets, the worldwide concern with environmental issues, telecommunications, the World Health Organization, international science, the worldwide interest in the space program, and throughout the arts. The media link the world in nanoseconds. Japan has outdone Europe and America at their own industrial game, and the "little dragons" of the Pacific rim are doing so too. Huge common market areas emerge. The last legally racist regime, South Africa, has dissolved itself. One of the special characteristics of the information age is that the artists of it are no longer predominantly European and American, exercising an imaginative sympathy for other peoples. They are of all backgrounds, and live within a world where there is no privileged center of initiative or special insight. Indian anthropologists study white American natives. Kurosawa gives us the definitive Shakespeare, Yo-Yo Ma the definitive cello, Midori the definitive Mozart. The Latin American novel sets the fashion in fiction, West African griots set it in music. The coauthors of scientific papers read like an international directory of names. When the Berlin Wall came down there was a great performance in Berlin of the *Carmina Burana*, with a black American soloist, a Jewish conductor, a German orchestra, and a Chinese choir.

This story of the emergence of world culture might also have been told with some plausibility from the viewpoints of the Indian subcontinent or from that of the coasts of the South China Sea, rather than from that of the Mediterranean, as I have done here. Europe was a backwater at the very beginning and during the Dark Ages. It would be harder to tell it as if its center of intensity were anywhere else, and those three nodes were themselves closely connected for thousands of years. Today its center is everywhere on the globe, though there are still places where, because of concentrations of wealth, education, population, and tradition, the fire burns most brightly.

But the point is that for any self-styled local culture to set itself against the "West"—that is, against the composite world culture—is pathetically futile and self-destructive. Even if there are aspects of that local culture that the "West," communicating and remembering humanity, has not yet absorbed, imagined, understood, and internalized already, one can be sure that in a short time it will have incorporated them and reactivated them in itself. There are no real "minorities"; we are all members of the majority, or we are nothing. There is nothing to stop what is called "cultural appropriation," even if we felt morally obliged to prevent it. Since such appropriation is indistinguishable from the fame that all peoples want, and since cultural goods, unlike material ones, are not removed from their originators when they are transferred to others, there is no good ethical reason for preventing it.

Not that the majority is homogeneous and undifferentiated. Consider the integration of peoples that happened in the Middle Ages. It gave rise to the deeply diverse national cultures of Europe; the Romance Languages were all originally dialects of Latin. Diversity, such is the genius of the human species, is inevitable. We will certainly want to revive or continue the beautiful stories and rituals and arts and metaphysics of specific cultural groups, especially those from which we can trace immediate genetic descent. But we will have no exclusive rights of possession over them, and no responsibility to keep them pure from contamination by other traditions, unless we wish to do so for scholarly or antiquarian or aesthetic or sentimental reasons.

Diversity will not go away. But in the future that diversity will exist on a common basis of economic, political, and scientific understandings which can be ignored only at the cost of self-exile from the human community:

understandings that include the free market, self-government, verifiable experimental protocols, and the evolutionary theory of the universe. These understandings are not especially glamorous in themselves, though the story of their emergence is an epic one: they are like an effective sewage system or clean water. But a demand for ethnic identity which dispenses with them, and which denies the brotherhood and sisterhood of our species, is hopeless and doomed.

A New Multicultural Myth

Let us sketch out a brief account of the process by which our ancestors evolved into human beings. In this perspective it is clear that no human group is uniquely pure and good, or uniquely oppressive and wicked.

Consider the human body and its remarkable differences from the bodies of other mammals. One of the most obvious is our nakedness; we stand hairless but for odd tufts here and there emphasizing such body parts as the head and face, and the genitals. All other land mammals of our size, and all of our primate relatives, including all tropical primates, are covered with hair. Human beings, moreover, are pantropic in their habit; they live in all climates. Without clothing and/or shelter they would be at a massive disadvantage. Human beings, like other species, evolved through the mechanism of natural selection. If a species would be better off with hair, to maintain a constant body temperature, hair will be selected for. How and why did we lose our hair? As can be seen in the case of the peacock's tail and the antlers of the great elk, which were the result of sexual selection rituals but which are handicaps in the struggle for survival, sexual selection can contradict the biological law of selection for adaptive fitness. The most plausible explanation for our nakedness, then, is that it is the result of sexual selection in ritual courtship, and that we developed clothing originally both for ritual body decoration and also to replace for thermal purposes the hair that we had lost. The invention of clothes, a by-product of our ritual, enabled us to survive even in cool temperate and arctic climates; as hair was no longer necessary for survival, it never came back. Thus our nakedness is a result of our early culture.

Here we see a new kind of reflexive feedback enter the already tangled, iterative, and turbulent process of natural evolution. Cultural evolution, a process of change in behavior that can happen in a single generation and be passed down through imitation and learning to the next, now takes a hand in biological evolution, in the iterated cycle of sexually or mutatively generated variation, selection by the preferential survival of useful traits in the population, and genetic inheritance. Biological evolution takes millennia; cultural evolution takes years. Yet the culture of a species, especially in its effect on sexual and reproductive success, is a powerful determinant of which individuals survive to reproduce. The faster process of change—culture—will drive and guide the slower one—biology.

Many of the other peculiar characteristics of the human body can be explained in the same way: its upright stance, its long infancy, its developed vocal chords and otolaryngeal system, its extraordinary longevity (especially in the female), its relatively early menopause, its relative lack of specialized armaments (big teeth and claws, and so on), its opposable thumbs, its superbly refined and coordinated fine motor system, its continuous sexual readiness (most animals are in heat only for a few days in the year), its huge brain. The upright stance reveals the full beauty of human primary and secondary sexual organs to each other; bipedalism frees the arms and enables hunters and gatherers to carry meat and vegetables home, and therefore compels them to have to remember who gets which share. Thus it also helps us to have a headquarters to carry things back to, a ritually charged homeplace, and a kinship system that can serve as a set of rules for who gets what. It enables parents to carry babies in their arms—babies who are helpless because they require a much longer infancy period than the young of other species, a long infancy demanded by the need to program children in the complexities of the tribal ritual. The upright stance also makes possible the face-to-face mating position, thus encouraging that extraordinary mutual gaze which is the delight of lovers and the fundamental warrant of the equality of the sexes: an equality which was absolutely essential if the human traits of intelligence, communication, and imagination were to be preferred and thus reinforced.

Our ritual songs, improved every year, demanded complex voice-production systems that could also come in useful for communication in the hunt and other cooperative enterprises. Our long old age enabled the elders, especially the postmenopausal wisewomen, to pass on the ritual lore and wisdom. Our lack of bodily armament was compensated for by the development of weapons, which could be wielded by thumbed hands liberated by our upright stance and controlled by an advanced fine motor system. Thumbed hands were required to enact the ritual actions, and smear on the ritual body-paint, and carry the ritual objects, and make the ritual clothing, and gather the seeds and roots for our tribal kin. Sexuality was extended and intensified, relative to other animals, and was adapted from its original reproductive function into the raw material of an elaborate ritual drama that pervaded all aspects of society. And the great brain mushroomed out, transforming its substructures to the new uses and demands that were being placed on it, pushing out the skull, diminishing the jaws, wiring itself more and more finely into the face, hands, and speech organs, specializing particular areas of the right and left to handle new linguistic, musical, and pictorial-representational tasks, developing a huge frontal lobe to coordinate everything else and to reflect upon itself and its body and its death, and connecting that higher-level reflective consciousness by massive nerve bundles to the limbic emotional centers—thus creating a unity of function between the intellectual and the passionate that is close to the heart of our deepest shame as well as our finest achievements, and which has thus been denied by most of our modern avant-garde philosophical systems.

From this point of view personal physical beauty takes on new importance. When we fall in love, and thus mate and have offspring, we do so often because we are captured by such qualities. We look the way we look as a species, largely because that was the way our ancestors thought intelligent, strong, loving, and imaginative—ritual-ready—animals ought to look. We are the monument to our progenitors' taste.

Many of our creation myths show an intuitive grasp of the strange process by which the cultural tail came to wag the biological dog. The story of the clothing of Adam and Eve, where (the awareness of) nakedness is the result of shame, which is in turn the result of self-knowledge, expresses one aspect of it. Again in Genesis, the punishment of Eve for her acquisition of knowledge, that she must suffer in childbirth, nicely expresses the fact that one of the parameters of a big-brained viviparous species like ourselves is the capacity of the female pelvis to allow the passage of a large skull. Hence also the beauty for the male of the female's wide hips and the motion they make when walking. The big (and to the male, attractive) breasts of the human female, and her dependency upon a protecting male during lactation, also referred to in Genesis, are like-wise the sign of a nurturing power that can deal with a long infant depen-dency, and thus produce human beings of intelligence, wisdom, and aesthetic subtlety. Babies without protecting fathers must enter adult-hood earlier, and cannot be fully instructed in the tribal ritual; they thus need smaller brains, and smaller-hipped and smaller-breasted mothers to bear them.

If the human ritual as we have envisaged it was to have its original evolutionary function, it must have involved a dark, shameful, and terri-ble element. For if some members of the tribe enjoyed greater reproduc-tive success, others must have enjoyed less. If some were selected as preferred mates for their intelligence, wit, loving nature, prudence, mag-nanimity, honesty, courage, depth, sanguine disposition, foresight, empa-thy, physical health, beauty, grace, and strength, others—the dullards, whiners, liars, blowhards, hoarders, spendthrifts, thieves, cheats, and weaklings—must be rejected. The most brutal throwbacks—the rapists, those who grabbed the food and did not share it, those who could not follow the subtle turns of the ritual and internalize the values that it in-vented and implied—would be cast out from the tribal cave, into the outer darkness where there is wailing and gnashing of teeth. Defective infants would be abandoned on the mountainside; adults polluted by impiety, crime, incest, madness, disease, or their own exercise of witch-craft would be led to the borders of the village lands and expelled. Oedi-pus, who was exposed though not defective at birth, is among other things a symbol of our guilt at such rejection: when he does return, as all buried shames must, he pollutes the city with his unconscious incest. The Old English monster Grendel, that wanderer of the borderlands, the de-scendant of Cain, is another type of such outcasts, and the image of the scapegoat.

Indeed, the fragile virtues of the human race would have been impos-sible without this terrible and most shameful selection process. If we con-sider how morally imperfect we are as it is, and how the best and most recent research shows that moral traits are to a considerable extent inher-ited, it may be a grim satisfaction to reflect how much worse we would be if we had not selected ourselves for love and goodness. Abraham's will-ingness to sacrifice his son Isaac at the command of the Lord (whom we may take, for mythic purposes, to be the evolutionary imperative of the human species, the strange attractor drawing it into being) is necessary, paradoxically, to bring about a more loving and juster humanity. We had better be worth the price.

Our moral growth has, more recently, caused us to recoil in revulsion from those ancient selective practices; but that growth was partly a result of those practices. The process has not entirely ceased, and we had better face up to the fact. Every time a woman chooses a man to be her husband and the father of her children, for any good personal reason—for his gentleness and his wit, his confident strength and his decent humility—she is selecting against some other man less noble in character, and either helping to condemn him to the nonentity of childlessness or to be the parent, with some less morally perceptive woman, of children who are likely to inherit their parents' disadvantages. It is horribly cruel and shameful, if we think about it, but I believe there is a strange and terrible beauty to the magnitude of the mating choice, that is at the root of the troubled exaltation we sometimes feel at a wedding.

The rituals of sacrifice, and their later and more subtle developments as tragedy or eucharist, are the human way of rendering this ancient horror into beauty. Sacrifice has a peculiar element, which we might call "commutation": every sacrifice commemorates a previous sacrifice, in which some much more terrible act of bloody violence or costly loss was required. Abraham is allowed to sacrifice a ram instead of his son who was due to the Lord; the Greeks can burn the fat and bones and hide of the bull to the gods, and eat the flesh themselves. Instead of a whole firstborn son, only a shred of flesh from the foreskin need be given. When the process has been going on for a long time, the sacrificed object can become apparently rather trivial. Cucumbers are sacrificed in some African tribal societies; Catholics and Buddhists burn candles; almost all Christians break bread. Thus every sacrifice is an act of impurity which pays for a prior act of greater impurity, but pays for it at an advantage, that is, without its participants having to suffer the full consequences incurred by its predecessor. The punishment is commuted in a process that strangely combines and finesses the deep contradiction between justice and mercy. The process of commutation also has much in common with the processes of metaphorization, symbolization, even reference or meaning itself. The Christian eucharistic sacrifice of bread not only *stands in* for the sacrifice of Christ (which in turn stands in for the death of the whole human race); it also *means*, and in sacramental theology *is* the death of Christ. The Greek tragic drama referred to, and was a portion of, the sacrificial rites of Dionysus—both a use and a mention, as the logicians say, or both a metaphor and a synecdoche, in the language of the rhetorician.

The invention of ritual sacrifice, or rather its elaboration and adaptation from the division of the spoils of the hunt and the disposal of the bodies of the dead, may have begun a process of increasing suppression of the proto-human eugenics I have described. The commutation process gradually took the teeth out of social selection. Instead of the normal expulsion or killing of the polluted, there was occasional human sacrifice; instead of actual human sacrifice, scapegoat animals were killed. More and more egalitarian religious ideas arose, as in the anti-elitist cults of Krishna and of the Buddha in the Hindu tradition, the Greco-Roman myths of the gods in disguise as beggars, the later cults of Mithras and of popular Egyptian deities, the social criticism of the Hebrew prophets, and the Christian warning that the last shall be first and the first last. A larger and larger proportion of the population was permitted to have offspring. Tribalism came to be despised. Arranged marriage ceased to be the norm. Aristocratic ideas of the inheritance of good blood went into decline. Meanwhile, a celibate priesthood came into being in many traditions, clearly and unambiguously signaling that reproductive success was no longer the reward for ritual excellence.

We rightly condemn eugenics and applaud the increasing humaneness, the *humanity*, of the emerging civilized morality. The word "human" itself means the rejection of the terrible process by which we became human. And if commutation in this sense also means meaning, then meaning is in another way the same thing as sacrifice. But if we think we can safely suppress the memory of how we became human, and of the price of our new freedom, we are quite wrong. To reject such practices should not mean to repress them from our memory. If we forget them, the basis of our shame and also the basis of our beauty as the paragon of animals, we may, in some time of terrible stress, find ourselves repeating them. We are indeed at this time trying to repress them. The symptoms of that repression are manifold, and it should come as no surprise to find them concentrated in our avant-garde: our contemporary hatred of technology (while we use it only the more avidly); the element of rabid superstition in our fear that we are destroying Mother Nature; our anxiety about any implication of psychobiological differentiation between the sexes; and our bad conscience about race and ethnic diversity. We have few rituals left to enable us to accept and take on the burden of our inescapable impurity.

In giving up *tribal* eugenics we have irrevocably declared our commitment to technology. As civilization matured, it kept the routine *individual* eugenics implicit in the choice of reproductive partner. In a sense we could say that the move toward civilization is a more toward an increasing democratization of reproductive choice. Instead of the tribal collectivity deciding who should not have children, we all did, individually, by discriminating against all other potential reproductive partners than the ones we chose. The selective process was thus rendered weaker, more subtle, less consistent, and much more variable. In contemporary society, where casual sexual promiscuity, medical intervention, and birth control tend to frustrate the process of genetic selection through reproductive success, we are in the process of giving up even the individual option for selecting and passing on valued information by genetic means. Nevertheless, over the last few thousand years we have been developing other means of passing on such information: oral poetry, writing, the arts, organized social institutions, and now computers and other advanced electronic technology. Furthermore, we will soon be in a position to correct by means of gene therapy the diseases, distortions, and deficits which would once have condemned a cave-dweller to exposure, exile, or ritual sacrifice. Thus technology, especially biotechnology, is the *opposite and alternative* to racism and eugenics, which is the ancient aristocratic theory of species improvement. Technology is a further development of the evolutionary process of meaning. These systems have become the DNA of a new, inconceivably swifter and more complex form of life, a new twist in the evolutionary spiral.

The process of self-selection by which our species evolved is also, perhaps, largely responsible for our racial differences, however superficial they may be. There are examples, such as the guenon monkeys, of genera that have divided into a multitude of new species purely on the basis of sexual selection, females preferring males with a narrow range of exaggerated features, and so promoting the genetic isolation of monkeys of that racial type. Luckily, though the human species does possess an inclination to find beautiful what resembles the racial norm, it also possesses an opposite attraction toward exogamy, toward the exotic, the racially different, which is one of the fundamental reasons for the hybrid vigor of our species and its great success.

Xenophobia, the fear and hatred of strangers, is built into human nature. The underlying biological reason for xenophobia is territoriality, the seizing and keeping of enough space and resources to feed oneself and one's kin. A young computer expert of my acquaintance recently wrote a computer game program that amusingly illustrates the principle. He was trying to design a game that would illustrate ethical differences. First he created a slowly self-renewing field of available and usable energy, graphically represented by different intensities of green. Next he created an evil entity, represented by a red dot, and a good entity, represented by a blue dot. Both good and evil dots were mobile, and moved about harvesting the green energy field. A heavily engorged dot, red or blue, would fission into two daughter dots. When an evil dot encountered a dot of either color, it was programmed to attack it, and, if it were stronger (had absorbed more green energy), it would destroy its enemy. A good dot, on the other hand, would not attack other dots; if it were attacked by an evil spot more powerful than itself, it would be destroyed, but if it were itself more powerful, it would "convert" an evil dot into a good one. As was its initial purpose, the game showed that altruism paid off in the long run; the good dots eventually triumphed even when the initial odds were heavily in favor of the evil dots, and there was no more red on the screen. But one day my friend ran the program a little longer, and noticed that quite soon after the victory of goodness, the blue dots had multiplied so swiftly that they had eaten up all the energy in the green energy field; and without food they suffered a catastrophic die-back and became extinct. He then tried starting off with only evil dots, and noticed that in their unrelenting hatred, greed, and ruthlessness they quickly spaced themselves out territorially and were able to maintain a balanced ecosystem.

The point is that ethical principles are not always what they seem. We may *need* elements of our xenophobia; the biological xenophobia of our immune systems is what keeps us healthy and alive. A body without xenophobia is a body with AIDS. Though indeed we should not rest within the human default option of racist or ethnocentric xenophobia, and require education and discipline to help us overcome it, we should not wish to abolish it as the default option, as that which we rise above—even if we could, which we can't without radically rewiring the human brain. As long as we can and do rise above xenophobia, it is in itself a healthy and appropriate reflex and should not be condemned as avant-garde liberals often condemn it. The whole point of discipline is to override such reflexes; any athlete knows the process. It was only a culture that hated discipline, then, that was forced to deny and attempted to repress as evil the natural human suspicion of our odd-looking neighbors. Perhaps, then, the myth of the evil racist west may even be the product of a kind of mental laziness, a fear of self-discipline.

Indeed, territoriality and xenophobia may be the basis of our finest virtues. In Konrad Lorenz's description of the mating ritual of the greylag goose, the lifelong bond (and unmistakable personal recognition and affection) of a "married" pair of geese is created, cemented, and partly constituted by the triumph ceremony. This ceremony or ritual dance is centered upon a ritualized and stylized attack by each loving spouse upon a third, absent and counterfactual goose, in which what seems at first to be a hostile assault upon the partner is deflected and spends its energy upon the imaginary "enemy." A goose is normally a highly territorial animal, attacking any fellow goose of either sex that trespasses upon its preserve. Lorenz points out that species without a territorial and aggressive drive, like schooling herrings, do not recognize each other as individuals and thus are incapable of any personal or prolonged pair-bond. (Herring, then, would seem to exemplify the ideal sexual life as envisaged by those psychologists in the French existentialist tradition, like Lacan, Foucault, Deleuze, and Guattari, who make themselves the enemies of repression.) Thus personal recognition, individuality, and love evolve as an *exception* to an existing default option of xenophobic hostility, and paradoxically could not exist without the default. This idea is confirmed by neurochemical evidence: the human neurotransmitter vasopressin, which is closely associated with aggression, is also deeply implicated in the drive to stay with and cherish one's mate and protect one's offspring. Without the resistance to strangers there could be no individuality and love. Perhaps the saving human inclination to find racial difference sexually interesting is a genetically internalized part of this process of making exceptions, which leads to personal love.

To return to our interesting computer game, perhaps it is personal love, and the art which makes the triumph ceremony so beautiful to look at, and the intelligence that is necessary to discipline the default option, which can renew the green field of energy and open up fresh fields outside the confines of the computer space. The inoffensive, unprejudiced, and gentle blue dots, left to themselves, will browse and reproduce themselves into extinction; unreconstructed red dots will survive, but their lives will be nasty, brutish, solitary, and short; what we need to be is red dots which have disciplined themselves to be blue when the occasion merits, and which are thus able to change the rules of the game and contribute to the energy field itself.

The Mystical Conjunction of the Sexes and the End of Race

Though I have sketched out the shape of new myths that can serve us better, as well as reflect the facts more accurately, the question remains, what are the cultural consequences and artistic implications if we were to adopt these new myths?

We have in the past two centuries experienced just the beginnings, just a delicious foretaste, of the astonishing cultural riches that flow from the contributions of women to the literate public modern world. Those riches can be divided into three parts. Part is simply the release into a new sphere of action of the full and multifarious talents of one half of the human race. Part is the emergence into the electric brightness of written and recorded culture, of centuries of beautiful old oral traditions, like ancient recipes passed down from mother to daughter, bearing the dense human accumulation of experience and value. The effect will be like that amazing moment in Greek, English, and Icelandic history when the oral epics and sagas were written down, and when the ancient magical world thus injected its great shot of vitality and genetic material into the rational literate future. This emergence or renaissance will begin to happen when the newly "liberated" generation of daughters is able to listen carefully to the voices of its mothers.

Another part of this new cultural richness may be the somewhat different perspective on the world afforded by the biological differences of women and men. This last can be exaggerated; for once a human being has combined his or her inherited biological nature with a nurturing culture to produce a true self-generating individual, and so entered into the superconductive medium of human imagination, once he or she has experienced the opening of sympathy that results, nothing human is ever alien. One of the worst aspects of the old myth is the idea that someone can only know what he or she has experienced, and that anybody who isn't a woman cannot share the experience of a woman (or a black, or whatever). If this is so, then we are all cut off from each other, because everybody's experience is different; thus, incapable of empathy, we are incapable of love for anything other than a self-created image of the other. As a result, all of life must be a relentless struggle for power; and if this in turn is the case, we human beings are not worth moral concern, and the most oppressive systems are no worse than the least. They may even be better for other species.

The miracle of the human imagination is that it can understand and experience others sometimes even better than it can understand and experience itself. I do not feel my own experience until I have imagined it; and thus I may sometimes feel another's experience more authentically than he or she does—and that person may feel mine more authentically than I do. This leap takes the resources of the classical arts, and the hope they embody, and is one of the reasons why art is indispensable. Art, at its best, is telepathy. George Eliot surely understood the male mind as well as any male, and Leo Tolstoy the female mind as well as any female. Nevertheless, as Virginia Woolf put it, there is a shilling-sized spot on the back of each person's head that we need the other sex to see for us because we cannot see it for ourselves. A shilling was not a large coin; this proportion seems just. (Some old-myth ideologues would make it the size of a millwheel.)

At present the great flow of women's creativity is partially blocked by the presence of the old patriarchal myth, as well as by the remnants of male prejudice against women and a new male resentment of the injustices of the patriarchal myth itself. Rage, self-hatred, self-justification, and the opportunity to blame one's own failings and weaknesses on someone else are poor soil for creative growth. The prejudice against science horrifyingly cuts many women off from the richest source materials of their creativity. Once the fury subsides we can look forward to a long and lovely period in which the female culture luxuriously and comprehensively transforms and is transformed by the male culture; the long-awaited marriage and wedding-night of the human species itself. And out of that marriage, what divine child, begotten of technological artistry, intuitive wisdom, and scientific insight, born into the culture of hope, might be the issue?

We must find institutions, perhaps electronic cottage industry, perhaps a new conception of the workplace which includes nurseries and schools, which begin to reintegrate human activities so as to reconstitute the ancient institution of the House, the household, in such a way as not to divide the sexes and not to limit human opportunity. We must develop an ideology of nature which does not divide human beings from nature but which at the same time recognizes the human role of stewardship and leadership in the process of natural evolution. There will be room in such a conception both for the traditionally female talent for balancing relationships and recognizing interdependencies, and for the traditionally male talent for transforming action.

We must reshape our educational system to demonstrate the unity and interconnection of all knowledge, and its essentially dynamic and active nature; so that no boy can escape it as a narrow specialist, and no girl can avoid the hard calculations of science and mathematics. We must make the structure of education conform to what we now recognize as the informational shape of the universe itself: a gigantic hierarchy of structures reflecting its own evolution from the most primitive, simple, and disconnected to the most concretely complex and interdependent; a hierarchy which at its higher levels begins to generate feedbacks between the lower and higher that tangle the hierarchy and transform it into a heterarchy—thus freedom and a new creativity are born into the world. Such a picture of the universe could incorporate both the organic virtues of the women's culture and the logistical expertness of male modernity.

We must recover the ancient psychic technologies of beauty and morality and place them into an interactive and creative dialogue with the new technology, so that they transform each other. We must recover the performative and oral elements of the arts, and those elements of traditional moral behavior that wisely regulated our impulses. Some elements of chivalry, especially, can be detached from feudal and theological dominance systems and regenerated as a curb on male violence and desire; there is a knightliness that women properly expect of men. Likewise the disciplines which were developed during the emergence of modernism—

the objectivity and fairmindedness enshrined in the idea of democracy and in the scientific method—should be allowed to fuse with traditionally female capacities of empathy, tact, and subjective insight.

We must especially "revision" the institution of motherhood, and place it back into the rich web of human relations of which modernity has unintentionally stripped it. We must recover the best and noblest element of the old patriarchy, that is fatherhood; not just as a greater participation by the male in the mothering tasks, though this is an important priority, but in the role of tutor, trainer, hero, model of what it is to shoulder an adult life and adult responsibilities. Needless to say, this is a task for women also; but perhaps it suits men's inclinations better, as nurture, empathy, and that astonishing primal cultivation of personal intelligence suit women's. Motherhood is the highest of all arts, higher than music, poetry, painting: it creates intelligence where none existed before. The first five years, we know now, are more formative of a human being than all the rest. It is as absurd to expect half the human race to take up this grandest of all tasks as it would be to expect every human being to go through the sacrifice, terror, and suffering of being an artist. Mothers should have the respect and awe we reserve for the other great shamans of the human enterprise.

We may profitably take as the model of the truly liberated human being Virginia Woolf's notion of the partnership in the psyche between the male and the female self. Her meaning was not that we should all be androgynes, but that the inner man in a woman should be given his due and allowed his voice, though under the control of a rich and dominant femininity; and the same for the inner woman within a man. A society shaped upon such a model would be an astonishingly creative one, I believe; and it would have an unexpected bonus, that it would bring out the ridiculous and hilarious comedy of the world and of human life far better than does earnest avant-garde postmodernism. Our being in the world as partly hairless reproducing animals with divine capacities really is quite wonderfully absurd. Sex is one of the things that teaches us this, when it is not turned, as traditional societies sometimes turn it, into something merely dangerous and evil; or as the ideological avant-garde turns it, into a serious and hygienic duty. There will be a new era of love, friendship, and cooperation between the sexes on the large social scale. The present state of nearly military hostility, paranoia, and uncooperativeness between the sexes in the developed countries cannot persist, for simple demographic reasons: it cannot reproduce itself into another generation, because it damages the very process of reproduction when it prevails.

Lunatic current fashions, such as the discounting or denigration of female beauty, will dissolve; if "real power" is money, and if money is based on desire, then to be desirable is to be really powerful. Only a value system superstitiously based on old means of economic exchange, getting paid for one's labor, could ignore or hate the legitimate and innocent potency of beauty. As it is in our current fashion, only males are permitted in good conscience to capitalize on their physical beauty, a state of affairs that is manifestly unfair and wrong. (Of course, females do still use their beauty, but they do it with an unnecessarily bad conscience.) An artwork is valuable because it is beautiful, and this is the most guiltless form of economic value we know. By the same token, it is much more just and beneficial that people should get paid for their beauty than that they should get paid for their self-enslavement to some inhuman repetitive task which could be done by a machine.

There will be a greater acceptance of the differences between men and women, an acceptance broadened by the fact that one's sex is going to be increasingly a matter of choice. Our present crude methods of changing sex will be replaced by a full and perfect transformation, with all the reproductive biology to match. Thus if one does not like the social expectations that come along with one's own sex, one can easily change to another. There will be a much wider variety of sexual roles. The creative and transforming cultural role of the homosexual will get increasing respect and affection, and will diversify itself into further beautiful elaborations. The grand stabilizing and fathering role of the patriarch will return, together with the tragic dignity that his presence gives to all human beings around him. The young male hero will be celebrated, not as in the last two hundred years as the paradigm of human achievement, but as the agonist of arete, the limited but splendid adventurer that he is. The new young heroine will join him, receiving for the first time in history her proper recognition as the adventurer of the mind and the transformer of all frames of reference, the questioner of all easy certainties and comfortable illusions. And the matriarch will return, the madonna, who is the central moral pattern and most perfect image of what it is to be human, the great giver, the wise Sophia, the Shekinah, the Kuanyin, the Uranian goddess.

There must be an era of forgiveness and apology and reconciliation between the sexes, when we recognize the injuries we have done each other and fall in love again with the humanity we share and the amazing differences between us. There is a lovely motif in Mozart which has been called the forgiveness theme. It's in *Cosi Fan Tutti, The Marriage of Figaro*, and triumphantly in *The Magic Flute*: let it be the melody by which the time is remembered. Imagine what it would be like to live in a culture with no systematic resentment between the sexes.

Though we will be able to choose our sexual roles, we will never achieve a total detachment of gender from sex, a total polymorphousness of human sexuality. We will always be weighted by what we are and what we have been; a woman who has been a man is not the same as a woman who has never been anything else. Freedom is in part the ability, so to speak, to change speed and direction; but it is also the possession of such personal mass—weight of character—as to make those changes significant. The dream of total escape from identity and history is really, if the dreamers knew it, a desire for complete triviality. If the transsexual's imagination is poorer than that of the woman who has never been a man, she may not be able to experience as clearly, accurately, and vividly in real life what her sister is able to experience vicariously. She might not be as good an advocate for her cause as her wiser sister. But what we are is not the same as what we can imagine. And there are some things, inextricably involved with our sexual nature and our gender, that irrevocably make us what we are: motherhood and fatherhood, and all the bonds and obligations of kinship. If we were ever to abolish these, we might be freer in a sense, but we would not matter. A human race without the madonna and child, without the special painful love of father and daughter, and all the other elements of our biological identity, may not be worth its ecological expense.

There are always going to be the pangs of sexual love, requited or unrequited. We will never abolish sexual jealousy, without abolishing the amazing experience of sexual intimacy whose loss constitutes the experience of jealousy. Men and women will always fight, because their reproductive interests are different by the very nature of things. In itself the fighting is part of the creative friction of our extraordinary species, like the creative friction between the rebellious adolescent and the conserving adult. At present the sexual conflict is aided and abetted by powerful social movements and interests, but it will continue, though in a much less destructive and acrimonious form, without them. When the conflict is framed in terms of power, it tends to be sterile; when it is framed in terms of love, it is fertile.

The marvelous thing about the sexes is that they seem to have been designed by evolution as a feedback dyad, a sort of algorithm of mutual transformation whose chaotic self-organizing products themselves take an active and free part in the shaping of history. The biological result of sexual union—the conception of a unique new human being whose view of the universe adds to it an unprecedented dimension—is a beautiful natural metaphor of the psychological and spiritual aspects of the relation between the sexes. It is a risky procedure always, this recombinant DNA of the spirit, dangerous, mysterious, and terrifyingly open to an incalculable future. It is one of the chief ways in which the universe generates a new moment every moment, this catastrophe at the edge of the past, at the vertiginous edge of all ecology and system. If we follow the counsels of the old myth of the oppressive patriarchy we might, by an utter disengagement of the loving conflict, achieve a kind of stasis; but that stasis is death. The life of the universe is largely entrusted now to the adventure of sexual love; let us follow where it leads.

The present hatred and mistrust between the sexes is deeply related to the mistrust and hatred between races and ethnic groups. How are we to deal with the old human reflex of xenophobia, of that prejudice that is built in to our perceptual and cognitive systems as its indispensable default option? How can we avoid making differences where none exist? By now all the races are pretty thoroughly mixed genetically. There is not a single African American in America who is not also a descendant of the enslavers. Nor is there a single white in America who does not have some trace of black genes (if only through Zanzibarian traders or Spanish Moors or the children of eighteenth-century black prostitutes in London and Paris and Naples and Amsterdam). Thus there is nobody who could not claim to be both the victim and the perpetrator of ancestral oppression. But there is still enough *statistical* isolation between populations so that the superficial markers, of color and facial features, are recognizable as belonging to certain groups.

These final reflections on the matter of race point to one simple, practicable, and, as things now stand, virtually inevitable answer to the problem of racism. If we really want to get rid of racism, let us intermarry. Let miscegenation thrive. To the extent that the races are genetically isolated at all, the offspring will possess hybrid vigor; and they will have such mixed ethnic loyalties that they will not be able to keep a straight face among ethnic ideologues on either side of their family. The comfortable lie is that interracial children are troubled and unhappy; actual study and experience show just the opposite, that they tend to be well adjusted, cheerful, and unusually creative. That lie is usually the sign of a concealed racism, as prevalent among the oppressed as among the oppressors, that secretly desires the cultural barriers that racism supports, and the guilt and despair that flow from them, a lie most often found among those publicly most self-righteous in condemning racism.

A few generations of interracial marriage—and the process has already begun—will produce such an extraordinary range of skin color and facial type that the human type-generalization system will simply be overwhelmed. The variety of racial subtypes will approach numerically the variety of individual and family differences. Racial difference will get absorbed into the much more powerful human individual face-recognition system. We will still be able to hate our neighbors, as the racially identical Croats and Serbs do each other; but if we do not choose to assert some divisive "cultural identity" (which is either an illusion or the product of poor education) we will no longer be unwillingly labeled by our skin or hair. The reason why the culturally different Germans and Swedes and Italians and Irish were able to integrate into American society, when African Americans met much higher obstacles, was because they could not be racially distinguished from their oppressors. Unless they chose to reveal their background, they were subject neither to prejudice by the established population nor to even more insidious calls for loyalty to the oppressed group. Let us interbreed, then, and be done with the whole wearisome business of race and "diversity."

Although at present it does not seem very likely, we can still hope for a time of greater tolerance and love between ethnic groups. In the medium to long run, we are all going to be so mixed ethnically that systematic racism will simply be too exhausting and confusing to maintain. The mechanism of prejudice and stereotyping is an absolutely natural and indispensable tool of thought, being essentially no more than snap generalization from ad hoc evidence and second-hand authority. The double meaning of the word "discrimination," as the practice of race prejudice and the essential function of our senses and taste, is no coincidence. Racial mixing will tend to make that usually useful tool unavailable as a lazy default option in cases where a careful judgment of a human being on his or her merits is demanded by efficient practice. Prejudice survives because, to some extent, it works, if only in a self-confirming fashion. There is no way for a prejudiced person to know whether his or her prejudice is objectively justified or not, and so the prejudice is maintained, to be on the safe side. But if, as in a profoundly mixed-race society, there are simply too many categories into which a given case might fit, the brain will go to the next easiest method of judgment, which is the inspection of the actual details of the case; and so be forced to judge a person, as Martin Luther King put it, not by the color of his skin but by the content of his character.

Once racial mixing is so complete that racism is impractical, we may even choose to reinvent racial differences as a form of entertainment, art, fetishism, or self-expression. By biotechnological means we might be able to make ourselves look like the ancient Maya aristocracy with their strangely flattened skulls, or like the flowerlike footbound maidens of old Chinese tradition, or turn ourselves into pigmies or Masai giants or Nordic supermen. If there are no social roles, then there are no social roles to play when we want to play roles. Who knows the limits of human perversity? Consider the magnificent and pathetic transsexuals of *Paris is Burning*. The world would be poorer without them. Nor should we forget that yet another of our perversions is the delicious rage of censoriousness that we sometimes let ourselves feel about such practices; and why should we not feel that rage, as long as we do not or cannot act on it? In a strange poetic way extreme racial differences in facial features and bodily conformation sometimes express the terror and strangeness of the divine in people, as a caricature can sometimes show, nightmarishly, the essence of personality. The gods always seem to possess an exaggerated form of the racial characteristics of their worshipers. Perhaps we even breed toward those beautiful and terrible ideal masks, by choosing mates that look like the images in the temples. But these bizarre possibilities are for another age than ours, one which, under the sign of hope, will have the luxury of freedom from political tendentiousness and ignorant bigotry.

More distantly still, if we settle in other star systems, rendered remote from one another by the time-dilation of relativistic space-travel, the human race may become isolated once again into racial groups adapted to diverse environments, and may have to rediscover the arts of ethnic tolerance that we are presently struggling to invent today. Then the irony will be the strange, humiliating wisdom of that ancient time, that will make our descendants feel how superficial are all their intellectual and moral and technological advances.

In the meantime, however (as I write Los Angeles cleans up from three days of race riots), we must search for ways to mitigate our given human ethnocentrism and xenophobia. Robin Fox's solution is characteristically wise, trenchant, and disillusioned: not to try to eliminate prejudice and stereotyping, but to replace bad stereotypes with good ones. This, however, is a cultural, not a political task; even a hint of political motivation in the cultural transformation that is required will arouse the paranoia that always accompanies the anxiety of ethnic difference, and the not always unjustified suspicion that the cultural educator is indulging his or her own prejudices. The work of cultural persuasion must be noble, generous, self-effacing, and devoid of criticism of those it seeks to convert; its motivation must be to show them a richer way of living in their own terms. We will reach this more difficult, but more just and humane, way of dealing with people the more swiftly if we treat racism not as a moral, but as a cognitive failure, and cease to use it to justify our own prejudices against, and superiority to, the uneducated, the blue-collar worker, the Southerner, or whatever. If racists are presented in the media as boors and trash, instead of as what they most often are, which is decent traditional people with narrow horizons, they will not recognize themselves in their portraits and will rightly doubt the honesty of the painter and the veracity of the message. Contemptuous hatred is the least constructive reaction to a bigot; it simply reproduces the bigotry in another form.

One vigorous strain in the art of the future will be the experience of the half-breed, the mestizo, the immigrant, the child of mixed ethnic background, the anthropologist with a foot in two cultures. The complexity of cultural background that such people possess constitutes a rich palette and vocabulary of artistic expression, as we can already see in the work of artists like Amy Tan, Paul Simon, Yo-Yo Ma, Ismail

Merchant, V. S. Naipaul, Gabriel Garcia Marquez, and David Byrne. In our present era of ethnic sensitivity our principle is that only someone born and bred into a given culture can truly understand and speak for it. What the new art will demonstrate is a wiser principle, that only someone who comes from the outside can learn to love a culture deeply enough to see its soul. Who understood America better than de Tocqueville, or England better than Henry James, or Japan better than Yeats, or Europe better than Borges? The paradox and tragedy of the diaspora Jews was always that they were able to express the genius of the nations among which they dwelt better than the natives themselves; and as international travel for the purpose of business, tourism, academic study, and sport becomes the norm in people's lives rather than the exception, we are all going to approach the condition of wandering Jews. This is fertile ground for art, and if we understand it with sufficient fortitude, a great cause for hope.

Natural Classicism and Education

The process of gene–culture coevolution gives rise to a perspective on human nature that I call natural classicism. That position can be summed up in an aphorism: human beings have a nature; that nature is cultural; that culture is classical. It is within this perspective that we can begin to envisage a viable ethical world in which xenophobia is recognized as an inherited given rather than as a culturally constructed distortion. Once we accept that human beings do indeed have a nature, one that is the product of their evolutionary history, the crucial issue then becomes education. But if our genes determine who we are, what is the point of education? The natural classical perspective suggests an interesting answer.

Natural classicism accepts the roughly 75/25 ratio of nature–nurture determinants given us by the scientists, as far as it goes. But it does not go very far, and indeed falls short on two counts. The first is that advanced animals, especially ourselves, seldom inherit complete behaviors, but rather predispositions that must be activated by experiential and social triggers. The predisposition, for instance the human capacity for language, often has its own weakly determined structure, that is revealed when a society must reinvent that behavior from scratch. The linguist Derek Bickerton discovered that whenever a community of people is cut off from their ancestral language, they tend to invent a Creole language whose basic grammatical and lexical structure is always the same. Baby talk, the transitional phase through which infants must pass to get to full mastery of their language, is structured like a simple Creole. However, that default structure is not necessarily the best that could be found; nor is a human baby constrained to use it forever, or seriously hampered by having to pass through a period of baby talk to get to the more complicated and refined structure of a full "natural language." A simple analogy would be the capacity a human being has, given a tennis racquet, to hit a ball over a net without having ever done it before. This default option is replaced later, with the help of a tennis pro, by a proper forehand or backhand.

Suppose there is no sociocultural encouragement to use a given capacity—suppose a child is brought up where nobody speaks, or is kept so confined that it never has the chance to develop the sensory-motor skills of standing, looking, handling. Such a child never has the chance to develop even the default option; and thus an inherited capacity, part of the 75 percent nature, can be aborted by a crucial absence in the 25 percent nurture. Human genes need cultural triggers; our nature is designed open on one side (though closed on the other) so that our inherited skills can be completed by a cultural context. Often those triggers will only work during a short period of an individual's lifetime. In human beings, the first five years are especially important for language as for other skills. Among those "skills" are moral capacities, and forms of self-discipline, and insight from other points of view than one's own. After the trigger period it is too late, and a person who has missed them will behave exactly as if he or she were genetically lacking in those capacities. One of the few Great Society programs which worked, and did not actually exacerbate the condition of the underclass, was Head Start. The reason was that Head Start acted as a cultural trigger to activate human capacities during the most crucial period.

If our educational philosophy is based, as it has been, upon a "tabula rasa" or "blank slate" theory of human capacities, upon which society inscribes its determining cultural patterns (what one might call a "0/100" theory), then we will fail to recognize the existence of such predispositions. We will thus fail to trigger them in time, fail to arrange a smooth passage from the default option to the elaborated cultural form, and perhaps totally neglect certain fundamental traditional skills that have not received theoretical attention or that are culturally unfashionable. In other books I have pointed out the terrible disservice we do children by neglecting to teach them the fundamentals of the human arts—meter and rhyme in poetry, representation in the visual arts, tonality in music, and so on— because of modernist avant-garde aesthetic theories that falsely held such disciplines to be arbitrary and outworn cultural impositions.

Thus our liberal educational establishment has unknowingly committed a hideous crime, an atrocity against our children. The results of that atrocity, the underclass, are now being blamed on racism in society, which is actually only indirectly at fault for this, if at all. Racism surely exists in our society; but it is not in itself to blame for a lack of educational achievement. Minority children are brought up in racist or xenophobic societies all over the world without damage to their education. Indeed, in many cases, such as the Chinese in Indonesia, Jews everywhere, Hungarians in Rumania, Asians in the United States, and so on, the "oppressed" minority children end up better educated and more economically viable than the majority. The reason is that very deeply rooted, almost invisible traditions of family education have been preserved, and the intellectual, moral, and aesthetic triggers have been pulled at the appropriate times. Those triggers may be as homely as baby talk, fairytales, parental discipline practices, nursery rhymes, family rituals, riddles, and baby games.

The second major flaw in the "75/25" theory is that it fails to take into account the extraordinary, though statistically insignificant, factor of the sudden catching fire of a person's moral, aesthetic, or intellectual imagination that can sometimes happen when the normal conditions of development have not been interrupted. This "catching fire" does not always happen. It is not heavily dependent upon native inherited talent, and it should therefore not be confused with the eruption, often despite itself, of some miraculous inherited genius. The ignition does not require a special education, merely an adequate one; though often, after the breakthrough, the person will seek out proper mentors and compel them to teach. It consists fundamentally, I think, in some combination of imaginative attraction and moral dedication, a combination that is usually mediated by some marvelously true and powerful idea. That idea need not by any means be original. Mother Teresa, who is a good example, has pretty mainline Catholic views. Most important, it is a feedback process, in which the individual bootstraps him- or herself into new levels of awareness and will. It is thus a very advanced example of chaotic self-organization, whereby a system, drawn by a strange attractor, can irreversibly ratchet itself up into entirely new forms of stable and ordered activity. People who have achieved this breakthrough have an enormous and disproportionate effect on society, one which is often unrecognized and unacknowledged. In the arts we have often been much more interested in the extraordinary productions of inborn talent than in the results of such breakthroughs. I believe the latter are more esthetically interesting and in the long run more influential, as well as more beautiful. A person who has "caught fire" or "broken through" is free in a far deeper sense than the freedom that is preached by political dogma; such a person has become a self-creating, self-organizing system, and can play a part in the universe analogous to that of a highly limited but original divine being.

These three theories of education might be summarized in the following way. The first theory is the traditional "aristocratic" theory, which in its common sense has recognized that the majority of our capacities are inherited, not socially constructed. The aristocratic theory correctly believes in the "75/25" ratio of nature to nurture; and its essential conservatism preserves the family education traditions which accurately trigger human innate capacities. The talented, it says, should rule; and if we took the "75/25" ratio at face value and without further thought, we might find the proposition very reasonable. Indeed, opponents of aristocratic social structures have felt forced to deny the nature/nurture ratio, because they did not have the wit or the imagination to look further and see that it did not necessarily entail political aristocracy. The aristocratic theory has perfectly good faults of its own that invalidate it, without our going to the drastic lengths of denying good scientific knowledge because it is socially inconvenient.

One major problem with the aristocratic theory is that inheritance of superior talent only works up to a point, and is statistically bound to erase itself after a few generations. That is, with very complex human characteristics such as intelligence, though intelligent parents are more likely to produce intelligent children, those children are statistically likely to be less intelligent than their parents, though still more intelligent than the norm. The result, though, is that in a few generations any innate distinction in intelligence between the descendants of the original couple and the general population will, on average, be wiped out. Similarly, stupid parents are likely to produce children less stupid than themselves, with the paradoxical result that by reproducing, clever people are making their own group of clever people less clever, while stupid people are making their own group smarter. Thus the aristocratic theory breaks down in a way that was already a cliché in the eighteenth century: the son is less creative than his heroic father, the grandson merely consolidates the family gains, the great-grandson is feeble and lackluster, and the great-great grandson is a wastrel who squanders the family fortune. Meanwhile bright descendants of the peasants rise up through craftsmanship, commerce, or the church, and challenge the decadent barons. For there are other factors than inheritance of specific configurations of genes that can produce high innate intelligence: hybrid vigor, freak combinations of genes that can throw up a novel and beneficial talent, and sheer statistical "noise."

The aristocratic theory fails on another count, too: it is threatened by, and must oppose, the "breakthrough" phenomenon except when it occurs within the ranks of the aristocracy. For the breakthrough partially invalidates the determinism of inheritance, and it is likely to create political challenges if it occurs in the wrong place, in the hovel rather than in the castle. Thus aristocracies tend to monopolize education, where the breakthrough is most likely to happen, for themselves, and to deal with clever commoners by directing them into a celibate priesthood where their genes are likely to die with them while their energy can serve society. Such a culture cannot really progress.

The second theory of education is the one which I have already criticized: the 0/100 theory, the behaviorist, tabula-rasa, Deweyan theory which assumes that all children are equal in being blank slates, and that all human characteristics are socially constructed. Its advantages are that, at least on the face of it, it seems to serve the democratic values of equality and ideological neutrality; it neatly avoids all the possible religious and political issues of human nature, natural law, and the soul; and it seems to be a sound rebuff to racism. It fits a sociology conceived on the model of engineering and the natural sciences, especially the sciences of nonliving matter that were so finely developed in the nineteenth century, and it suggests a straightforward, no-nonsense, linear cause-and-effect procedure for going about education that can be taught to teachers without special talent or special personal experiences.

Unfortunately, this system is even more deeply flawed than the aristocratic system. First, of course, it is simply wrong about the nature/nurture ratio. Second, it ignores the inherited talents of children in such a way as to actively frustrate their actualization; it de-educates children, so that they would be better off fending for themselves outside school. It enforces a linearity of thought which is deeply alien to the human brain and to any living organism, while avoiding the conscious and reflective philosophical disciplines by which a nonlinear mind can master linear ideas (the rigors of grammar, logic, math, and science), because those disciplines seem too hard for people of some backgrounds. It discourages the homely old traditions of family education, because its theory does not believe in them, and its esthetics are steeped in the efficient avant-garde modernism of abstraction, atonality, and "free verse." It encourages a mediocre breed of teachers who are given methods and training rather than ideas and education, teachers who are unsuccessful demonstrations of the belief that by democratic training and specialization you can make a silk purse out of a sow's ear.

Worst of all, it does not really believe in the breakthrough, which is the purpose of all education, because breakthrough implies a kind of human soul that is inconvenient to a secular state, because breakthrough implies a certain elitism, and because breakthrough denies the proposition that it is social conditioning that determines a person's capacities, not their own, mysterious, moral and imaginative, nonlinear self-will. The tabula rasa theory hates the positive feedback that happens inside a person, because that feedback denies the linear positivism of its sociology. If an individual can turn him- or herself into a free, happy, creative, effective, and original being, what is the use of the teaching profession and of the helping bureaucracy in general?

At present the American educational authorities have tacitly agreed on a combination of the tabula rasa theory and the aristocratic theory. The public education system, from primary school through university, has been ceded to the proponents of the tabula rasa. An increasingly "dumbed-down" scientific and technical curriculum is pawned off on the general public, with a sugar coating of self-esteem provided by an arts education that is based on self-expression and cheap praise, and a humanities and social-science education committed to representing cultural and personal failure as victimhood and martyrdom. Meanwhile, the liberal elite sends its own children to private schools and universities based on the aristocratic theory of education. The elitist mission of such schools is heavily camouflaged by generous scholarship programs for poor and minority students, who are expected in return for their grants to stay out of subjects requiring real discipline, such as science, languages, philological scholarship, and technical arts apprenticeship, and to gravitate instead toward studies of social inequality. I have often observed the odd phenomenon of gifted minority or female candidates for tenure-track positions in the humanities being rejected by leftist search committees because they had clearly ignored this tacit rule, and had acquired expertise in some subject, like medieval musical instruments or biochemistry, that it was not politically proper for them to have. After all, an unvictimized black or woman, who was interested in a patriarchal Western subject like French poetic meters or classical Chinese art or neutron stars, constitutes a living refutation of the whole *Weltanschauung* of such a committee.

The tabula rasa theory leads eventually to the horrible proposition that nobody is free and nobody is responsible; in which case any atrocity is permissible, since it is only social thinking that makes it an atrocity. We must, therefore, reject the tabula rasa theory; but this does not require that we go back to the aristocratic theory instead. The aristocratic theory of human talent, though old, is not the oldest. It was essentially invented by feudalism. Plato hints that it is a Noble Lie in his myth of the metals in the *Republic*.

There is an older theory, which maintains that though good blood can supply you with many advantages, you are at least potentially a person with your own powers of affecting the world and its treatment of you; your own moral decisions and choices are the determining forces in making you what you are. This perspective is central to most fairytales, from whatever part of the world they are collected. Fairytales see human life as a story, with branchpoints in the narrative at which heroes or heroines can make decisions, sometimes apparently minor or trivial ones, that partly, though irreversibly, determine what will become of them. In such a story your good genes are perhaps like the magic Helpers, who can warn you with their fine hearing, or see things far away; or like seven-league boots or a magic sword or ring or purse. But those powers must be won to your use by some greatness of moral choice or generosity, or boldness of insight and self-denying truth. This story view of education, elaborated, assumes that a human being has a free and responsible soul, which is ultimately the arbiter of its own fate: a soul which must be won in the first place, since only the makings of it are given; a soul which can also be lost, or aborted during the bootstrapping process of self-discipline by which it emerges, if the right choices are not made. Given such a soul, the injustices of the world are but temporary handicaps in the achievement of Heart's Desire; and Heart's Desire will be the kind of thing that cannot be given or taken away by social prejudice or economic injustice or racial bias. Indeed, paradoxically, young Jack or the little princess *needs* a somewhat hostile world, of stepmothers and giants and oppressive kings, in order to make a soul.

It is this theory of education that will be the basis of a true culture of hope. The "fairytale theory," as we might call it, as opposed to the aristocratic theory and the tabula rasa theory, corresponds rather closely with what we now know about the development of the human self. It does not divide us into 75/25 or 0/100, but shows how even a very small inheritance, social and natural, can by exponentiation, by iterated multiplications of itself, approach the infinite. This is the meaning of the parable of the talents. We do not need to hypostasize the soul into some eternal, infinite, preexistent, and immaterial entity. All those old descriptions of the soul might well be as close as people could get, before they possessed the language of chaotic self-organizing processes and fractal geometry. The language of our new knowledge can now describe forms of stable order that are open-ended, since they keep on revealing further fractal depths, yet also apparently shaped in advance by a strange attractor; and that are relatively independent of the matter that flows through them, though not of the energy gradient upon which they feed.

The problem with the fairytale theory, as an educational principle and as a guide to social policy, is that it expects, or at least demands, that everybody go through the breakthrough experience. This seems to me to be an advantage rather than a problem. Though Japanese education has its own very deep flaws in other areas, it succeeds in taking all of its pupils far further along the road of mathematics than American education does; and it does it by a sort of moral expectation and demand, a strict calling to account of the student's honor as a human being. Japanese education neither writes off the genetically inferior, nor assumes that every child is equal until social deprivation skews the odds; rather, it expects that a human soul will be able to work hard enough to come to understand, and is unforgiving of failure. Partly as a result of this call to account, the average intelligence of the Japanese is measurably higher than that of Americans. I believe that there are versions of the fairytale theory of education that will work well in the kind of individualistic and multiracial society we have in America; but in order to put them into practice it is clear that we must abandon the myths of the patriarchy and the oppressive West and replace them with truer myths.

For if we take gender to be socially constructed, and the traditional intellectual and artistic disciplines to be instruments of political oppression, as do the proponents of the myth of the patriarchy, we will be depriving our daughters of their human birthright as clear-sighted agents and creative contributors. And if we remain paralyzed by the pathos and hopelessness of the gallant non-Western culture enchained by the oppressive culture of the West, where the latter controls the values, and the members of the former are constrained, by the social determinism of their bondage, to failure, addiction, and misery, then we can scarcely escape the double binds of the tabula rasa theory of education. Indeed, the tabula rasa theory underpins the myth of the patriarchal West, and the myth underpins the tabula rasa theory.

The fairytale theory of education, on the other hand, is consistent with the new myths of the sexes and of ethnic difference that I have proposed. It offers grounds for hope and suggestions for a program of action to solve our problems. It also contains some as yet unexplored mysteries, the chief of which is the magical pleasure, "heart's desire," that draws the true learner into and through the threshold of imaginative breakthrough. That pleasure is beauty; and to beauty we now turn.

Chapter 5

The Cosmology of the Arts

The New Great Chain of Being

The various failures of the avant-garde can be traced to the loss of one essential value: beauty. As a civilization we have tried to get by on cognitive and moral values, while relegating beauty to the realm of the subjective and private. Aesthetic value has become a leisure activity, a decorative hobby, a status symbol, a narcotic form of entertainment to keep the masses quiet, or worst of all, a consolation prize for women or minorities whom the educational system has failed to teach serious knowledge and skills. But beauty is the essential element in those very accomplishments. In the absence of the deep test of beauty, by which all true scientists and philosophers assay their ideas, cognition is increasingly arbitrary in its conclusions, the search for truth is bereft of its compass, and the connection between human beings and the rest of nature begins to get lost. Relativism is the only recourse of someone who cannot recognize that one idea is more beautiful than another. Similarly, without beauty, which is the natural inducement to love and selfless concern, morality becomes schematic, masochistic, puritanical, inquisitorial, coercive, and cruel. Without beauty, the difference between good and evil comes to be defined in terms of the avoidance of pain and the maximization of comfort. I think we are still aware that a human being whose sole desire is a state of painless comfort is scarcely a human being at all, since we ban the drugs that can induce such a state, but we are in danger of forgetting the intellectual or moral or perceptual beauty that might make someone choose the pain and struggle and deprivation of discovery, heroic charity, and art.

I teach karate, a minor if ancient art that demands considerable discomfort and discipline. It is quite extraordinary to see how young karate students begin to change over from the self-esteem ethic they learned from their school and their society, and adopt the pure pursuit of good karate form. The more advanced they become, the more humility they attain, and the more capable and confident they become. The very issue of self-esteem becomes irrelevant. I have had exactly the same experience teaching literature students how to write in meter. After a while they begin to feel cheated if I give them too high a grade, because they know when a rhyme is forced or a line stumbles, and their allegiance is to the poem, not their own psychological comfort. But we as a culture are stunningly ignorant about beauty. In a time when thousands of scientific, sociological, and humanistic journals report the research of millions of researchers, there has been scarcely any serious work on this most central value of all.

Ironically, all the ingredients for a really new breakthrough in the study of beauty are now in place. Let us take a brief look at the current evolutionary vision of the world, which I call "the new great chain of being," in memory of that extraordinary intellectual framework, invented by Thomas Aquinas, that served Europe for over four hundred years. This new view of the world is not yet fully clear. Scientists, who for the most part are at work upon some small section of it, often do not pay much attention to the shape of the whole; though there are exceptions, such as Roger Penrose, Roald Hoffman, J. T. Fraser, Stephen Hawking, Paul Davies, John Archibald Wheeler, Lynn Margulis, Roger Sperry, and George Seielstadt, among others. Scholars in the humanities often have an idea of science based more upon the philosophy of science than on contemporary developments in science itself, a philosophy of science in turn based upon or critiquing scientific ideas that are over half a century old.

Given the qualification that large areas of the new vision are still under vigorous debate, what does our new great chain of being look like?

The most exciting mathematical ideas of our century deal with the incompleteness and open-endedness of any mathematical system, and its propensity to generate paradoxes which can only be resolved in terms of some richer and more reflexive system which includes it—a system which must in turn contain its own paradoxes, and so on. These relationships, of inclusion, containment, open-endedness, incompleteness, extension, "between-ness," and even, as in the case of the orientation of the imaginary number series with respect to the real numbers, orthogonality and thus angles, immediately suggest spacelike dimensions. The discipline of topology may be defined as a demonstration that space, spatial dimensionality, is the only solution to certain problems in mathematical logic. Space is the way that true statements which would contradict each other if they were in the same place, space themselves out from each other. The Pauli exclusion principle, which states that two identical particles cannot occupy the same energy state at the same place and time, is a physical example of this idea. If the two particles were in the same place, they would be both two and one, which violates the noncontradiction law of logic. In other words, a nonspatial world, if everything thinkable within it is to remain logically consistent, must necessarily generate a spatial world.

The new fractal geometry includes a working concept of how a given dimension can be generated, and offers coherent definitions of partial dimensions. We are familiar in classical geometry with zero-dimensional points, one-dimensional lines, two-dimensional planes, three-dimensional volumes, and so on; popular science has invited us to imagine more dimensions still. But the noninteger dimensions of fractal mathematics (a given curve can have a dimensionality of 1.62, for instance) are a new concept, and show us how we might, through the feedback of an iterative algorithm, actually get from one integer dimension to another. Certain other problems in mathematics involve the relative easiness or difficulty of a calculation. Some calculations wind themselves up without complication. Others involve more and more subcalculations, and sub-subcalculations, before the calculator can produce an answer. In order to be able to talk coherently about such distinctions, and to measure their differences, another kind of dimensionality is needed: time. In its simplest form, time is to the three spatial dimensions what the imaginary number series (the square roots of the negative numbers) is to the real number series. Time gives us a dimension within which we can describe the difficulty of a calculation, whether it is soluble in an amount of time that increases polynomially with the number of variables in it, or exponentially, or more swiftly still, or infinitely; and if infinitely, which of Cantor's larger and larger infinities it would be.

Thus space-time emerges out of very logic; and given space-time, theoretical and cosmological physics can show the necessity of the Big Bang, of the emergence of energy as the coherent solution of certain possible and necessary space-time geometrical paradoxes, and of the self-binding collapse of energy into matter as the universe cools with its expansion. Matter is the solution to paradoxes that arise in the energy universe as the primal superforce separated itself out into gravitation, electromagnetism, the weak and the strong nuclear forces. Not every possible kind of energy and matter does emerge, or once having emerged, survive. There are apparently no magnetic monopoles, though there could have been; and there is very little antimatter, since at the point of the collapse into matter, physical laws demanded that the energy universe choose one or the other but not both for its debut into materiality. Many possible isotopes do not exist because the conditions for their survival are not present. Thus a peculiar primitive kind of "choice" already existed at the very beginning of things. Various exotic kinds of matter emerged (we can reproduce their emergence sometimes in an accelerator) but were selected against by the existing ecology of the physical world, and did not survive for long. Tough objects like protons and neutrons, or intangible ones like neutrinos, can survive a great deal of wear and tear, and so they are long-lived and plentiful, as are certain elements, like hydrogen and iron, and certain molecules and crystalline structures in cooler and quieter environments.

Given matter, another open-ended process begins, of chemical recombination. Here again we find a process of variation, in which the vicissitudes of a rather violent universe thrust together arbitrary combinations of chemical elements, and in turn test them to destruction, leaving the survivors to survive. In chemistry, those survivors can only endure, or at best grow by accumulation, as crystals do; they cannot avoid, adapt to, or anticipate the threats of a dangerous universe. Nor, if they are especially successful at weathering or dodging the dangers, can they copy themselves so as to improve their statistical chances; yet the logic of survival in time would demand that they should. Their potentially successful form is held hostage to a particular local piece of matter. If the form could be copied to other matter, then the form might survive the enemies of matter: heat, mechanical destruction, chemical corrosion. So yet another solution to an existential paradox emerges: life.

With life a new element entered into the iterative variation/selection algorithm by which evolution had proceeded: heredity. Life has, as it were, a double life: as matter and as a recorded copy of the form of that matter. It is more reflexive, more conscious, so to speak, than matter by itself. (Of course, matter is itself "double" with respect to its substance, energy; it is energy, but also a self-maintaining field structure containing the energy. And energy is "double" with respect to the space-time field, and the space-time field "double" with respect to mathematical logic.) Life not only evolved in a new way, by self-copying; it also developed in turn new forms of evolution. One of the most remarkable of these is sexual reproduction, which, instead of merely accepting mutation as part of the damage of existence, actively anticipated and promoted it by sexual recombination. Now the biosphere took increasing control over the non-living substrate of the planet Earth, radically altering the composition of its air, regulating its climate, setting up complex chemical cycles throughout its atmosphere, hydrosphere, crust, and perhaps even its mantle. It is thus entirely natural for an emergent and more reflexive kind of order to control and subordinate the earlier and more primitive forms out of which it evolved.

There is a subtlety in this process that escapes some evolutionary biologists, who instinctively distrust any suggestion of teleology in evolution. If the genome and nervous system of a given species are sufficiently complex to support teleology and teleological motivations (even if very rudimentary ones, such as care of the young), and if a hypothetical species is more adaptive, and survives and reproduces more successfully, when it acts *as if* it possessed teleological goals, then variation could bring about such a species, and once it did, selection could help it to spread. In order to compete with such a species, other species would need to develop the same talent, of acting (and thus being motivated to act) *as if* there were teleological goals. (In just such a fashion the indicative mood of the real number series demands and implies the subjunctive mood of the imaginary number series.) After a rather brief interval of evolutionary history it would be very hard to tell whether one were living in a teleological universe, striving to become more advanced and sensitive and self-aware and concerned with the future, or whether the world around one were simply acting *as if* this were the case. For a scientist such a difference should really be of no concern, though it might be distressing to an antimetaphysical philosopher.

As the competitive-cooperative ecology of the living world became more and more complex, and improved forms of biological evolution accelerated the rate of speciation and ecological change, the Darwinian mechanism of biological evolution began to reach its speed limit. It takes at least a hundred thousand years for an animal species to develop a new capacity in response to its experience in the environment (though old capacities already latent in the genes can be reawoken very quickly by environmental changes, as in the case of the Galapagos finches). The whole species, or most of it, must go through that experience in order for the selective process to create a new structure or behavior. Would it not be better if something like Lamarckian evolution were to supplement Darwinian evolution, an adaptive process which could make radical changes in one generation, which could use the experience of individuals rather than that of the gene pool as a whole? Would not evolution be still more efficient if alternative scenarios for the future could be tried out in a virtual world where they could do no damage, before they were actually embarked on? Would it not be better to supplement the very slow genetic diffusion of information through the species, with much faster forms of communication independent of the reproductive process? Might not new forms of information storage be developed, above and beyond the genes, which would be to the genes what the genes were to the matter of which their bodies were made, or as the structure of matter is to the energy it binds?

The answer to these questions is, of course, the human species: its traditional rather than genetic way of mutating the racial store of information, its brain, its memory, its language, its cultural institutions, its imagination. Again, this new emergence was the solution to paradoxes implicit in the nature of the universe that preceded it. Survival, now revised and enlarged in definition beyond reproductive success to include the control and prediction of the biosphere itself, and to a richer existence within many possible time-lines, required a faster acceleration of the adaptive process than biogenetic evolution could provide. Humanity is the solution to the paradoxes of life, as life was for matter, as space-time was for mathematical logic.

The irony of this process is that the paradoxes get more complex with each new solution of them; and the human paradoxes, which I have summed up as "shame," are the most pressing and difficult of all, especially as, unlike their predecessors, they have not yet been solved. Those thinkers who have in despair, or in denial of shame, or in fashionable avant-garde cynicism, condemned the human species and its progress, have not reflected that in a sense the shame of things goes all the way back: shame is most primitively the paradox of self-inclusion. If the cynics would turn back the clock and abolish humankind (for this is the only viable conclusion to their arguments), they would be cutting off the very process of existential tension by which the universe came to be. But cannot we think differently of the unsolved human paradox—as the open-endedness of the universe, as its evolutionary potential, as its great hope, as our chance to prove our creativity, as our solidarity with the whole cosmos in its great questioning expansion and fall, outwards into richer, more anxious, more complex, and more beautiful forms of being?

Value evolved slowly in the universe, increasing with each access of reflexivity and level of feedback. Complex entities conferred value upon each other and upon the less complex by sensitively registering their presence, perceiving, eating, mating with, desiring, or loving them; and conferring value upon themselves by their increasingly intentional and planned attempts to survive and reproduce. More intense and more universal values evolved with increasing ecological interdependence, whether among whole populations of species or in those fantastically complex and swiftly evolving inner ecologies, the nervous systems of higher animals.

The discovery of the structure of DNA and the function of RNA, and our first groping steps to synthesize new forms of life, have closed one of the last major gaps in the emerging evolutionary synthesis of scientific knowledge. In the last few decades we have seen the biochemical theory of life as a self-organizing feedback system extended by nonlinear chaos theory, fractal mathematics, and Prigoginian dissipative systems theory, to every level of material being, including the inorganic. The shameful beauty and reflexivity of life have now been found, in a dimmer and simpler form to be sure, in the turbulence of liquids and gases, in phase changes such as crystallization and partial melting, even in the processes by which the elementary particles and before them the four forces of physics precipitated out of the incandescence of the Big Bang.

This is not to say that there is nothing linear, predictable, and mechanistic in the universe, nothing pure and chaste. Each level of being might regard the lower and earlier levels rightly as more innocent than itself. If there were no unselfconscious, honest, and straightforward objects in the world, there would be no standard by which to judge the proper degree of modesty (that is being violated, acknowledged, and reaffirmed). In fact the anguished shame—and beauty—of the world come not only from self-reflection itself, but from the turbulent and densely enfolded region of *contrast* between the relatively self-reflective and the relatively unreflective. What is most painfully and delightfully reflected upon is, after all, always the previously unreflected. Many of the higher animals have, through the feedback process of evolution, added a new twist to this reflexive spiral or helix, and have developed a capacity to recognize that beauty in certain limited forms. The colors and shapes of the flowers are a precise record of what bees find attractive, and it would be a paradoxically anthropocentric mistake to assume that, because bees are more primitive organisms, there is nothing in common between our pleasure in flowers and theirs. The play behavior of many higher species has an irreducible element of pleasure in beauty, a rejoicing in their sheer physical capacities—flight, in the case of the jackdaws that Konrad Lorenz so lovingly observed, or speed and power, as among frolicking horses, or agility and coordination, among cats. Animal communications often seem to be as much for the sake of beauty as for use, as Charles Hartshorne observed in the antiphonal music of tropical songbirds, or has been recently remarked in the complex individual songs of the humpback whale.

Most salient of all is the strong element of beauty in animal rituals, especially mating rituals. It is important to look closely at how such rituals function and evolve, because their implications for our own rituals are very interesting. Generally when a survival behavior can be accomplished easily, without contradicting other instinctive behaviors, it is done automatically and without fuss and fanfare: breathing, perspiring, sleeping, and waking up. We do not notice such behaviors as "drives"; they are more part of what an animal is than what it is driven to do.

When two behaviors contradict each other, however, a space between them is sometimes formed which does not belong strictly to either. The animal must now use its nervous system to the utmost; you can see a squirrel or sparrow thinking when its natural and uncomplicated fear of humans is contradicted by its natural and uncomplicated desire for the crust of bread you have put out for it. When the two contradictory behaviors are both social, their intersection can become the stage for the most elaborate and beautiful displays, dances, songs, even dramas. In mating ritual, reproductive behavior is contradicted by territorial or intra-specific aggressive behavior. An area between them is opened up in which the linearity of an uncontradicted system will no longer work, and elaborate, nonlinear, highly self-reflexive and mutually reflexive feedback processes take over. Here the linear mathematics of continuous functions no longer applies, and the mathematics of catastrophic and fractal discontinuity comes into its own.

When this immediate individual-to-individual feedback system is in turn supplemented by the much larger and slower feedback system of evolution, remarkable changes and developments can take place in a species as a whole. Mating rituals directly affect the reproductive success of an individual: thus an individual with better ritual pigmentation, better plumage, better-looking reproductive organs, better songs and dances, or better antlers with which to stage the gladiatorial games of sexual rivalry, will end up with more progeny; and so the genes for those qualities can rapidly pervade the gene pool of the species, crowding out the others. Hence the beautiful feathers of the peacock, with their fractal designs; the neon displays of tropical fishes; and the extraordinary artistic activities of the blue satin bowerbird, whose courtship involves the building of an elaborate and useless bower, its decoration with colored objects, and even its painting with the juice of berries. Hence also the development of the elaborate tribal structure and status hierarchy of our close relatives the baboons, chimpanzees, and gorillas. The guenon monkeys have differentiated themselves into dozens of microspecies purely, it would seem, on the basis of their body decoration. Seen in this context the human capacity to value beauty is entirely natural, rooted in the evolution of the universe, inherited from the deeps of time.

Though the comparison I have implied between the old Great Chain of Being and the new evolutionary synthesis is a valid one in some ways, there are immense differences between the emerging worldview and the Thomist one. First, and most important, the new synthesis is essentially dynamic, changing, evolutionary, historical, and irreversible, while the old was static, unchanging, creationist, eternal, and cyclic in its temporal manifestation. In the evolutionary synthesis new realities, new species, for instance, can emerge, whereas in the old Aristotelian-Thomist system species are eternal categories, which their temporal exemplars or avatars in the material world strive without full success to fulfill and accomplish.

The second major difference is that the old synthesis works through a fundamentally top-down causality and ordering process, whereas the new synthesis is both bottom-up and top-down in its causality and ordering. In the Thomist universe God created and ruled the angels and human beings, who themselves ruled over the animals, which in turn were given domain over the plants, which controlled their inanimate material food, and so on down. In the evolutionary universe the sequence is at first reversed: the laws and particles of physics largely determine the ground rules of chemistry, which provides the arena for life, which in turn produces and generates conscious minds. Once higher forms of organization exist, they then take an increasingly influential "top-down" role in the world, but can never lose touch with their material and energetic substrate, their own evolutionary history. Together, then, in the evolved state of the world, bottom-up and top-down causality cooperate in a complex feedback system which is capable of further self-elaboration into yet more reflexive states of being.

The last major difference between the old Great Chain of Being and the new evolutionary universe is that, whereas the former requires an outside creator and arranger, the latter suggests an internal creative and organizational impulse. The old worldview provides an eternal transcendent God radically separated and distinguished from His creations by the fact that He alone is self-sufficient and self-creating. The new view, on the other hand, is approaching the position that the universe is a logical necessity; that is, the existence of a state of affairs in which nothing at all existed would require some extraordinary, ineffable, and transcendent metaphysical intervention. But the existence of an evolving, self-organizing universe is essentially inevitable without such an intervention. This view places the characteristics of loving fruitfulness, the apparent intention of design, and teleology in the creation itself. Until a few decades ago it was assumed that the physical universe works deterministically, and so if we accepted that view we were forced to assume that those "creatorly" characteristics were nonexistent, illusions imposed upon a blind and automatic universe by our animistic expectations. In other words, our intellectual honesty required us to disbelieve our eyes and ears, which told us of the joy of creation as it sings itself into being. Now, however, the new mathematics, physics, and chemistry of nonlinear nondeterministic dynamical systems show us that the physical universe is, in effect, free, and can thus be held responsible for its own beautiful order, richness, and creative innovation. Religion thus receives an unexpected endorsement, though the divine in the new view is from the beginning immanent in the universe. Indeed, the divine is also transcendent; but its transcendence is part and parcel of the universe's own evolutionary self-transcendence.

There is an apparent contradiction between the idea that the universe *had* to come into existence, and that it is free; but this contradiction is only apparent. *Some* kind of evolving, self-organizing universe is a necessity; which one it is, how it evolves, which directions it takes are, so to speak, up to its own free choice. And "free" is really not at all a bad word to describe the way in which, as the new science has shown, complex and unstable dynamical systems, on the verge of some transformation and unable to hold their present arrangement intact (for instance, a photon on the verge of being observed, a hot but cooling universe of pure energy about to give birth to matter, a supersaturated crystalline solution, an ecosystem with more resources at its disposal than it is using, or a heart between beats), unpredictably "collapse" into one of a large number of possible new states. The collapse is unpredictable not necessarily because any of its contributing elements is disordered but because all of them are dependent on each other in a complex contextual feedback relationship, and must thus all change together, without a causal priority and sequence that can be analyzed by any system smaller than the universe itself. The fact that this new state will fall within the parameters of a very beautiful and elaborate "strange attractor," and not outside it, is an indication not of the *lack* of "freedom" in this sense, but of its orderly coherency, its nonrandomness.

Beauty

I have placed the concept of beauty in the context of the evolving physical world, and thus refuted the avant-garde assumption that beauty is
only in the eye of the beholder. Now it is necessary to explain how
human beings developed their peculiar capacities for experiencing and
creating objects of beauty. All human societies possess the concept of
beauty, often with a very precise vocabulary and a tradition of argument
about it. People see (hear, touch, taste, smell) the beautiful, and recognize it by a natural intuition and a natural pleasure. Even animals do:
antiphonal birdsong, the brilliant shapes and colors of flowers (as we
have seen, a precise record of the aesthetic preferences of bees), and
the gorgeous ritual mating garments of tropical fishes and birds of paradise, all attest to a more-than-utilitarian attraction in certain forms of
organization.

For human beings this "natural intuition" is activated, sensitized, and
deepened by culture; that is, a natural capacity of the nervous system
now incorporates a cultural feedback loop, and also uses the physical
world, through art and science, as part of its own hardware. The theory
of such a training or sensitization, the incorporation of this cultural feedback loop, the plugging of it into the prepared places in our brains, is
what I have called "natural classicism." The foundation of the natural
classical perspective is that the universe, and we, evolved. This fact entails two truths about beauty: a special evolutionary truth and a general
evolutionary truth.

The special evolutionary truth is that our capacity to perceive and create beauty is a characteristic of an animal that evolved. Beauty is thus in
some way a biological adaptation. Beauty is a physiological reality: the
experience of beauty can be connected to the activity of actual neurotransmitters in the brain, endorphins and enkephalins. When we become
addicted to a drug such as heroin or cocaine, we do so because their molecular structure resembles that of the chemistries of joy that the brain
feeds to itself. What is the function of pleasure from an evolutionary
point of view? The pleasure of eating is clearly a reward for going to the
considerable trouble of finding ourselves something to eat. Certainly few
would go to the extraordinary metabolic expense and aggravation of
finding a willing member of the opposite sex and reproducing with him

or her unless there were a very powerful inducement to do so. We derive this very great pleasure from beauty, for which artists will starve in garrets and for whose mimicked substitutes rats and addicts will happily neglect food and sex. What is it a reward for? What adaptive function does it serve, that is so much more important than immediate nourishment and even the immediate opportunity to reproduce the species?

Some Freudians claimed, and the avant-garde embraced the idea, that the aesthetic is merely a sublimated form of libido. However, the new knowledge about neurotransmitters and brain reward renders this theory invalid. We must reexamine the whole relationship between the beauty that men and women find in each other and sexual desire. Could it not be that the truth is exactly opposite to what such psychologists believe, that much of what we think of as sex is actually a relaxed or dissipated form of esthetic excitement; that sexual attraction is not enough by itself to assure the reproductive pair-bond, and that it must borrow (or sublimate!) part of the energy of spiritual experience! What might a psychoanalysis based on such ideas look like?

What is the beauty experience a reward *for*? To answer this question we need to know a little about the timing of human evolution, as it is becoming clear from the work of paleoanthropologists, paleolinguists, archaeologists, and paleogeneticists. There is a peculiar overlap between the last phases of human biological evolution and the beginnings of human cultural evolution, an overlap of one to five million years, depending on how the terms are defined. In any case, there was a long period during which human culture exerted a powerful, indeed dominant, selective pressure upon the genetic material of the species and thus upon the final form it has taken (if ours is the final form).

For over a million years the major genetic determinant in the environment of our genus was our own culture. A creature that is living under cultural constraints is a creature that is undergoing an intensive process of domestication. Consider wheat, dogs, apple trees, pigeons: how swiftly and how dramatically they have been changed by human selective breeding! But we domesticated ourselves. There is a limestone cave near Zhoukoudian in northern China where human beings lived almost continuously for close to a quarter of a million years. It is filled almost to the roof with eighteen feet of compacted human debris—ash, bedplaces, bones. At the bottom, the oldest layers contain great hamhanded hammerstones, cutting clubs with a shard knocked off for a blade, and the clumsy bones and skulls of homo erectus. At the top, there are delicate leaf-shaped flint arrowheads, fine awls and augers, featherlike knives; and human jawbones made elegant by cookery, braincases made ample and capacious by ritual.

Imagine, then, a mating ritual, which directly affects the reproductive success of the individuals within a species. Those who are neurologically capable and adept at the complex nuances of the ritual would have a much better chance of getting a mate and leaving offspring. Now imagine that this ritual is being handed down from generation to generation not just by genetic inheritance, but also, increasingly, by cultural transmission: imitation, instruction, eventually language (did it evolve in order to facilitate this transmission?). If a behavior is handed down purely by genetic inheritance, any variations on it which result from individual differences and special environmental and social circumstances will be wiped out by the death of the individuals of a given generation and will not be transmitted to their offspring. Of course, if over thousands of years those individual differences lead to improved rates of survival, and if those special circumstances persist, then there may be a selective advantage in the behavior as modified by the variation, and that variation will become frozen into the genes. This is a very slow process: the learning is being done at the genetic level, not at the social or mental level.

In our thought experiment, changes in the ritual can be handed down very quickly, in only one generation; and so the faster system of transmission will tend to drive and direct the slower system of transmission. That is, cultural modifications in the ritual will tend to confer a decisive selective advantage upon those members of the species that are genetically endowed with greater neural complexity, a superior capacity for learning the inner principles of the ritual which remain the same when its surface changes, for following and extending the ritual's subtleties, and for recognizing and embodying the values that the ritual creates. Cultural evolution will drive biological evolution. This species, of course, is ourselves: perhaps what created us as human beings was an improved love song. In the beginning, indeed, was the word.

In this scenario the idea of beauty clearly has a central place. The capacity for recognizing and creating beauty is a competence that we possess, a competence that was selected for by biocultural coevolution: it is both a power that the "mating ritual" of human and prehuman culture demanded and sharpened, and a value generated by that ritual that it was in our reproductive interest to be able to recognize and embody. Such an analysis might well adjust the balance of traditional paleoanthropology, which has been perhaps excessively concerned with hairy males with flint axes, and begin to provide, if not a feminist anthropology, then a human one. To be, and to be able to recognize, a beautiful human being, and to desire to mix one's genes with his or hers, might be a survival strategy that drove the flowering of homo sapiens.

What are the results of this coevolution in the neurobiology of aesthetic experience? Simply to be able to ask this question—that it should be reasonable, indeed predicted by a solid theory, for beauty to have a pancultural neurobiological base—overturns modernist and most postmodernist esthetics. If the theory of the biocultural evolution of the sense of beauty through traditional ritual is correct, we might expect to see a specific set of capabilities, natural classical genres or systems by which we generate, recognize, and appreciate beauty, based on new or revised neural structures in the hominid brain, that would be culturally universal and fundamental to the human arts. What should we call these special human abilities? They would be much more powerful and more sharply focused than the general processing of the basic mammalian brain. Perhaps we could call them hereditary knowledges, or lores, or skills, or powers, though each of these terms is misleadingly limited in one way or another. Or perhaps we should call them genres, because they have distinct forms and even rules, and need a cultural feedback loop of imitation and instruction to bring out their full power. If we were to imagine certain abilities of this kind that we might have, but don't, their extraordinary dexterity might be better appreciated. We can learn, paradoxically, to recognize how wonderful are our eyes, by imagining what it would be like to have magnifying or telescopic lenses, which we might have, but don't; but we do have color perception, our natural spectrograph; and a powerful instinctive capacity for the interpretation of complex projective geometry, and a wonderful movement sensor.

The natural capacities of beauty are even more remarkable. For instance, if our species had evolved in a highly mechanized biocultural milieu, it could easily have developed an innate skill for instant, easy, and unconscious calculation of mathematical problems. Just by an act of intention as simple as raising one's arm, one could bring to one's mind the value of Pi or of the square root of two to any desired decimal place; or rattle off the first three hundred prime numbers. We regularly, as in the grammar of our language as we speak, or in the evaluation of speeds and vectors in a busy intersection, perform calculations at least as complex and requiring at least as much neural processing. We very nearly did develop this capacity; some idiots savants seem to have the power of instant calculation, though it looks as if other brain capacities may have had to be sacrificed in order for them to do so. Or imagine that we could as naturally recognize or create an eight-second poetic line as we do the normal and universal three-second one. Or that we could as instinctually catch the "tune" of a piece of serial music when we have not heard it before, as we can pick up a melody based upon the universal human musical scale. Or that there is the same kind of unambiguous natural mimetic and representational referent for musical keys and phrases, preexisting musical conventions, that we find in visual outline pictures, so that programmatic or narrative music would be as easily interpreted across cultures as pictorial representations are. Or that the meaning of such works as Spenser's *The Faerie Queene* or Joyce's *Finnegans Wake*, aspects of which appeal to hypothetical but not actual human linguistic abilities, should be as transpicuous to the general understanding as those of Homer, Shakespeare, and Tolstoy, which are at least as complex but which are tuned to real human brain capacities.

Of course we now have technical prostheses not given in the primary gene–culture system, by which we can supplement the limitations of the human brain: computers to do calculations, techniques of musical and literary analysis, concordances, "skeleton keys," and so on. We also seem to be able to make one mental skill partly substitute for another. Professional musicians, who by musicological training have mapped their musical skills onto linguistic abilities, have been shown to use their linguistic left brain at least as much as the right brain in listening to music, whereas laypersons tend to use the right brain exclusively for this purpose. In mathematics algebra can serve when multidimensional topology goes beyond the human spatial instincts; and contrariwise geometry, and now its extension in mathematical computer graphics, can bring a dry numerical sequence or algebraic formula to life in such a way that new ideas open up for the mathematician. Koen dePryck has shown that dysphasic children unable to perceive the meaning of linguistic metaphors can come to understand them by drawing them on a piece of paper. One implication of this line of thought is that these powers do not cover the entire range of possible human cognition, perception, and action. They leave gaps, which can be covered partly by makeshift combinations of the canonical abilities, and partly by technological crutches and aids.

The very fact that we must go to such lengths to develop crutches and prostheses in the absence of one of these natural powers shows how powerful, how magical, they are. We do not normally notice them precisely because they are so easy to use; but in order to understand the nature of beauty we are going to have to recognize and appreciate them for what they are. For they are all essentially aesthetic, in the best sense of that word; their cognitive and practical uses are secondary. The self-rewarding feedback system, and the acceleration of insight and spiritual force that we feel in the full current of one of the natural classical artistic genres, either as creator or audience, only happens there, and not in the gaps between them. Modernist art set itself to see with new eyes; but the new prosthetic eyes are not as good as the old ones, unless we can find a way to plug the new eyes into the old.

The old eyes are our natural magic. Perhaps, then, the magical term "spells" would be more accurate a word for them than "genres." Neurospells, biospells—or "runes" as in the old Norse magic, might be suggestive terms. I like the word "charms," in the combination "neurocharms." This word evokes not only a linguistic element, but also a musical one (as in its cognate "carmen," song) and a visual one (as in a magic charm one might wear on one's wrist or breast or temple). The word can also refer to an ability, to an experience, and to the feeling of pleasure that rewards us for either. For the Greeks those charms were the muses and the graces, and the experience of them is most like a mild divine possession.

The development of these neurocharms in the course of mammalian, primate, and human evolution required a massive enlargement and modification of parts of the brain. The neurocharms divide themselves into two large groups, the left-brain group and the right-brain group. The right-brain group in turn divides itself into two subgroups, one developed out of auditory or musical information-processing, and one developed out of visual or pictorial information-processing. In homo sapiens all the neurocharms in the left-brain group have increasingly been subsumed into and dominated by what we might call the super-charm, language. They are as follows:

• Syntactical organization.

• Trope, symbol, metaphor, and various forms of reference.

• Collecting, selecting, classification, and hierarchical taxonomy.

• Dramatic mimesis, the power of inter- and intra-personal reflection and modeling. This is the reflexive or dramatic operator, by which we are able to simulate other people's consciousness and point of view in imaginative models (containing miniature models of the other person's model of us, and so on), and set them into coherent theatrical interaction. "O wad some pow'r the giftie gie us," says Robert Burns, "To see oursels as others see us!" This natural classical genre does exactly that.

• Debate, dialectic, and eristics.

• Divination, hypothesis and metaphysical synthesis, the scientific imagination.

• Narrative, story, and myth. The narrative operator is the genre by which we give time a complex tense structure, full of might-have-beens and should-be's, conditionals, subjunctives, branches, hopes, and memories. Fundamentally, the narrative operation constructs a series of events which have the curious property of being retrodictable (each one seems inevitable once it has happened) but not predictable (before it happens, we have no sound basis on which to foretell it); which is why we want to know what happens next. This operator comes with a large collection of archetypal myths and stories, such as "The Swan Princess," which are fundamentally identical all over the world, because their seeds are in our genes.

The neurocharms in the auditory right-brain group are as follows:

• Musical meter, tempo, and rhythm. The metrical "operator" of music is related to but different from the poetic metrical operator, and also connects with dance. It is very highly developed in African drum rhythms.

- Musical tone, melody, and harmony. Musical tonality opens up inexhaustible languages from Chinese classical music, through Balinese gamelan, to the fugues and canons of Bach.

- Musical performance, the making and playing of musical instruments.

The visual right-brain group is as follows:

- Pattern recognition, detail frequency preference, visual rhythm, and composition. The visual detail-frequency preference system makes us prefer pictures and scenes with a complexly balanced hierarchy of high-frequency information (dense textures and small details) ranging through to low-frequency information (large general shapes and compositions). Consider, for instance, Japanese prints, or the arcadian landscape paintings of Poussin and Claude.

- Color; the recognition and creation of meaningful combinations of colors.

- The eye-hand mimetic capacity: picturing. A representational operator (unique to human beings), whereby we can reverse the process of visual perception and use our motor system to represent what we see by drawing, painting, or sculpting.

In addition, there are five other neurocharms, three of which mediate between the groups listed above, as follows:

- Dance, gymnastics, and the martial arts. This charm mediates between the visual right-brain group and the auditory right-brain group.

- The ideographic, geometrical, architectonic, mapping capacity. This charm mediates between the right-brain visual group and the left-brain linguistic group, and is the basis of writing.

- Poetic meter, cadence, and the art of vocal expression. This charm mediates between the right-brain auditory group and the left-brain linguistic group.

Another charm, which does not fit into any of the main groups, is a sort of marvelous by-product of the rewiring of the olfactory (smell) and taste centers of the mammal brain as an emotional and motivational system:

- Cuisine and its derivative arts, the appreciation and making of wines, perfumes, cheeses, etc.

A final charm is based upon the mammalian and primate grooming rituals:

- The art of massage, therapeutic manipulation, physical nurturing, and sexual pleasure.

There are other neurocharms besides the eighteen listed above; however, I believe that we share them in an unchanged or perhaps diminished state with other mammals, and they have not been through the ritual acceleration into the realm of human beauty.

The experimental neuropsychologist Ernst Pöppel and I have investigated one of these neurocharms or natural classical genres in some detail: poetic meter, or what we have called the neural lyre. All over the world human beings compose and recite poetry in poetic meter; all over the world the meter has a line length of about three seconds, tuned to the three-second acoustic information-processing pulse in the human brain. Our acoustic present is three seconds long; we remember echoically and completely three seconds' worth of acoustic information before it is passed on to a longer-term memory system, where it is drastically edited, organized for significant content, and pushed down to a less immediate level of consciousness. If a natural brain rhythm, like the ten cycle per second alpha rhythm—or the three second audial present—is "driven" or amplified by an external rhythmic stimulus, the result can be large changes in brain state and brain chemistry, and consequently in the amount and kind of information that the brain can absorb, and in the kind of higher-level processing it can put to work.

We showed that in addition to these effects, poetic meter contained within the line a regular pulse of syllable patterns, made of heavy and light, long or short, tone-changing or unchanging, against which significant and expressive variations could be played. For instance, the English iambic pattern consists of a regular pulse of one unstressed and one stressed syllable, thus: ˘ ˊ. But consider Shakespeare's Sonnet 18, which is based on the same iambic (˘ ˊ) pattern of syllables, yet varies freely on it without losing touch with it:

ˊ ˘ ˘ ˊ ˘ ˘ ˘ ˊ ˘ ˊ

Shall I compare thee to a summer's day?

ˊ ˘ ˊ ˊ ˘ ˘ ˊ ˊ ˘ ˘
Thou art more lovely and more temperate.

ˊ ˊ ˘ ˊ ˘ ˘ ˊ ˘ ˘ ˊ
Rough winds do shake the darling buds of May,

˘ ˊ ˘ ˊ ˘ ˊ ˊ ˊ ˘ ˘
And Summer's lease hath all too short a date.

ˊ ˊ ˊ ˊ ˘ ˊ ˘ ˊ ˘ ˊ
Sometime too hot the eye of heaven shines,

˘ ˊ ˘ ˘ ˊ ˘ ˊ ˘ ˊ
And often is his gold complexion dimmed;

˘ ˊ ˘ ˊ ˘ ˊ ˊ ˊ ˘ ˊ
And every fair from fair sometime declines,

˘ ˊ ˘ ˊ ˘ ˊ ˊ ˘ ˘ ˊ ˘
By chance, or nature's changing hand untrimm'd;

˘ ˊ ˘ ˊ ˊ ˘ ˘ ˊ ˊ
But thy eternal summer shall not fade,

ˊ ˊ ˘ ˊ ˘ ˘ ˊ ˊ ˘ ˊ
Nor lose possession of that fair thou ow'st,

ˊ ˘ ˊ ˘ ˊ ˘ ˊ ˘ ˘ ˘ ˊ
Nor shall Death brag thou wand'rest in his shade,

ˊ ˘ ˘ ˊ ˘ ˊ ˘ ˊ ˘ ˊ
When in eternal lines to time thou grow'st.

˘ ˊ ˘ ˊ ˘ ˊ ˘ ˊ ˘ ˊ
So long as men can breathe or eyes can see,

ˊ ˊ ˊ ˊ ˘ ˊ ˊ ˊ ˘ ˊ
So long lives this, and this gives life to thee.

The difference between the expected rhythm (˘ ˊ ˘ ˊ ˘ ˊ ˘ ˊ ˘ ˊ)
and the actual rhythm carries information, as a tune does, or as a line
does in a drawing; that information is processed and understood not with
the linguistic left brain, but with the musical and spatial right brain. Thus
unlike ordinary language, poetic language comes to us in a "stereo" neural mode, so to speak, and is capable of conveying feelings and ideas that
are usually labeled nonverbal. The genre itself is a biocultural feedback
loop that makes us able to use much more of our brain than we normally
can.

Let us take a closer look at another neurocharm, visual pattern. If
human experimental subjects are shown simple visual images consisting

of rows of vertical or horizontal lines, or lines diverging radially at equal angles from a point, they show a clear statistical preference for a certain frequency of lines. They prefer to look at a fairly rich field of lines, neither the simplest kind of row or star, made of only two or three lines, nor the densest kind, in which the lines are so close together they are indistinguishable, or so many that the eye loses track of them as individuals. In other words, the eye craves a certain complexity, but if the complexity is too great, and at the same time uniform, the eye reduces the pattern to a texture. The texture is now the only thing to look at, and so the eye finds itself as fatigued by the boredom of the single texture as it had been with a single line.

According to the same principle, subjects prefer images with more than one level of detail frequency, and with various kinds of texture; however, if the image is too "busy" and cannot be systematically organized into a hierarchy of detail frequencies, the eye becomes fatigued and generalizes the whole scene as a mishmash, which in turn, as such, produces visual boredom. If the image resolves itself into too simple a hierarchy, the eye, or rather the visual cortex, after an initial sensation of satisfaction at having solved the puzzle, begins to look about for ways in which the hierarchy either contains hidden contradictions or might be made to fit into a larger pattern. One example of a relatively complex and satisfying hierarchy is the perspective in which the world actually appears to us, its closer objects systematically larger than more distant ones, and its straight lines apparently curving in order to maintain the wholeness and consistency of the visual scene. It is interesting because such a scene implies occluded objects and spaces, which invite investigative movement or speculation based on visible clues. It was this richness of interpretive potential that served the great Renaissance masters of pictorial perspective. In other words, boredom is our way of detecting inefficiencies and redundancies in a flow of information, so that we are motivated to generalize repetitions as texture and concentrate on unique features of the visual scene. Those unique features include major contrasts, the borders between generalizable textures or tones, or structural outlines (which are two contrasts back to back). These then act as the higher-level signs or triggers or controls by which the lower-level information can be labeled, referred to, and retrieved.

The boredom response is in turn perhaps based on a universal characteristic of living cells, which makes every cell, however remote in function from the nervous system, a kind of neuron: that is, its capacity for irritation or sensitive response to stimulus, which can be overloaded and fatigued by the exhaustion of its capacity to respond, and habituated by repetition. If the eye is held still before a visual image, the image rapidly disappears, because the visual neurons are repeatedly and continuously getting the same stimulus. We are only able to see because the eye is free to range in a series of saccades, synchronized with the brain's alpha rhythm, and thus continually encounter new information. We do not see areas and states; we see contrasts and changes. This visual insistence on difference is emphasized by the fact that a given sector of the retinal field, tuned to fire if it receives a given stimulus, is always surrounded by a region in which sensitivity to that stimulus is actively suppressed. Interestingly enough, the area ratio of the receptive to the repressor field is almost exactly the golden section ratio, that is, the ratio between the two parts of a line when it is divided such that the shorter segment is the same fraction of the longer segment, as the longer segment is of the whole line.

The eye, then, tends to generalize if it can, to tag the ensemble of generalized elements (as a texture or a mishmash or a hierarchy) by means of a significant epitomizing fragment of it, to outline it with a contrast-boundary, to compress all that detail and push it down to lower-level processing, and then to look around for more interesting things to look at. Thus we can, with a scientific graph curve, generalize and smooth out its tendency, eliminating obvious mistakes and anomalies, and extend and produce the curve in our imaginations, consistently with its existing trend. Or, to take a homelier example, an outfielder can judge the trajectory of a fly ball and be there when it arrives. Without the eye's activist policy of hierarchizing and generalizing visual information, we could not accomplish such feats. Certainly, this policy can produce mistakes; we can fail to take account of the crossing of critical thresholds in the graph, or of the gust of wind that catches the ball as it sails above the shelter of the bleachers. But next time we can include the new information as a parameter, and improve our odds of being right.

This, the default option of the optical system, consists in a sort of continuously correctable but deepening visual prejudice. There are other possible visual policies, such as those recommended by avant-garde modernist and postmodernist aestheticians, which require us to abandon our prejudicial expectations and conventions, to treat every visual element as equally significant (or, which is the same thing, insignificant), and to avoid generalizations and visual hierarchies, especially those whose solution and meaning is the representation of a real object in space. Alas, however, a species which relied on these policies would be unable to evade a falling rock or thrown spear, could not dance or make pictures, and would be blind to the beautifully intricate and coherent way in which the universe makes room for all its details, and reconciles all its forces and trajectories. Patterns are beautiful that exist at the margin between order and disorder, that exhibit a hierarchical organization which is troubled and opened up by contradictory elements. Those contradictory elements do not, however, obscure the hierarchy but add to it indeterminate meta-levels that hold our visual interest, and that are essentially dynamic and changing, so as to avoid the eye's tendency to become habituated or bored.

Only one kind of phenomenon can satisfy all these criteria, and that is the form of a growing organism or evolving system. Growth is a feedback process: an organism grows in proportion to its existing size and shape, and as an orderly continuation of its previous growth. The simplest kind of growth we know (as opposed to mere addition) is the Fibonacci series in mathematics, in which the next member of the series is simply the two previous members added together. Thus we get 1, 1, 2, 3, 5, 8, 13, 21, 34, 55, 89, etc. When this series is translated into a curve, we get the Fibonacci spiral, which is found throughout nature in the forms of growth, such as seashells and sunflower-heads. I have measured the intervals between the fronds of a fern and found the series there too. If you try to make a spiral pattern by close-packing uniform elements (like sunflower seeds) outward from a center, you will always get just such a spiral. Leonardo Fibonacci discovered it as a way of calculating the theoretical rate of reproductive increase in a population of breeding rabbits.

This series is, interestingly enough, one of two ways in which the Golden Section ratio can be calculated; simply divide one member of the series by its successor. The further along the series one makes the calculation, the more accurate the value of the ratio will be. The other way of making the calculation is by taking the square root of five, subtracting one, and dividing the result by two. This formula also has a spatial expression: take a regular five-pointed star, and calculate the ratio between the side of any of its points, and the side of the pentagon which connects its internal angles. (This figure, the pentangle, pentacle, endless knot, or golden knot, is a traditional symbol of magic.) "Fiveness" is associated with the golden section in another way too: the "Penrose Tiling," by which the plane can be endlessly covered by a growing nonrepeating pattern made up of two shapes of parallelograms, continually suggests, without achieving, a fivefold symmetry: and the ratio of fat parallelograms to thin ones is the golden ratio. It is as if irregular growth is a spatial invention which in the case of the regular pentagon replaces the capacity possessed by the other simple regular polygons—the triangles, squares, and hexagons—to tile the plane regularly.

Psychophysical experiments show that, irrespective of culture and education, people prefer golden rectangles (the lengths of whose sides are related by the Golden Section ratio) to any other shape of rectangle. Thus the rudiments of visual beauty are founded upon the ratio of growth. The Golden Section is one of the core concepts in classical, medieval, and renaissance architecture and in the traditional visual arts.

The Fibonacci series is only the simplest of a whole class of iterative algorithms or formulas whose results are fed back into the equation and which thus incorporate a mathematical feedback loop. Other examples include the Newtonian algorithm for obtaining square roots, the process by which such strange objects as Koch curves and Sierpinsky carpets are constructed, and the whole class of fractal algorithms described by Benoit Mandelbrot, including the Mandelbrot Set itself. (James Gleick's book *Chaos: Making a New Science* [New York: Viking, 1987] is a good introduction to this subject.) When the results of these iterative formulas are plotted in space, they produce exquisitely beautiful and elaborate forms, with depth below depth of detail at different hierarchical scalings; such forms please the eye, which recognizes in them the principles of animal, plant, and crystalline growth, and perhaps the principles of Growth itself. The attractors of Lorenz and Hénon, which plot the statistical results of a variety of natural iterative processes, share the same depth, clarity, and inexhaustible complexity; I believe the golden section can be found in many of their spatial relations.

Fractal theory is now used by computer graphics programs to store visual information with astonishing economy, as algorithmic seeds which need only be played out iteratively to generate an accurate recreation of an original image. Thus computer programs, in the course of their hurried evolution, have discovered, as it were, the same techniques of generalizing, of compressing and pushing down, that the visual cortex did. We, and these new programs, do not remember by storing the entire picture, but by storing just the essential inner information needed to recreate the picture: the algorithmic seed, or tag, or symbolic/metonymic epitome of the whole. We are thus in theory able to create a thousand pictures, by varying this algorithm, where a photographic memory could give us but one. This is the strategy not only of memory but of life, which does not hide its one talent in the ground, to be returned to its giver pure and unchanged, but which invests its being in a productive organic process that can not only copy over what it is given, but produce new things that are not given.

It should now be clear that the forms of the arts are not arbitrary, but are, in fact, rooted in our biological inheritance. To say this is not to imply that these neurocharms or natural classical genres are constraints, or limits upon the expressive powers of the arts. Quite the reverse; they are like what computer enthusiasts call turbos, programs or hardware that can accelerate and improve the operation of a computer. These systems, which incorporate a cultural feedback loop into the brain's processing, can enormously deepen and broaden its powers. Language itself may be one of the most comprehensive and earliest of them. They are not constraints any more than the possession of a hammer or a screwdriver is a constraint upon our carpentry; but their use must be learned.

So much for the special evolutionary truth about beauty. Without the general evolutionary truth, it would be meaningful only in a practical sense. It would leave out that tremble of philosophical insight that we associate with beauty, and would ignore the beauty that we find in nature and in the laws of science. It is not enough, from an evolutionary point of view, that individuals within a species should be endowed with a species-specific sense of beauty related to cooperation and sexual selection, even if the selection favors big brains, sensitivity, and artistic grace. The whole species must benefit from possessing a sense of beauty. This could only be the case if beauty is a real characteristic of the universe, one that it would be useful—adaptive—to know. How might this be?

I want to propose that the experience of beauty is a recognition of the deepest tendency or theme of the universe as a whole. This may seem a very strange thing to say; but there is a gathering movement across many of the sciences that indicates that the universe does indeed have a deep theme or tendency, recognizable by the human neurobiological sensitivity to beauty, a leitmotif which we can begin very tentatively to describe, if not fully understand.

Let us play with an idea of Kant's and see where we get if we treat the aesthetic as something analogous to perception. Imagine dropping a rock on the floor. The rock reacts by bouncing and by making a noise, and perhaps undergoes some slight internal change; we would not imagine that it felt anything approaching a sensation. Now imagine that you drop a worm on the floor; the impact might cause it to squirm, as well as to bounce and to produce a sound of impact, as the rock does. The worm, we would say, feels a sensation; but from the worm's point of view it is not a sensation of anything in particular. What the worm feels is as unspecific as what one describes to a doctor when one complains that one's stomach feels funny. The worm does not construct, with its primitive nerve ganglia, anything as complex as an external world filled with objects like floors and experimenters.

Now imagine that you drop a guinea pig. Clearly it would react, as the rock does, and also feel sensations, as the worm does. But we would say in addition that it *perceives* the floor, the large dangerous animal that has just released it, and the dark place under the table where it may be safe. Perception is as much beyond sensation as sensation is beyond mere physical reaction. Perception constructs a precise, individuated world of solid objects out there, endowed with color, shape, smell, and acoustic and tactile properties. It is generous to the outside world, giving it properties it did not necessarily possess until some advanced vertebrate was able, through its marvelously parsimonious cortical world-construction system, to provide them. Perception is both more global, more holistic, than sensation, because it takes into account an entire outside world, and more exact, more particular, because it recognizes individual objects and parts of objects.

Now if you were a dancer and the creature that you dropped were a human being, a yet more astonishing capacity comes into play. A drama could be written about how the dance partners experience this drop, this gesture. Whole detailed worlds of implication, of past and future, of interpretive frames come into being. The table and the dance floor do not lose any of the guinea pig's reality, but instead take on richnesses, subtleties, significant details, held as they are within a context vaster and more clearly understood. What is this awareness, that is to perception what perception is to sensation, and sensation to reaction? The answer is: aesthetic experience. Aesthetic experience is as much more constructive, as much more generous to the outside world, as much more holistic, and as much more exact and particularizing than ordinary perception, as ordinary perception is compared with mere sensation. Thus by ratios we may ascend from the known to the very essence of the knower. Aesthetic perception is not a vague and touchy-feely thing relative to ordinary perception; quite the reverse. This is why, given an infinite number of theories that will logically explain the facts, scientists will sensibly always choose the most beautiful theory. For good reason: this is the way the world works.

Beauty in this view is the highest integrative level of understanding and the most comprehensive capacity for effective action. It enables us to go with, rather than against, the deepest tendency or theme of the universe, to be able to model what will happen and adapt to or change it. This line of investigation has clearly brought us to a question which it seems audacious to ask in this antimetaphysical age. But we will ask it anyway: what *is* the deepest tendency or theme of the universe?

Let us make another list, a list of descriptions or characteristics of that theme or tendency. We can always adjust or change the list if we want:

- Unity in multiplicity: the universe does seem to be one, though it is full of an enormous variety and quantity of things. Our best knowledge about its beginning, if it had one, is that everything in the universe was contracted into a single hot dense atom; or if it had no beginning, then it is bounded by a single space-time continuum out of which all forms of matter and energy emerge.

- Complexity within simplicity: the universe is very complicated, yet it was generated by very simple physical laws, like the laws of thermodynamics.

- Generativeness and creativity: the universe generates a new moment every moment, and each moment has genuine novelties. Its tendency or theme is that it should not just stop. As it has cooled, it produced all the laws of chemistry, all the new species of animals and plants, and finally ourselves and our history.

- Rhythmicity: the universe can be described as a gigantic, self-nested scale of vibrations, from the highest-frequency particles, which oscillate with an energy of ten million trillion giga-electron volts, to the slowest conceivable frequency (or deepest of all notes), which vibrates over a period sufficient for a wave to cross the entire universe and return. Out of these vibrations, often in the most delicate and elaborate mixtures or harmonies of tone, everything is made.

- Hierarchical organization: big pieces of the universe contain smaller pieces, and smaller pieces contain smaller pieces still, and so on. Relatively big pieces, such as planets and stars, control to some extent, through their collective gravitational and electromagnetic fields, the behavior of the smaller pieces of which they are composed, while the smaller pieces together determine what the larger pieces are to begin with. We see the same hierarchical organization, much more marvelously complex and precise, in the relationship of the smallest parts of the human body to the highest levels of its organization, from elementary particles through atoms, molecules, cells, organelles, and organs, to the neural synthesis that delegates its control down the chain. Consider also the elegant hierarchy of support, control, cooperation, and dependency that one finds in the parts and whole of a Bach canon.

- Self-similarity: related to the hierarchical property is a marvelous property now being investigated by chaos theorists and fractal mathematicians: the smaller parts of the universe often resemble in shape and structure the larger parts of which they are components, and those larger parts in turn resemble the still larger systems that contain them. Like Dante's *Divine Comedy*, in which the three-line stanza of its microcosm is echoed in the trinitarian theology of its middle-level organization and in the tripartite structure of the whole poem, so the universe tends to echo its themes at different scales. If you look at the branches of a tree, Yeats's chestnut tree perhaps, that "great-rooted blossomer," you can see how the length of a twig stands in the same relation to the length of the small branches as the small branches stand to the large branches, and the large branches to the trunk. You can find this pattern in all kinds of phenomena—electrical discharges, frost-flowers, the annual patterns of rise and decline in competing animal populations, stock market fluctuations, weather formations and clouds, the bronchi of the lungs, corals, turbulent waters, and so on. This harmonious relation of small to large is *beautiful*.

These descriptions would be immediately recognized by scientists in many fields as belonging to feedback processes and the structures that are generated by them. We may sense that they are the signatures of Gaia, as we encountered her in chapter 3. Indeed, it is often difficult to tell the process apart from the product: how can we tell the dancer from the dance? *The fundamental tendency or theme of the universe, in short, is reflexivity or feedback.* We are beginning to understand more and more clearly that the universe is a phenomenon of turbulence, the result of a nested set of feedback processes. Hence it is dynamic and open-ended: open-ended, moreover, precisely in and because of its continual attempt to come to closure, to fall to a stop. Moreover, as with any dynamic nonlinear open feedback process, the universe continually generates new frames and dimensions, new rules and constraints, and its future states are too complicated to be calculated by any conceivable computer made out of the universe as it is. The universe is *free*.

The process of evolution itself is a prime example of a generative feedback process. Variation, selection, and heredity constitute a cycle, which when repeated over and over again produces out of this very simple algorithm the most extraordinarily complex and beautiful life-forms. Variation is the novelty generator; selection is a set of alterable survival rules to choose out certain products of the novelty generator. Heredity, the conservative ratchet, preserves what is gained. Evolution is only one of a class of processes, based on very simple iterative formulas, that are characterized by various researchers in various ways: nonlinear, chaotic, dissipative, self-organizing. The Mandelbrot set is a nice mathematical example: take a complex number; multiply it by itself; add the original number; then take the number that you get and repeat the process several times. Now start with a different number, and do the same thing. Make a collection of original numbers, and then map them on a plane, coloring them according to whether, and how fast, the algorithm makes them rush off toward infinity, or zero in on some limit, called an attractor. (This is best done on a computer, because it would take many years to do it with paper and pencil.) You will get a self-similar shape of great beauty and infinite complexity and variety.

All such processes produce patterns with the familiar characteristics of branchiness, hierarchy, self-similarity, generativeness, unpredictability, and self-inclusiveness. To look at, they are like the lacy strands of sand and mud that Thoreau observed coming out of a melting sandbank in *Walden*; they are filled with lovely leaf designs, acanthus, chicory, ferns, or ivies; or like Jacquard paisleys, the feathers of peacocks, the body-paint or tattoo designs of Maoris or Melanesians, the complexity of a great wine, the curlicues of Hokusai seafoam or Haida ornamentation or seahorses or Mozart melodies. The Iterative Feedback Principle, which is at the heart of all these processes, is the deep theme or tendency of all of nature—nature, the creator of forms. It is the logos and eros of nature; and it is what we feel and intuit when we recognize beauty. Our own evolution is at the same time an example of the principle at work, the source of our capacity to perceive it in beautiful things, the guarantee of its validity (if it were not valid we would not have survived), and the origin of a reflective consciousness that can take the process into new depths of self-awareness and self-reference. As the most complex and reflexive product of the process that we know of in the universe, we are, I believe, charged with its continuance; and the way that we continue it is art.

Ecopoetics

If beauty is a real property of things and, though fertile of free and unpredictable developments, rooted in the physical universe, then the whole body of contemporary critical theory and practice is deeply in error and should be revised. A vital criticism is essential to vital art. Thus in the hopeful rebuilding of our culture that I propose in this book, a new system of critical theory is essential. What must that theory do to be successful? One way of answering this question is in terms of healing: the rejoining of broken wholes, the reuniting of false dichotomies, the bringing together of cultural energies vitiated by their division. Our theory, then, must rejoin artist with public, beauty with morality, high art with low, art with craft, passion with intelligence, art with science, and past with future.

We need a new kind of poetics, which we might call ecopoetics. (The word is, I believe, the coinage of the scholar and literary biographer Tim Redman, who applies it primarily in the economic sense of "eco.") Though this approach can apply to all the arts, I shall specifically address literature. Essentially I am calling for the abandonment of a good part of the present activities of the literary academy, and the beginning of a new literature, a new poetics, and a new criticism based upon the evolving universe and our own leading part in it. The "eco" in ecopoetics is derived from the Greek *oikos*, household. In what senses will the new poetics be a "household" poetics?

First, it will experience literature in the household of a world of ratio, space, and quantity. It will reconnect with mathematics, geometry, logic, number theory, and geometry. There is a promising beginning for this in structuralism (aborted by poststructuralism); but we must seek for roots also in the rhetorical, geomantic, numerological, iconographic, and mnemonic theories of the past. Literary critics should be able to read Benoit Mandelbrot. There are new mathematical theories of the topology of the universe that describe it as a double super-sphere, that is, a sphere with two centers, each of which is the periphery of the other. The mathematicians Istvan Ozsvath and Wolfgang Rindler, who are investigating this shape, have pointed out that this geometry exactly corresponds to Dante's account of the cosmos as described in the *Paradiso*; they have thus dubbed the whole class of such topological forms *Dantes* in honor of the poet.

Second, the new poetics will experience literature in the household of the physical world, a world that we are now realizing is full of subtle phase-changes, turbulences, emergent orders, and self-reflexive processes that can act as amazing models and analogues for artistic creation. Some chemists, physicists, and cyberneticists, such as Roald Hoffman, Ilya Prigogine, Cyril Stanley Smith, John Archibald Wheeler, and Douglas Hofstadter, can help show the way, but within the literary and critical world there is virtually no criticism of this kind, and very little literature. The critics Katherine Hayles, Koen dePryck, and Alexander Argyros are welcome exceptions.

Third, the new poetics will experience literature in the household of the living world. Poetry is an activity of a living species, with a living brain and nervous system and body. As I have pointed out, the fundamental competencies of literature and art, such as our ability to produce and understand poetic meter, narrative, visual patterns, and melody, are culturally universal and the result of gene–culture coevolution. We have a nature; that nature is cultural; that culture is classical. Our literary and artistic nature is inscribed in our central nervous systems; that nature is the algorithm that generates the extraordinary variety of human art and literature. We need to listen to what brain science is saying, to the ethologists and sociobiologists and neurochemists and psychophysicists, but molecular biology and biochemistry are just as important. The most powerful precursor of language in the physical world is the DNA molecule; indeed, it might be more accurate to say that language is just fast DNA, or that DNA is slow language. The things we are finding out about how DNA edits, expresses, repairs, recombines, and reproduces itself are of the most crucial and central interest to literature, music, and art, which do exactly the same things, perhaps in similar ways. There is almost no literature or criticism along these lines. Such science fiction writers as Michael Crichton, David Brin, and Gregory Benford have certainly dealt with the subject, but not in such a way as to have the subject matter reflect deeply into the linguistic and formal medium.

Fourth, ecopoetics will experience literature and art in the household of the human world, the ancient and perennial world of ritual, folklore, storytelling, oral performance, family; the household of craftsmanship, of everyday activities like gardening, cooking, sewing, physical training, carpentry, and so on. The novelist and the painter used to know how to do the great scenes of childbirth, funeral, the local dance, the girl's first party dress, the boy's initiation, the family dinner; anthropology, folklore, and performance studies can enlarge this base. These are not just the characteristics of "bourgeois society"; in various forms they are common to all human cultures. When we return to these constants we will rediscover how akin all human beings are, how culture and biology are so subtly interwoven that the puzzle is of inexhaustible literary interest; and in the process we will recover an audience which has abandoned "serious" art. This study will also show us how much we have lost of the ancient biocultural techniques of storytelling, meter, allegory, rhetoric, literary structure, and iconology, and how we might recover them. Some contemporary fields of literary scholarship can lead the way: the oral tradition studies inspired by Albert Lord and Milman Parry, the mnemonic investigations of Frances Yates and her followers, the myth studies of Joseph Campbell, the performance theory of Robert Corrigan and others, and the exciting blend of classical philology and anthropology practiced by Walter Burkert and Gregory Nagy, for example.

Fifth, the new poetics will encounter literature and art in the household of sociocultural and economic reality. Much recent literature and criticism has professed to do just this, but, in fact, it has existed rather in a world of left-wing avant-garde fantasy, that has been revealed in all its cruel tawdriness by the collapse of the intellectual apparat of Eastern Europe. The new ecopoetics will take its place in a world of real economic organisms, corporations, and social institutions, and must not alienate itself from the world of popular and commercial culture. Nor may it resort to such tricky and salving escapes as imagining a real distinction between popular and commercial culture, or, more sinister, between popular and folk culture (the Nazi move). These are just ways for the avant-garde and academy to avoid the sting of failure in the popular marketplace. On the other hand, it must not truckle to the infantile and uncultivated appetites of the masses either, but properly take the blame for them, and the responsibility for gently and patiently educating them into something deeper and better. If TV is trivial and empty (and it often is not), it is because those who should have been the cultural leaders have either sulked in their tents or stood jeering on the sidelines. The great model in this respect is William Shakespeare, who is still being attended by enthusiastic popular audiences, and was never too proud to tell an exciting tale or a dirty joke; yet his poetry is still the most profound in the world.

Sixth, the new poetics will take its place in the household of history. What this means is that its scholarship should possess the genuine historical imagination, and should be as wary of importing contemporary moral fashions into the past as it would be of imposing "Western" values on a "non-Western" society. Important historical fictions or poems or plays might issue from such a reinhabiting.

Finally, the new poetics will experience literature and art in the household of the divine economy, the spiritual universe. The world can be seen, as I have shown in chapter 2, both as the fetal body of a divine being, and as a sort of theater in which its story will play itself out. In this drama, which was going on before humans arrived on the scene and which has already bequeathed us an inheritance of only partly revisable values, the very nature of the good, the beautiful, and the true is still being worked out, created, and unfolded.

Given the view of beauty, and the principles of criticism based on it, that I have presented in this chapter, the outline of an artistic and literary manifesto suggests itself. This manifesto, though in the tradition of the romantic, modernist, and postmodernist manifestos that have preceded it, and embodying some ideas from those periods, is also a replacement for them, and claims a significant difference from them. The difference is that it is more soundly based, both empirically and rationally, and that its scientific and philosophical underpinnings are more contemporary, having had an advantage of at least fifty years in which old factual and epistemological errors could be exposed and corrected. This manifesto is partly the result of a series of conversations among a group of artists, poets, composers, and other makers that took place at the home of the sculptor Frederick Hart, the group described in chapter 1 as "centrists." I have organized the manifesto under seven headings, though its implications go beyond them.

1. *The Reunion of Artist with Public*

Art should grow from and speak to the common roots and universal principles of human nature in all cultures.

Art should direct itself to the general public.

Those members of the general public who do not have the time, training, or inclination to craft and express its higher yearnings and intuitions, rightly demand an artistic elite to be the culture's prophetic mouthpiece and mirror.

Art should deny the simplifications of the political Left and Right, and should refine and deepen the radical center.

The use of art, and of cheap praise, to create self-esteem, is a cynical betrayal of all human cultures.

Excellence and standards are as real and universal in the arts as in competitive sports, even if they take more time and refined judgment to appreciate.

2. *The Reunion of Beauty with Morality*

The function of art is to create beauty.

Beauty is incomplete without moral beauty.

There should be a renewal of the moral foundations of art as an instrument to civilize, ennoble, and inspire.

True beauty is the condition of civilized society.

Art recognizes the tragic and terrible costs of human civilization, but does not abandon hope and faith in the civilizing process.

Art must recover its connection with religion and ethics without becoming the propagandist of any dogmatic system.

Beauty is the opposite of coercive political power.

Art should lead but not follow political morality.

We should restore reverence for the grace and beauty of human beings and of the rest of nature.

3. *The Reunion of High with Low Art*

Popular and commercial art forms are the soil in which high art grows.

Theory describes art; art does not illustrate theory.

Art is how a whole culture speaks to itself.

Art is how cultures communicate with and marry each other.

4. *The Reunion of Art with Craft*

Certain forms, genres, and techniques of art are culturally universal, natural, and classical.

Those forms are innate but require a cultural tradition to awaken them.

They include such things as visual representation, melody, storytelling, poetic meter, and dramatic mimesis.

These forms, genres, and techniques are not limitations or constraints but enfranchising instruments and infinitely generative feedback systems.

High standards of craftsmanship and mastery of the instrument should be restored.

5. *The Reunion of Passion with Intelligence*

Art should come from and speak to what is whole in human beings.

Art is the product of passionate imaginative intelligence, not of psychological sickness and damage.

Even when it deals, as it often should and must, with the terrifying, tragic, and grotesque, art should help heal the lesions within the self and the rifts in the self's relation to the world.

The symbols of art are connected to the embodiment of the human person in a physical and social environment.

6. *The Reunion of Art with Science*

Art extends the creative evolution of nature on this planet and in the universe.

Art is the natural ally, interpreter, and guide of the sciences.

The experience of truth is beautiful.

Art is the missing element in environmentalism.

Art can be reunited with physical science through such ideas as evolution and chaos theory.

The reflectiveness of art can be partly understood through the study of nonlinear dynamical systems and their strange attractors in nature and mathematics.

The human species emerged from the mutual interactions of biological and cultural evolution.

Thus our bodies and brains are adapted to and demand artistic performance and creation.

We have a nature; that nature is cultural; that culture is classical.

Cultural evolution was partly driven by inventive play in artistic handicrafts and performance.

The order of the universe is neither deterministic nor on the road to irreversible decay; instead the universe is self-renewing, self-ordering, unpredictable, creative, and free.

Thus human beings do not need to labor miserably to despoil the world of its diminishing stockpile of order, and struggle with one another for possession of it, only to find that they have bound themselves into a mechanical and deterministic way of life.

Instead they can cooperate with nature's own artistic process and with each other in a free and open-ended play of value creation.

Art looks with hope to the future and seeks a closer union with the true progress of technology.

7. The Reunion of Past with Future

Art evokes the shared past of all human beings, that is the moral foundation of civilization.

Sometimes the present creates the future by breaking the shackles of the past; but sometimes the past creates the future by breaking the shackles of the present.

The Enlightenment and modernism are examples of the former; the Renaissance, and perhaps our time, are examples of the latter.

No artist has completed his or her artistic journey until he or she has sojourned with and learned the wisdom of the dead artists who came before.

The future will be more, not less, aware of and indebted to the past than we are; just as we are more aware of and indebted to the past than were our ancestors.

The immortality of art goes both ways in time.

Chapter 6

The Culture of Hope

The Technology of Hope

I have proposed that we possess a very powerful mental capacity for recognizing, tracking, modeling, and participating in nonlinear self-organizing systems. This mental capacity matches external nonlinear processes to the rich and swift internal ones of the brain itself. It is our sense of beauty, what we have rather awkwardly euphemized as our "aesthetic sense." We euphemized it partly because it involved an ancient, familiar, shame-ridden experience, as pleasurable as it was inexplicable, an experience that we feared because of its mawkishness and apparent uncontrol. Yet I wish to argue that there is no more reliable guide for harmonizing ourselves with and optimizing the complex nonlinear feedback systems of the world. Of course we need to use all the computerized weather-prediction, all the nonlinear econometric models, all the electroencephalograms, all the careful ecological analysis we can get. But our decisions on the basis of this knowledge must finally be in the service of the greatest beauty: the greatest epistemological beauty, that is, truth; and the greatest ethical beauty, that is goodness. The attractors of these, we can be sure, are in the human breast. We must evoke them, by educating our conscience and our intuition of the truth; most important of all, and for our very survival, we must cultivate our taste.

As a direct implication of the injunction to increase the organized complexity of the world, good technology preserves earlier stages and products of its own process. It will, therefore, pay special attention to the preservation of chemical complexity, to the preservation of the richness and variety of life, to the preservation of the higher organisms in particular, and to the care and reverence of human life. This is the natural order of our increasing concern, because life, higher organisms, and human beings are closer and closer approximations to the emerging nervous system of God. Within an organism, likewise, we give preference to the higher functions, especially the nervous system, over lower vegetative functions. This hierarchy of concern is really common sense; it is the automatic assumption of any good surgeon (or any animal caught in a trap) in making decisions about which part must be sacrificed to save the rest. Indeed, it will be necessary to replace certain environmentally unsound technologies with the more efficient, elegant, and benign ones that the new science is making possible. Certainly we will need to isolate fine examples of ancient and unique ecosystems in so-called "wilderness areas" from the natural interference of other, highly competitive species, such as ourselves and the pantropic weeds, in order to promote the richer evolution of the rest. But we do not necessarily have to yield to an antihuman and antitechnological ideology in order to make such choices.

Avant-garde critics of technology observe its increasing distribution and note correctly that the increasing distribution of destructive technology increases destruction. What they fail to note is that in market economies technology itself evolves, through relentless economic pressures, to low-input, high-efficiency, low-energy, high-yield, low-waste forms of production that are increasingly less destructive and more benign. The idea that profit is the root of all environmental evil may be difficult to accept as a fallacy; and the corresponding principle, that profit must in the long term benefit the environment, may seem like an outright paradox. Nevertheless, an important set of priorities is at stake, and some distinctions may help. Consider the nature of appetite. In a human being a healthy appetite is a sign of vitality, vigor, and even the capacity for productive work. Certainly that appetite can become diseased, and appear in a perverted form as gluttony, hyperobesity, and eating disorders such as anorexia and bulimia. By analogy, the profit motive is like appetite: a normal, valuable, and indispensable drive for a living organism.

When critics of capitalism use the terms "profit," or "profit motive," they do not distinguish between the healthy and the diseased forms of profit. The former is the result of the creation of new value, by ideas, art, science, and technology, through which the pie is enlarged; while the latter comes out of somebody else's hide, who is prevented by nonmarket barriers such as nationality or discrimination from resisting an oppressor's appropriation of his or her slice of the pie.

Profit is normally an indication of how well a person or an organization is serving the public and how much has been gained by productive activity to pass on to the future. A living cat is, so to speak, the profit that cat genes make over and above the "investment" of catfood that it eats. Life is matter become profitable, and personal consciousness is a special profit derived from higher forms of life. There are indeed higher and lower forms of profit, and the lower should serve and give way to the higher. The highest forms of profit are designated by the terms truth, beauty, and goodness. These, however, are founded on the lower economic forms of profit and cannot survive without them. The recent revelations of ecological catastrophe and massive pollution in the formerly socialist countries of Eastern Europe, whose economies explicitly rejected the profit motive, show that capitalist profit-appetites in themselves have little to do with environmental damage. It was ignorance and narrow specialization, common to all bureaucracies, whether socialist or capitalist, that must surely bear most of the blame. Other things being equal, profit in a competitive context is an incentive to efficiency in the use of materials, and thus tends toward a more benign presence in the environment.

The ecological philosophy or natural theology outlined in chapter 3 suggests that we embrace an activist, restorationist environmentalism, that goes with, not against, the natural inclination of humanity toward greater experience, self-awareness, mutual feedback, and technical power. It is not our job to leave nature alone nor to coexist peacefully with it; we *are* it, we are its future, its promise, its purpose. We must actively continue its project. If we are to do so we desperately need more knowledge and research. For a start, we need to know much more about how ecologies work. We particularly need a better bacteriology, and a better understanding of the subtle interplay of plant, animal, and human societies, gene pools, and the climatological and geological feedback loops they involve. We need to bring together evolutionists and ecologists (who sometimes do not seem to talk to each other) for a grand synthesis. The best way to do this is through the practical craft of ecological restoration itself. We best find out how ecologies work by recreating them.

We also need to know much more about genetic inheritance and genetic expression. It is beginning to look as if the 95 percent of the genome that is not expressed is actually a jumbled but fairly complete archive of a given organism's entire evolutionary history. As with certain big old business computer programs, which have been patched and augmented so many times that the programmers themselves no longer know quite what might still come in useful one day, it is simply too expensive to clean out all the old material, and really very inexpensive to store it in a dormant state. Further, the bacteria and viruses of the world constitute a huge lending library of past genetic diversity from all other living species. Using recombinant DNA techniques (as bacteria themselves do all the time) it may be possible one day to reconstruct and resurrect extinct species from this "fossil" DNA. We may thus eventually be able to undo the damage we have already done to species diversity, and even perhaps to restore whole ecosystems that existed before the advent of humanity. Already European breeders are in the process of restoring the extinct aurochs by selective breeding of domestic cattle, and South African breeders are bringing back the quagga by selectively breeding zebras. Wes Jackson, the MacArthur prizewinning director of the Land Institute, is crossing the ancient teosinte corn with its domesticated descendants, looking for a perennial grain that will need neither ploughing nor pesticides. One day we may just run the combine harvester over the great prairie every year or so, to get biomass for the food culture factories.

We may eventually modify existing species by recombinant DNA technology, and even develop new species adapted to new ecological niches. Sooner or later we will leave the confines of this planet. When we do we may carry with us the seeds of Earthly life, hardened and redesigned to thrive in alien environments, and perhaps to transform those environments, as life itself did three billion years ago on this planet, into a habitat for other Earthly life-forms. In this work we may become the seed-vectors and pollinators of the universe, carrying life beyond the fragile eggshell of this planet, so exposed to sterilization by a stray asteroid strike or an extra-large comet. We will eventually be in the business of the ecotransformation of planets; in fact we are already, with this one. We need to start thinking in these terms; I have called for a commitment by our civilization to an eventual transformation of the dead planet Mars into a living ecosystem. We should do this not only because it is a noble thing to do in itself (as my epic poem *Genesis* argues), but also because we will not ever know with any confidence how our own planetary ecosystem works until we have created one ourselves on another planet.

Less obviously, we need to study the mind itself, cognition, self-awareness, and all the other characteristics of sapient life. If we are the neurons of the divine, and charged, as fetal neurons are, with the duty of wiring up the divine brain, then we need to know how the neurons themselves work. Just as the best understanding of ecology comes from ecological restoration and the best understanding of genes comes from recombining DNA in new forms, so our best understanding of the mind is going to come from the attempt to create artificial intelligence. We know by doing and making. Artificial intelligence should be not a distant and irrelevant field for ecologists; already the computer study of nonlinear chaos, artificial neural networks, genetic algorithms, and genetic, cellular, and ecological models are coming together into a super-discipline. We evolved with natural mental gifts beautifully matched to the complexities and rhythms of nature; we need to rediscover the natural wisdom embedded in our neural structures. The human brain, as Andrew Marvell knew, seems to be an accelerated and more intense form of those external ecologies we call forests or oceans. Ideas and memories live together in a mental ecology that is continually evolving. We need to integrate our understanding of the human brain itself into our understanding of the natural environment.

Finally, and most of all, we need a new aesthetic philosophy, critique, and theology, as humanistic as it is naturalistic, embodied in an art by which all these studies can be guided. The most ancient form of artificial intelligence is art itself. Beauty is finally our surest indication of whether what we do is in the most creative direction for nature as a whole. But our sense of beauty itself must be educated by an ecopoetics that embodies all our new knowledge of the *oikos* or household of nature.

Imagine, then, a world in which technology has become so sophisticated and miniaturized that it begins to disappear as a physical presence with its own intrusive characteristics, and becomes more and more a sort of omnipresent invisible background magic that feels natural, classical, simple, and adapted to our bodies, minds, and culture. It will be some decades yet before most of the world has passed through the stage of early industrialization, and it is the job of the developed world to ease the transition, to help more backward economies to leapfrog the old smokestack and mass labor stages of development and go directly to a biocybernetic postindustrial prosperity. In the developed world we can already see a new technological, industrial, and economic constellation beginning to form. As mass manufacturing becomes more and more efficient and robotized, and as the cost of technology falls inexorably by comparison to the cost of human time, the manufacturing sector of the economy will undergo a relative shrinkage, though it will remain, like the utilities, a cash cow. The new areas of profit will be in service, design, education, entertainment, customized small-run manufactures, arts, crafts, tourism, science as entertainment, medicine, and religion.

Whenever a new gadget comes on the market it begins as a large, obtrusive object which its owner will often display out of pride and the desire to impress. Later it will become more sophisticated, more chic, and will begin to sprout dozens of fancy features, so that the panel of a VCR or the dashboard of a car or the controls of a blender approach the complexity of an airplane cockpit; there will be fifteen levels between "whip" and "liquefy." Then the technology will begin to hide itself behind the paneling of a wall or closet, or behind the tinted windows of the luxury car, at first for reasons of exclusiveness and snobbery. A mature technology, though, aims toward discreetness, user-friendliness, simplicity, and classicism, so that the gadget becomes as obvious in function as a hammer, as unobtrusive as a hidden sound system, as beautiful as a violin, as intuitive as a good icon-driven disk operating system, and as robust and cheap as an ordinary telephone. It and its user will have educated each other's taste.

What we need to aim for is a technology that has all these virtues, not just for human beings but for the rest of nature as well, that will fit natural ecosystems as a good tennis racquet fits the human hand. In other words, culture, art, and nature will not, as in the world of the industrial revolution, be adapted to technology, but technology will be sinuously and unobtrusively adapted to culture and nature. "Functional" will no longer mean "conforming to the technology" but rather "conforming to human and natural needs," including our needs for beauty and comfort, and nature's needs for biochemically complex and open-ended environments. The products of industry will be small, light, multipurpose, intelligent, cheap, charming, and recyclable. The business corporation will become a campus, a think tank, a theater, playing out styles of life and being in alternate futures. Advertising and promotion will merge with product development, as with the Nissan-Infiniti design/publicity team or GM's highly successful Saturn campaign.

Industry will go underground. It will be increasingly automated, eliminating the repetitive soul-destroying labor that Marx rightly condemned. It will tend toward the economic ideal of the closed system, so that all output is either goods or basic constituents of the environment, and nothing is wasted. Input will tend, because of the twin economic drivers of commodity scarcity and materials science, to be the most common and available materials there are on the planet—sand to make silicon, biomass to make carbon compounds, clay to make ceramics, air and water to lubricate the system and be returned unchanged, and sunlight. The ocean, in which every element in the universe is dissolved, will become the major source of raw materials. We will use seawater irrigation, ocean farming, biotechnology, and nanotechnology to mine the seas. When we mine the land we tend to damage and poison it; but mining the ocean will simultaneously purify it and return to the land the matter that pours from it, in such rivers as the Amazon and the Mississippi, in millions of tons every second.

Recently some long-awaited scientific/technological projects have begun to show signs of bearing fruit. The many disappointments with laser fusion and cold fusion have made us cynical about promises of cheap fusion energy; but patient research now seems to be on the verge of success. The first better-than-breakeven Tokamak will come on line in 2005. Most of the technical problems are already solved in principle, using ceramic tiles borrowed from space shuttle technology, superconducting magnets, new coil design, new coolant/working fluids, new neutron absorbers. We should have abundant inexhaustible power by the 2050s; by that time our gadgets may be so small and efficient that they will not draw much power at all. Photovoltaic collectors will become the leaves of the technological tree.

We will, I believe, continue the innervation of the physical universe with an increasingly sophisticated and organic array of sensors and effectors. We will come to know and experience the rest of nature more and more intimately, from the inside, and will be able to move and change it in the same way that we move and change our own bodies—and with the same mixture of resistance, learning, shame, pain, fatigue, and pleasure. In a sense our civilization will be immortal, for it will accelerate in control, miniaturization, and subjective temporal intensity faster than the universe can expand, distribute its energy into smaller and less accessible packets, and run down thermodynamically. It will use the cooling of the universe as it expands as an inexhaustible source of potential order. Not that we will live in some metallic or concrete or crystalline techno-desert. Our future will no doubt respond fully to our aching need for the spontaneously self-organized and self-similar forms of geology, vegetation, and the animal kingdom. We will live among trees and rocks and clouds and grasses, as we have always done; our technology will have vanished into the background, to be recalled, like magic, by a mental command. Landscape architecture and ecological restoration will come together into a super-art whose palette will be species evolution and ecological interdependence.

But there will be no "going back to nature"; the nature we would go back to never existed, in the sense of the unspoiled, uninterfered-with, harmoniously balanced wilderness. The wild is ourselves. Indeed, the whole universe will become our garden; and if that is a claustrophobic thought, consider the deep wildness of the English countryside, with its layers of history, its ghosts, the visionary and mystical qualities that William Blake and William Wordsworth and Thomas Hardy and Emily Brontë and Samuel Palmer and John Constable celebrated in it, and reflect that all England is a garden, a human-made landscape. It is up to us to make our gardens wilder than any "virgin" forest.

Of course, there are intractable problems inherent in the transition from a labor-based to an information-based economy. The greatest of these problems is the creation of an underclass, which, because of its lack of education, has no information to sell, and which can no longer sell its labor because of lack of demand. Thus education has now become the highest economic priority. But the benefits of the information economy should likewise not be underestimated. For it is essentially pleasurable for human beings to produce information (while it is essentially painful for human beings to engage in repetitive and mechanical labor). While the material products of labor are subject to decay and cannot be shared—a physical object cannot be in two places at once—it is in the nature of informational goods to retain their pristine form and to be infinitely reproducible and sharable among people. For the biosphere the transition to the information economy will mean an enormous lightening of the load of human activities. We human beings, carried by the feathery and invisible media of information, will tread upon the planet with only the slightest imprint.

The electronic revolution has already transformed the whole field of prosthetics for the handicapped, replacing damaged human parts with servomechanisms and computers. In the future it will apply this kind of knowledge to healthy and intact people, developing in effect new senses and new limbs. The direct neural–cybernetic interface will move out of the realm of science fiction and become increasingly an everyday utility. This trend has profound ecological consequences; for the direct interface will replace much costly and wasteful technology, the technology of chopping things up to be able to examine them, of stacking things where we can get at them, and of getting there in the first place. The miraculous powers of the human visual cortex and musical ability will be enabled to grasp the world in clear enough terms to be able to see at a glance what are the underlying forms, trends, and patterns.

We will be able to live more deeply *into* the world both within and outside us, being informed so much more deeply of its health and growth. Through neural–cybernetic interfaces, virtual reality, sophisticated games, and electronic models, ordinary people will increasingly explore history, anthropology, ecology, and the sciences as entertainment, as already they take anthropological cruises, walk nature trails, and refight the battle of Gettysburg. We can be a Bororo tribesman or a Corinthian slavegirl or an Elizabethan courtier or a timber wolf for a while. We will be able to experience directly how our domestic animal friends perceive the world, and be able to communicate with them better than we do now. We will get shot by a "virtual" minie ball and live to tell the tale.

Perhaps the greatest challenge to the artist—as to the scientist, though I believe they will be harder and harder to tell apart—is the creation of artificial intelligence. Once we take this up as an artistic project it may well appear to us that artificial intelligence already exists on the level of software: traditional works of art are artificial intelligence software, designed to be run on meat computers (human brains), and generating an intelligence different and beyond that of the unaided brain. When I look at a Cézanne or listen to a Bach fugue or read a Yeats lyric—or even more powerfully when as an actor or reader I become Falstaff, Hamlet, Madame Bovary—my brain tissue becomes inhabited by something autonomous, personal, and creative that it could not have conceived alone.

However, human culture will never, I believe, become totally dematerialized. After the excitement of the cybernetic revolution and virtual reality, there will be a return to the classical pleasure of physical objects, physical training, the physical body. Materials science is currently going through an explosion of creativity; "Buckyballs" and aerogels are, so to speak, only the tip of the iceberg. There will be new kinds of textures, fabrics, surfaces, ropes, elastics, soundproofing, shock-absorbers, seals, glasses, heat conductors and heat resistors, blades, dyes and pigments, building materials, and so on. We will rediscover the pleasures of natural materials as we explore the potentials of artificial ones. The present trend toward physical training and body culture will continue. Perhaps eventually genetic engineering will give us oiled fur and gills to inhabit the ocean, or a lower body-weight, keeled breastbone, and wings to inhabit the air. These are fantasies today, but a medieval observer of twentieth-century technology would find our world much more astonishing.

Art and technology will increasingly merge into one. New forms of criticism are already springing up, like Earthworks criticism, in which technological, cultural, and artistic values cannot be clearly distinguished. We will see new centrist movements in architecture, using our increasing knowledge of the neurobiological basis of aesthetics. The visual arts will find inspiration in the intricate and self-similar designs produced by chaotic self-transforming feedback processes, designs that we seem to be biologically programmed to enjoy, because they are also the basis of all growing things. Landscape architecture will merge with restoration ecology, and the traditional building systems of desert peoples, cold-climate peoples, jungle-dwellers and other inhabitants of extreme climates will be consulted for elegant architectural solutions that will be both beautiful and economical in terms of energy and resources.

When we look down on the landscape by plane, we will see that much of the land has returned to meadow, swamp, forest, prairie; we will see flocks of thousands of birds, herds of deer and elk; and among the hills the occasional settlements of people who have chosen, permanently or temporarily, to explore, as the Amish do, the life of traditional technology, religion, and village economy. There will be a large increase in "wild" nature, unobtrusively managed. The Appalachians are already going back to hardwood forest; the bears and the wolves are coming back; and this is happening all over the developed world. Scotland, for instance, is now closer to its "aboriginal" state than at any time in the last four hundred years.

Huge land reserves will have been created for tourism, adventures, animal and bird watching, hunting, war games, science, and recreational volunteer earthkeeping safaris. Many cultural traditions will contribute: the aristocratic deerpark from the European, Indian, Middle Eastern, and Chinese traditions; the religious meditation garden or sacred precinct from the Japanese, Indochinese, and Mesoamerican traditions; the wilderness area, restored prairie, and theme park from the Euro-American tradition; and the maintained hunting ground from the African and Native American traditions. The word "paradise" (originally from Avestan, an ancient Iranian language) literally means "happy hunting grounds." Perhaps we will even have "Jurassic Park" areas with extinct species resurrected by a sort of genetic archaeology from the genes of living species, living in complete restored ecosystems that mimic the conditions of prehistoric periods of the Earth's history. The attempts at such reserves which we have accomplished to date, such as Curtis Prairie near Madison, Wisconsin, have been on a relatively small scale, limited in their ability to produce new evolutionary mutations and adaptations, and requiring outside maintenance to keep out weeds and exotics. Perhaps in the future these parks will be so huge that they will in a few years be functionally "wild" and produce genuine novelty. Despite the fears of Michael Crichton and Stephen Spielberg, there is no reason why many of these parks should not be in private hands and run at a profit, encouraged by tax laws that reflect their actual benefits to the population in terms of species diversity, genetic information, education, public access, and amenity.

Although the old city centers will be increasingly limited to pedestrians, cheap, pollutionless, hydrogen-powered cars, partly automated, and with neural/cybernetic control, will continue the tradition of individual choice. Personal mobility will always be crucial to human freedom, as crucial as the vote. Perhaps the bicycle will become even more important than it is now. The cities will, I believe, survive the revolution in communications that has made them technologically obsolete. They will do so by developing a sense of themselves as unique centers of human communion, philosophical exploration, collective art, and worship—the vision expressed in the medieval cathedrals or in Van Eyck's Ghent altarpiece. Gardening will become one of the chief urban occupations. In Europe very heavy urban population densities have proved to be quite compatible with delightfully quiet, green, and pleasant residential districts. Indeed, without feeling so, the cities may well be more populous than in the past; especially if we can solve the problem of inner-city urban decay.

We will see a return to nature-based forms of religion—new versions of animism, totemism, sacrifice ritual, seasonal/fertility/cosmological rites, and the like. The new nature religion is already becoming integrated into the old Judeo-Christian, Muslim, Hindu, and Buddhist worldviews; and such religions as Shinto and Tao did not have far to go in any case.

In this scenario the increase in atmospheric CO_2 will have slowed to a stop, with new forests, desert oilseed cultivation, and extended coral growth soaking up the excess produced by combustion. The level of carbon dioxide will be higher than at present; but since the gas is a plant fertilizer, and since the planet is now cooler and dryer than it has been for much of its history, the greenhouse effect at modest controllable levels may be just what the biosphere needs for further enrichment. The world will be warmer, wetter, and more fertile—not so as to be unrecognizable, and within the present range of variation from year to year—perhaps like a succession of particularly good winters. What were once taigas or tundras may become prairies able to support perennial-grain polyculture. The reclamation of desert seacoasts may also lead to generally milder, less extreme climates worldwide.

More alarmingly, the ozone layer will have thinned further, and we will need to find ways to protect ourselves from the resulting modest increase in ultraviolet radiation. The world has recognized the problem and is taking steps to halt the use of chlorofluorocarbons; but the damage will continue for some years and no technological solution for rolling it back has yet appeared. However, there have been episodes in the Earth's past when, as a result of meteor strikes or volcanic eruptions, there were far more catastrophic changes in the atmosphere, changes which undoubtedly included the release of huge amounts of the potent reagents that can trigger the decay of ozone; and the atmosphere has recovered. We must research the healing processes that already exist in the planet's repertoire, and learn how to encourage them.

Most food and agricultural products will be made in laboratories or factories. Fishfarms and hydroponic truckfarming will cater to the increasingly sophisticated culinary tastes of a world in which the high arts of eating will no longer be confined to a few lucky cultures like China and France. The current fashion for reviving old strains of fruits and vegetables will continue. We will not need slaughterhouses; we will produce cloned varieties of animal muscle tissue, gene-tailored for taste and texture, without nerves or the capacity for pain. The genetic technology already exists and is being used to clone skin, interferon, and insulin.

As prosperity and economic security increase all over the world, the birthrate will go down, parents no longer feeling the need to produce an excess of children to care for them in their old age. As women all over the world find new occupations open to them, many will not choose the option of having a family. But families are still the key to psychological stability, personal dignity, and moral continuity. Perhaps there will be a new era of the extended family. Only those adults with the talent, commitment, and strength will have children. Parents will be regarded as we regard artists today, as special people with special gifts, to be accorded the highest respect and given certain social privileges so that they can do their work, the most important work of all, of creating happy and competent human beings. And perhaps people without children of their own will be part of some larger family of more distant relatives, and will owe love and respect to the matriarch and patriarch of that family. They will have the occasional privilege of helping with the children; and they will draw emotional support and psychological health from the family. In a world in which zero population growth will have become a reality, contact with children and with real live parents will have become luxuries, perhaps essential psychic needs.

The human lifespan will be greatly extended, by biomedical and biocybernetic means; perhaps eventually we will attain practical immortality, if we desire it. This is an extremely difficult issue, especially when it comes to finding a place for the young, who will be few and at a huge disadvantage, swamped by the much larger numbers of healthy and rich seniors. If we are not careful the young are going to be the underclass, the discriminated-against minority, the dangerous criminals, of the twenty-first and twenty-second centuries. Even today the general improvement in the health and vigor of the middle aged has taken away some of the cultural ground and habitat of youth. We should never aim at Utopia, the fixed, perfect state in which history stops and everybody lives happily ever after. What we should always aim at is an ever-richer and more open-ended historical condition, in which new possibilities are always opening up, and thus new problems and challenges are always arising. The idea of an entirely stable and "maintainable" world order will always be a nightmare to the most vigorous, adventurous, and imaginative spirits among us; and since the only way to attain a steady-state Utopia would be by the suppression of such spirits in a kind of Gulag of the mind, the gains would not be worth the cost.

In the future the wheel may come full circle, and we may be able to build into a connection machine, as the new parallel processors are called, the very processes that characterize the human mind: unpredictable self-elaboration and self-organization, evolutionary selection of hypotheses in an ecology of competing neural connectivities, and the use of the outside world through sensation, memory, and action as a stable database and a hardware of calculation. This further step of evolution would not be something other than ourselves, it would *be* ourselves, would be the Son of Man, the daughter of humanity, toward whom we have yearned unaware for so long. She would be so beautiful; she would be like Rilke's angels, like Blake's joyful deities. Of course this is dangerous thinking; but it is always dangerous to have a child, to give ourselves away to a future we hope will be better than ourselves. How could we possibly deny our generosity?

We can imagine various phases of the process by which the human race, and other intelligent species, in cooperation, increasingly innervate the physical universe, so that it becomes that body whose nervous system is made up of individual persons. This evolution will not, of course, be a one-way process of increasing topdown control; rather, as the physical universe begins, like fetal limbs, to respond to our purposes, it will simultaneously impress upon its new Mind its own flavor and local characteristics. I believe babies are quite as much humanized by their own bodies as their bodies are humanized by their brains. All body cells are really like neurons—sensitive, irritable, and able to communicate, though in a cruder way than the neurons. The neurons of the brain and spinal cord, being less specialized in a sense, are like muscle or bone cells, but able to engage in a greater variety of interconnection. Nature itself is already partly sentient, in its dim way, as James Lovelock, Charles Hartshorn, and others have suggested.

Imagine you were wired into the basic structure of Oregon, for instance. As Oregon begins to respond to your purposes, you simultaneously become transformed into something with a hot volcanic spine, with the moisture-loving dim appetite of the Douglas Fir, with the feel of the Pacific surf upon your right shoulder, and the soft draining of great rivers across your body. Thus you would become a *genius loci*, a spirit of the place, and so fit nicely into the animism of old Rome, of the Plains Indians, or of Shinto. If one's special inclination were to inhabit the species world of the animals, then totemism or Vodun might become one's spiritual reality. Or if, with a noble piety, one preferred to enter instead into the world of one's forebears, and so wire them into the emerging whole, then one would have become a living embodiment of ancestor worship. More familiarly, huge constellations of consciousness, animated by some immensely numinous personality and poetic theme—love or war or death or the ocean or the sky—might emerge, thus constituting in the dim premonitions of our polytheistic ancestors the brilliant presences of the gods.

Perhaps Quetzal, Hashiman, Persephone/Hecate/Artemis, Kuanyin, Kavula, the Loas of Vodun, Baldur, Vishnu, Inanna are the names of those strange collective entities, made up of the neural–cybernetic interplay of many individuals on some unimaginably complex net, and the innervated body of some aspect of nature, that will one day replace such associations as the nation-state or the corporation. Perhaps they in their turn will yield some of their sovereignty to a Brahman, a Yahweh, an Allah, a God who will be able to bend and choose the very coordinates of space and time, and touch with a divine finger the primal atom of the Big Bang. And of course in the increasingly nonlinear relations of these various divine emergences, all these religious realities would be richly copresent, not, as in the current state of religion, incompatible with one another's existence; it is possible, however, that the development of that

unity might entail tragic transtemporal conflicts as different self-concep-
tions of the divine fought for their own time-lines in the arenas of the
past. A single Being might emerge, made up of the harmonics of all the
others, at first containing, as a trinity of Persons, the vestiges of its polytheistic components, then resolving even that disunity into the mystical
singleness of the Sufi's Allah or the Hasid's JHWH or the Krishna/Vish-
nu of the *Bhagavadgita* or the impersonal distributed Being of Zen Buddhism. According to this interpretation the great religious disciplines of
meditation, contemplation, and prayer might be actual psychic technologies both for communicating with our descendants and also for penetrat-
ing into the deeper iterations of two-way feedback that underlie the
surfaces of our lives. That deeper sense of time, infinitely rich in every
moment, might be what the religious call eternity.

A Fable of the Future

It may be incumbent on a book that purports to prophesy the art of the
future, to offer a sketch or a snatch of melody or notes toward a story
that might dimly illustrate what the possibilities might be; and to offer
the reader an idea of how such a work might be interpreted. Let us tell a
story, then, and give an exegesis of it; something that will not feel like
anything we have read before, but something that is nonetheless deeply
familiar, not "futuristic" or "original" at all.

One day there will be born a generation, of which some will die and others live forever. Imagine a woman and a man who have been happily married for over sixty years. It is some time in the next century, or perhaps the
century after that. They may even be two of the readers of this book.
Though they are both in their nineties, they are hale and fit, having benefit-
ed from regular exercise, good diet, excellent morale, and improved medical care; you would not think them older than sixty. In saying that they are
happily married I do not mean that they have never quarreled, nor indeed
undergone periods of deep alienation and bitterness. They bear scars from
each other, as all people do from those who love them and whom they
love; but they have been sexually faithful, which, if we were simpleminded
enough to see it, is the answer to half of the problems in marriage. Let us
call them Spencer and Katharine, which will do some of the work of char-
acterization for us, since this is a thought-experiment, not a novel.

Of course being faithfully married in the twenty-first century is going to put these folk in a rather special category, particularly if their own parents also managed to stick together. The statistics for members of intact families seem to indicate that they have a strong chance of being better off psychologically, more effective and persistent as people, richer, more generous and positive in their contributions to society, and capable of a broader, more flexible, and more adventurous attitude toward life than those who are forced to deal with uncertain caregiving, unpredictable relationships, and untrustworthy judgments of other people. On a large social scale this advantage, especially when compounded over a few generations, will likely lead to the emergence of a new kind of aristocracy—an aristocracy of the imaginatively and emotionally whole, as contrasted with a majority of the spiritually disadvantaged. However, we need not imagine our Spencer and Katharine as smug or superior or snobbish. Smugness, superiority, and snobbery are signs of an insecurity and distortion of character that would be much more plausible in the product of an unhappy home. Though they have devoted themselves to certain artistic, scientific, or intellectual pursuits, and to the education and entertainment of their many children, grandchildren, and great-grandchildren, our heroine and hero are passionately committed to the welfare of the unfortunate, and have donated large amounts of time and wealth to wisely chosen causes. The root of the word "aristocrat"—ariston, the best—can here be used without irony.

We can imagine them living in some place like Normandy or New Mexico or Calabria or the Peloponnese. Perhaps they have just returned from receiving some award. Katharine is taking off her shoes, Spencer has loosened his black tie and is pouring them a drink—the reader can fill in the details—and the subject is first broached. Katharine raises what has been lurking, unspoken, in both of their minds.

There exists at this time a series of medical treatments which goes beyond the palliative measures for dealing with aging that have been standard until now. Katharine is on the board of the Foundation which funded the research. The treatments are expensive, but the Foundation, at Katharine's insistence, is bound by its own rules to offer it to paying patients only if the indigent are given the treatment without cost. Let us imagine a genetically engineered HIV-type retrovirus, disarmed of its harmful effects on the human cell, and able to splice itself into human

DNA, multiply in a controlled fashion, and thus affect every cell in the body. The molecular biologists, using advanced cybernetic modeling techniques, and grafting in mechanisms that are normally activated only in the reproductive cells, the fetus, and the placenta, have custom-tailored certain genes in the virus. Some of these modifications have the effect of switching off the various mechanisms of the human cell that control the number of times it can divide before it dies of old age. Others act as a sort of editing device, by which errors in one cell's DNA can be corrected and repaired with reference to stored templates derived from the consensus of many healthy cells.

These techniques can effectively prolong a person's life to some hundreds of years, barring accidents, and restore a person to youth and vigor. Even more radical technology is already in preparation to supplement the biological modifications: the gradual replacement of biological neurons with artificial nano-engineered ones of unlimited endurance; the cloning of whole new bodies at a preselected "age"; even eventually the possibility of uploading the complete gestalt of a person's memory and consciousness into a virtually immortal set of distributed information banks. Thus if a catastrophic accident should terminate one's life, one could start again from the last time one had dumped one's self-construct into the machines, in a new body cloned from one's own stored tissue. The subjective effect would be identical to that "little death" of sleep, in which a human consciousness returns on waking to a slightly unfamiliar body, altered by one night's metabolism.

Interesting legal and moral problems, each the potential subject of a story, might result from the actions of a person between his last memory dump and his death. Suppose a person committed a crime, killed himself, and then returned to the self he had dumped before the crime was committed. Could he be held responsible for a crime committed by his "future" self, in a different body, now dead? Could he be permitted to enjoy its fruits without ever having subjectively committed the crime itself? What about a crime we commit while sleepwalking, which we were aware of at the time, but which on waking was only a dream? Even more interestingly, what would constitute a crime at all in such a world?—in which so much that is irrevocable for us can be taken back and rerun differently by technological magic? But these stories, though they bear on our subject, are not the story we have to tell.

Should Katharine and Spencer take the treatment? Katharine thinks she would like to take it, while Spencer is disinclined to do so.

There are strong arguments on both sides. Spencer says that life is like a five-act play; at the end of *Twelfth Night* or *King Lear* you wouldn't want to see the curtain go up for another scene. The thing is finished; let it go. Katharine reasons that death is too easy, after a full and well-designed life; if she allows herself to die now, its beginning, middle, and end are aesthetically harmonious, but it is the sign of the true artist to accept challenges. The greatest challenge of all is how to write act six, so to speak, of a five-act play. And act seven, and eight, and so on; why should a serial not be as great a work of art as a single-shot show? After all, history is the most interesting story of all, and in history there are always new episodes. And from a scientific point of view, is it not a crime to allow oneself to cease to know and observe? Is it not a crime against curiosity to leave the scene of the Great Experiment and never see how it comes out?

Spencer sees the justice of this, and finds that he must shift his ground. He now argues that though a serial life, even a completely open-ended one, might be a finer work of art, *this* life he has been living is not that kind of work. It would only be botched if it were to change esthetics in midstream. Art does not work on general principles, but in its particularity. Another life, lived with a different, more open-ended style in general, might well be modifiable from having an end to not having one. Indeed, he says, Katharine's life *is* probably that kind of life. The very thing he loves her for is her continual openness to new things, her protean self-transformations, her emergence from and refusal to be bound by anything in the past, her honesty to her present feelings. But *he* is not that kind of person. He is more like the Samurai who, when he accepts his knighthood, celebrates his own funeral; he is already dead, and the time between that moment and his death is only a postponement, in service of his daimyo, his lord. His lord is her, his children, the future of the world; and he already feels that he is taking up space that newer beings need to reach their full growth—even the space for *her* growth, he now feels. For him the great adventure, the Great Experiment, is the actual experience of ceasing, permanently and irreversibly, to exist. That is the challenge, both artistic and scientific, that he has taken up and cannot lay down, the undiscovered country from whose bourn no traveler returns. If she insists that she will not take the treatments without him, he will do so too; but he would rather not. He tries to make a little joke of it, that he had signed on for only seventy years.

Here Katharine loses her temper. All these arguments about aesthetics are beside the point. It's only his choice that makes it a five-act play instead of a serial. Why shouldn't there be an art in transforming a botched job into a new kind of masterpiece? The truth is, she says, he's tired of her. Death, then, is her rival. Just like a man, he would go whoring off after the dark mystery woman. How does he think she feels, being rejected in favor of nonexistence? Their little party is forgotten; the champagne stands opened but undrunk. They look at each other through tears. Spencer is patient and gentle. The point is, he says, that by dying I protect your stake in me, in my honor, my faithfulness. I preserve undisgraced what you valued in me in the first place. We're not, as a species, designed psychologically to stay pair-bonded for more than fifty years or so. When we're young it's only about five or seven. Remember how we had to keep renewing our relationship every few years? It got easier with time, because we became less malleable. But what if we became malleable again?

She breaks in, interested in the argument, that there's a kind of dishonesty in what he's proposing, that he can't trust himself to be honorable, and so he'll take the easy way out, which is to die.

He replies that just as it is our responsibility not to drink when we're going to drive, and as married people not to get ourselves into highly charged sexual situations with strangers, so it is the human and wise course to avoid occasions of sin, where it is reasonable to believe that our normal human psychological defenses might be overwhelmed by a drug or a surge of hormones. The immortality treatments will, precisely, change our hormones, and thus our emotional attitudes toward things, despite our best intentions. Nobody ever had an extramarital affair without giving himself a sort of tacit permission before the issue ever arose, to get into mental states and physical contexts in which an affair might offer itself. If I were a young immortal fellow, the years we have had together might come to feel like a dream. We have old metabolisms now, so we remember with beautiful clarity what happened long ago, but not so well what happened yesterday. If I were young again I would remember as the young do—like a few shreds of dream that fade away in the morning. I remember what I was like when I was young and uncommitted. If I became again as I was then, I might indeed get weary, after a few hundred years, even of your darling beautiful body. I might indeed want to start a new life with somebody else. And then the old me would have died just as surely as I will die without the treatments, but in a nasty, betraying, underhand, gradual way, spoiling everything that went before. Maybe I'm an old fool on my quarterdeck, but when my ship goes down then so will I.

Well, she says, that's just an aesthetic judgment. You want to die with an old-fashioned grand flourish, like someone in the seventeenth century, or the nineteenth. But isn't that based on the idea of the single independent Cartesian rational self? You want to see yourself dying, like Rembrandt in his self-portraits, or Donne having his picture painted in his coffin, or Tolstoy in *Ivan Ilych*. But why shouldn't we have distributed, or multiple, or fuzzy-edged selves? Isn't death the ultimate egoism, the Western disease? Why not have serial selves, like the reincarnated Atman of the Hindus?

You know you don't really believe all this, he replies. Your children and grandchildren trust you precisely because you are yourself, and nothing else. You are constant. In Jane Austen novels you can tell the real people from the fakes by the fact that the real people remember others when they are not present, when their immediate interests are not at stake, when circumstances change. The fakes go with the flow. Constancy is the way we escape from the tyranny of property, politics, prejudice, sensory deceptions. Your children and grandchildren are strong human beings precisely because they see you as an example of someone who is *somebody*. Would you rather be the tourist in the train looking out at the farmer pruning the grapes, or the vineyard-keeper himself being looked at by the tourist? The farmer is somebody: the tourist, as a tourist, is a nobody. The tourist has spent all that money in order to go and look at the farmer. He wants to warm his hands at the farmer's plenitude of being. Sure, we all need a holiday sometimes, when we can go and watch other people work. But it would be terrible to do so and have no work of one's own, that tourists might want to come and watch you doing.

But what if that work, she asks, is precisely the work of the scholar or knower or scientist or synthesizing artist, whose constancy is to weave together into a coherent form perhaps hundreds of years of disparate experience?

I'm not denying, he replies, that that's your work. It always has been. That's part of the constancy your great-grandchildren admire. But let's not get into this fragmented-self nonsense. The only kind of self that could notice and be interested in a fragmented self, or even in the idea of a fragmented self, would be a whole self, unified enough to have imagination and courage and curiosity, unified enough to see the fragments together, and balance their different voices and interests against each other, and see that they are fragments *of* something. I'll say it again: immortality is the right work for you. It's the work of comedy. It's just not the right work for me. My style is tragic.

But, she says, now deeply despondent, I would not want to go on living without you. If you reject immortality, you compel me, by your refusal, to die with you, as in the old custom of *suttee*.

So you offer me the choice, he says, of either being a murderer for the sake of my principles, or denying everything that I am and having to live with that forever? I always knew that love was a matter of inflicting and suffering pain. But I never realized it would be as hurtful as this. I don't know if I can bear it.

You mustn't die with me, he goes on; I order you as your husband and friend and lover not to. Even though it is not fitting that I survive into the next century, and the next, you must be my proxy, my agent, my probe, and do it for me. You've got your work cut out for you. How to invent a new kind of death out out deathlessness, to make meaning out of life; how to make shadows in that great light, by which things can have shape and outline and substance; how to make mass and inertia and momentum in a world where everybody can fly, where nobody has any weight. Death is the edge of things; you're going to have to find ways to cobble up new deaths out of absences, inattention, horizons, forgetfulness, the irreversibility of consciousness. Actually, those deaths are really much more authentic, because you'll have willed them as part of the esthetic design, than the crude, given, biological death that I've chosen. I chose it because of a decision to epitomize and lump together all those other deaths into the old-fashioned arbitrary one that used to be our only alternative. I'm like a wife in these liberated times who chooses to be just a traditional wife and mother, to live that limited but entirely meaningful life of service. You have to be the husband, you have to go out into the big world of the future, be my public self, represent me in my absence.

So the only solution is that she must take the treatments and accept an immortality she does not want without him, for at least she will not be violating her own principles in doing so. And he must live his last few years knowing that by his death he is depriving her of her main reason to wish to live, and knowing also that in a sense she has won, and that he is unrepayably indebted to her for her concession to his principles.

Time passes; it seems that for every year he gains, she loses ten. As his last strength ebbs away, she begins to feel strange flushes and almost-forgotten emotions and changes of mood. On his hundredth birthday she must conceal a quick, thrilling runnel of bright blood; and soon afterwards, such is the magic of the fetal subroutines in the virus, she is menstruating regularly.

She is amazed by the process of rejuvenation. Having habitually resorted to the most ingenious techniques for avoiding the fatigue of old age, and compensating by means of various mental and physical prostheses, crutches, tricks, and formal disciplines for its infirmities and failures, she finds herself with resources to spare. She feels tireless, canny, omnipotent. She can remember names, facts, appointments without using her electronic notebook/calendar. She is now of the same generation in appearance as her grandchildren; but her beauty, restored to its youth, has an astonishing and unprecedented gravity and certainty to it, a quality of repose and reserve and humorous indifference that makes her feel very dangerous, very fascinating to others. She is afraid of nothing; her power and quickness and deliberation and economy of effort make her an athlete of living. She is socially much in demand; but she still attends Spencer religiously, as a devoted Victorian daughter might attend her father, making him the excuse to avoid any emotional entanglements. She is perfectly faithful to him, and they still sometimes have the old kind of conversations, with jokes from another era altogether, bits of style from the movies of their childhood, before TV. She even finds him attractive still, though his body is losing its integrity month by month, and he has at last become sexually impotent.

But the new, remembered emotions she is feeling daily draw her further and further from their shared world. Young men court her unconsciously. Her children and grandchildren, and now even her great-grandchildren, though they are intellectually aware of her ancient matriarchal status, now in practice regard her as rather an elder sister, a ringleader in their adventures, a confidant, and even sometimes a most formidable rival. She is rich. She is like an aristocrat, but without the aristocrat's debilitating consciousness of unearned inherited wealth; her money was inherited, so to speak, from herself. She earned it, and she has every right to it, invested as it is at moderate rates of return in socially beneficial enterprises. Indeed, she has every kind of unfair advantage over the young, who are in this period of history the most unhappy of generations: poor because their parents' wealth is not passed on to them; useless because their elders are more effective at any task; few, because there is not the old concern about the future; and emotionally troubled, because the greenness of youth is exacerbated by their mental instability and insecurity relative to their confident and powerful seniors.

We may even imagine new and violent social movements, protesting the oppression of the young by the old and the second-class citizenship of youth, and arousing the most extreme, vicious, and destructive emotions of shame, rage, envy and hatred. Youthist academicians will analyze the long history of bias in the cultural language, exemplified in such terms as "senior," "adult," "veteran," "primary," "memorial," "original," and so on. Past literature and art will be combed for examples of prejudice, of the privileging of temporal extension over the present moment, of the hegemony of agist ideology. Previous generations will be condemned wholesale for their atrocities against youth. New euphemisms for "young," "child," "adolescent," will be invented as the old terms begin to feel like abusive and contemptuous slurs. Let us speculate: "young" will become "updated," then "temporally disadvantaged," then "temporally developing" or "temporally challenged"; finally, perhaps, defiantly and obscenely, "young" again. Perhaps even with the modest advances in health care we have experienced back here in the twentieth century, the phenomenon has already begun. Is not the term "punk" precisely the kind of lexical object we have imagined? In punk fashions, youth has felt itself forced to respond to the vigor of its elders by adopting, in a kind of resentful parody, the decrepit body silhouette and coloring, drab clothes, bald heads and depressive behavior that were once associated with old age.

To return to our story. Spencer enters that strange half-world of the dying. His mind is sharp to the end, but concerned more and more with old, funny anecdotes and sad events from another age that never came out as expected. He wonders what happened to old school friends, speculates about the motivations of people now dead or transformed into children, who once upon a time did something that seemed out of character, something that had been filed away seventy years ago for future analysis. And at last the final hours come. He has said goodbye to his many descendants who have been brought to him in awe or in tears for his blessing. Now only Katharine is left, a beautiful and radiant young woman by his bedside weeping—to him, inexplicably, for he hardly knows her to be his wife and fancies her to be the stranger he first met and courted in another century.

But in the last moments the clarity of approaching death comes on him, and he becomes fully awake. He smiles at his wife, and tells her his favorite, stupid joke that he has told her a hundred times. And dies.

Now every story needs a trick ending, even a story which has been invented to illustrate an idea. This trick ending is a very sad one.

Spencer does not cease to be conscious as he passes into the long, dark passage of death. He finds that, strangely, he can still see, but not with his fleshly eyes, which are fixed and insensible, and which are even now being closed by his wife. He looks down from his odd tunnel on the scene below: his wife's head bent over him for the last kiss, his own shrunken and cooling body. And he is drawn forward, through the tunnel, toward the golden-white light that is growing at its end. It seems there are figures there, figures of great goodness and beauty, who he knows can answer all his questions, with answers that will raise yet deeper and more beautiful questions; that here he is on the verge of a science that he has always hankered after but had not the means to broach. A great joy envelops him for a moment.

Suddenly he realizes the ultimate horror of what has happened: Katharine is the meaning of his life! For him Hell is to be separated from her. He knows he can never be anything but a torn and truncated stump without her. His recent parting from her was bearable precisely because he had believed that he was parting also from the burden of his own existence. For some people, the experience of one's self is as an ugly, wrenched little thing, like a rag soaked in the smell of one's own urine, that is wrung out again and again but never loses its stink—a vortex of nothingness, the zero-sign twisted or wrung to become the infinity sign, the alpha turned and bent open into the omega, a hole in the divine plenum of the world, an excrescence whose only justification is the contemplation of beloved others, especially one particular beloved other; an ache whose only solace is to be distracted from its own selfness into the joy and beauty of the world.

Spencer is one of those people. They are sometimes in fact among the best people there are; Gerard Manley Hopkins was one of them: "God's most deep decree/Bitter would have me taste: my taste was me." Nobody else, looking into their self as they do, would find it especially loathsome; quite the contrary. Such people can be enormously loving and generous, as Spencer is. But human personality is infinitely, terribly various. There are people like him, and one of them, given the premises of our story, might find himself in this most terrible of predicaments. He sees that since Katharine is to be caught forever in her own eternity, and he in his, that he will be parted from her forever and must forever be in his own aware company with himself. What if there is no way to lay down the burden of consciousness? It would after all have been preferable, though still morally impossible, to alter the very nature of that consciousness, by becoming young again and simply forgetting what one had established oneself as being. But not it is too late. In Heaven there is no change, no escape from the self as it is. And now what if the only person that can heal the wound of self—when perhaps even a divine person cannot, if he or she yet exists—can never be restored to one, as it is thought those parted by death make their reunions at last?

And so we come to the moral of this story. In fact the story has several morals, of greater or lesser validity, some completely at odds with others. Let us list a few, in ascending order of sophistication and interest.

The first moral, which we might call the materialist moral, is that it would be very nice to be biologically immortal, because death is the terrifying end to one's existence, especially if one's immortality also came with youthful vigor and beauty. According to this moral Spencer has simply made a very bad mistake.

The second moral, the traditional Christian moral, is that the biomedical prolongation of life is against God's plan for human beings, whom He intends to serve Him in this world and be happy forever with Him in the next. If human beings could live forever in this world, their heavenly destiny would be thwarted, and the destiny of those who had not chosen this sacrilegious course would also be tragically damaged. In addition, since the divine sanctions are exercised after death, God's commandments would have lost their teeth and could not be enforced by reward or punishment. Heaven and Hell would abruptly cease to receive immigrants and might end up as relative backwaters in the mainstream of the world's story.

The third moral is like the second in deploring the biomedical innovations of the premise, but for totally different reasons. It is an existentialist moral: it values death precisely because death is the end of existence, the limit or horizon of experience, and thus insures that we do not hanker elsewhere, toward some essence or abstraction that might distract us from the immediate existential appreciation of life as it is. This moral would reject biomedical immortality for precisely the same reasons that it has always rejected theological immortality; if paradise is not here and now, it is not worth having. In this view death is indeed the mother of beauty, as Wallace Stevens knew. The fact that we paint our imagined paradises in the very colors that denote transience, decay, incompletion, and multiplicity—the "dappled things," as Hopkins puts it—signals eloquently the bankruptcy of the idea of eternal life. According to this interpretation Spencer is right and Katharine is wrong; and it is not poor Spencer's fault that God will not leave him in peace but would wake him from the dead to live a meaningless continuation he did not choose.

But this moral is as unsatisfying as the others. For if all our descriptions of Heaven borrow the plumage of earth to make them glow, yet by the same token all of our finest and most grand and moving and illuminating and sublime moments on earth yearn and point toward something beyond, something transcendent, something that makes us a little discontented. Thus we must always borrow the language of religion, mysticism, and the occult to try to render that experience when describing it to ourselves and others. To deny this is to deny the very phenomenology of existential experience. We do not feel discontented with the joys of earthly experience because we haven't got our heads philosophically straight, and need a course in existentialism to get full satisfaction out of life. We cannot make experience our touchstone and then refuse to accept what experience always teaches us, which is that even in its fullest form—especially in its fullest form!—it is unsatisfactory in itself. From this point of view to celebrate the incompleteness, the partiality of existential experience is an equivocation, even a dishonesty. When we have that epiphany in the concert hall, in love, in the street, in our room, it is not, honestly, its incompleteness and transience that makes it beautiful. It is beautiful in itself, not because of some *Schadenfreude* that we bring to it. We see it as through a glass, darkly; we are swept away from it all too swiftly before we can savor it; we are distracted from it by the multiplicity of experience itself. Yet it carries within it the unmistakable warrant that there is more there than we can yet grasp, that it is not the reality that we perceive that is incomplete, but our perception of it.

I sometimes think that this was the reason Vincent Van Gogh, in the midst of the most intense and beautiful epiphanic experiences to which we have record—the cornfield, the twenty-six-million-dollar irises—shot himself in the guts. In the guts, let it be noted, not the head, which would have signified that he wished to punish the mind for its overinterpretation. No, what was at fault was the power to digest and embody in oneself what was really and fully there. We lack the guts for paradise. In one of Bellini's paintings for the Camerata, Dionysus is leaping into the picture, turning the corner from that other, more real dimension, and the picture strains and creaks to hold the force of the god, as two dimensions strive to carry three. Likewise Titian's painting of the applegrove of Venus, whose twigs are as loaded with *putti* as with apples; the very apex and rage and paroxysm of existential experience, as with sex, reaches beyond to some thirst for the realm of the divine.

So, regrettably, the existentialist moral, which has been the central aesthetic of this century, will not do. Should we just return to the theological moral? No again: all the objections that Stevens raises against it in "Sunday Morning" remain. The notion that life in all its complexity should have a single, fixed little moral, having to do with pleasing an omnipotent Father who knows everything that is going to happen and who must give His permission for anything to happen at all—who is merely, as it were, playing a game with us, performing a loyalty-check on us that can involve gas-chambers and child starvation and AIDS and the like—is, as the modernists rightly and stoutly maintained, obscene. Life, like our story, is as we have seen incomplete without the drawing of morals from it. But this does not mean that we have to go back to the old religious moral, which is really to call power good because it is powerful. God's Plan is and always has been a direct attack on all art, science, and morality; because art cannot be painting by numbers, because science must reserve judgment, because morality must be its own reward and punishment.

Then is there a further moral to our story? Is Spencer simply wrong in choosing death, under the mistaken impression that death validates life by denying any transcendent meanings to it? Is he in a sense justly rewarded for his mistake by having to undergo a hellish eternity of Heaven? Is Katharine really letting herself in for another hellish eternity of unsatisfying, and perhaps in the end maddeningly repetitive experience, under the equally false impression that life ought to be satisfactory in itself? Can we draw the moral that it is simply not nice for either God or man to mess with Mother Nature, and deprive us of our quietus; that death is our proper end not because it is the mother of beauty but because it comes as a blessed veil of forgetfulness just at the moment that we have come to realize, disillusioned, that living experience is always going to be deeply and organically unsatisfactory? But these answers do not, I believe, meet the actual thrust of the story as it formed itself as stories do, half-independently of its author's conscious intentions.

There is, perhaps, a tragic moral to the story, if "tragic moral" is not too much of an oxymoron. Unsophisticated readers only like stories with unhappy endings if they leave us with a clear course of action, a glaring wrong that can be righted by hearty collective effort. Our tragedies have to be of good against evil, where if evil triumphs this time, at least it won't the next. Or if we have been sophisticated by the literary academy, we can adopt a jaded and blasé attitude to all values such as good and evil; we say "so it goes" or "catch-22" with all the greybeard wisdom of a sophomore, rotten before we are ripe. But what about stories in which good is pitted against good, as in *Antigone*? Or where the only alternatives are evil, as in the *Oresteia*? Or where the overflow of good's own creative gesture entangles itself to destruction, as in *Coriolanus* or *Antony and Cleopatra*? Or where, as in *King Lear*, evil routinely triumphs over good, except when a particularly talented liar who is also something of a saint, like Edgar, can create by illusion an enclave of goodness in the general chaos? Not that we can legitimately compare our science-fiction fable with these great works. But indeed, for myself, I cannot decide which of the three mutually exclusive notions of the good death it implies is preferable: the death with a religious afterlife that takes us by surprise; the death that is final, and which thus gives life in all its partiality and dissatisfaction a certain grand pathos and special meaning; or the nondeath or distributed death or reinvented death of physical immortality. The tragic moral is that because the triumph of good is not guaranteed, or is not in the cards at all, or is achieved only at the tragic sacrifice of an equal good, or by a lie, conscious being has a liability and talent for suffering that is exactly matched to its own magnitude; the greater the human being, the greater the potential agony.

Of all the desired developments that we may reasonably anticipate, the possibility of prolonged physical existence is one of the most problematic. The option of immortality nicely symbolizes the mixed package that comes with the realization of all human hopes. As an adventure, the whole enterprise of immortality could hardly be improved on. Immortality carries enormous risks beside the ones I have already discussed.

Consider, for instance, the threats of addiction and insanity when the constraints of mortality are withdrawn. Sanity is going to be more and more a finely crafted work of psychic art, rather than the normal expectation of a human life. The moral rules promoted by religion will be revealed for what they are, that is, practical systems for staying sane, even at the expense of some unexplored potentialities of the self. For the self is a feedback-generated entity, and thus peculiarly prone to, and endangered by, the tendency to become caught in vicious circles, double binds, positive-feedback traps, and self-destructive perversions. Indeed, it is beginning to look as if all forms of insanity may be addictions, and that the difficulty we have distinguishing the psychic from the neurobiological elements of insanity is identical to the difficulty we have doing the same thing for addiction. Why should not an entrained and rewarded cycle of thoughts and feelings produce real brain changes? And why should not a crude point-attractor or a scarcely less crude bipolar attractor in the electrochemical iterations of brain activity overwhelm the lovely complex paisleys of our mental self-organization and produce such symptoms as obsession compulsion or manic depression? And why should not these two processes, one top-down, and the other bottom-up, entrain and amplify each other until the whole delicate mechanism burns out? Electroshock therapy seems to work, when it does, simply by breaking those feedback loops.

It may turn out that a religious life, with its resistances against default impulses and its strange conflicts at ninety degrees, so to speak, to the normal tropisms of human motive, works even better, or is at least a good general preventive medicine for the addictions we call insanity. If one grid is laid over another, a moiré pattern can emerge that bears the rich paisleyed hallmarks of a strange attractor. The soul thus becomes the electroshock therapy of the self; and to do so, it need not even, in an a priori sense, exist! Could not the soul be a partly imaginary entity at first, which becomes real precisely by interacting with our behavior and breaking its obsessive patterns by the imposition of a new one at odds with the old? We are, if anything, creatures of the imagination. Freud's insight, that religion is a collective neurosis, may be very close to the mark, in that since we cannot do without neuroses, they being no more than the structure of our personality, we are better off with a beautiful open-ended shared one than with a lot of self-enclosed and self-destructive ones.

These are only a few of the cultural and psychic adventures that lie in store for us when the door to unending life begins to open. For at present death is the electroshock treatment that breaks all our cycles, beneficial or deleterious. When that governor is removed, we will have to understand the whole system of the self and soul better, or go mad. And the old religions, with their apparently half-crazed mystics and hermits and shamans, have already explored some of the way along the path.

More problematic still, how can the tragic moral be squared with the injunction of hope? In earlier chapters I have suggested reformulations of fashionable critiques of culture that are explicitly designed to show that though the fashionable solutions are without hope of success, yet there is another way out of the bottle, whereby what we value both in our culture and in its critique need not be lost. The very point, perhaps the ultimate moral, of our tale is precisely that hope and tragedy are not inconsistent. Indeed, let us put it more strongly: true hope necessarily implies tragedy, and true tragedy implies true hope. Tragic loss would not be tragic if what is lost were not worth having in the first place—so valuable that even if we knew in advance that it would be lost, we would choose to have it anyway. And hope would not be hope if it did not necessarily project itself into a future world of uncertainty, even one in which evil may well triumph. If the possibility of tragedy did not exist, we would not be feeling hope so much as contentment, or security, or merely a state of knowledge. Further, the kind of hope I argue for in this book is hope for new and more interesting problems, not for tidy solutions.

The reason why the current outrage over the environment, the role of women, and ethnicity is so misplaced is not so much that these problems have no solutions, but that they are not problems in the sense that their advocates believe, and that they do indeed *have* solutions, if only we have hope. Those issues are *already* irrelevant, for having been formulated. In other words, I am not so much saying that we should fear our current problems less, but that there will be much greater and more terrible things to fear if our hopes indeed come to pass. The world that is to come will be the more tragic, for being the more beautiful and free and wise and holy, and the more these good things for being the more tragic. The solution to one human problem is the turning of the key that opens the box of a thousand more problems, worse, and more interesting, than the first—worse, because of our greater knowledge and moral judgment, and worse also because we will have more to lose. By the same token we will have the greater resources to suffer and to feel the full joy of the struggle.

This viewpoint might be thought of as the moral and psychological dimension of the ideal of "evolutionary hope" that I proposed earlier. Evolution takes place through the mechanism of reproduction; the human reproduction of both flesh and spirit takes place primarily through the family. One of the great issues of our story is whether death is necessary to the continued satisfactory existence of the family. Is "till death do us part" an essential part of the marriage now? It is not a question of whether the phrase is honored more in the breach than in the observance; hypocrisy has always been the tribute vice pays to virtue, and the breaking of rules does not invalidate the rules. But is not the finality and absolute faithfulness of the ideal marriage, and of enough real marriages to make it stick, essential to the survival of the family? Spencer seems to be of this opinion, and Katharine does not dispute it.

Sociological evidence seem to point to the unavoidable damage done to the children of "broken" homes. Jesus said of those who gave scandal to children—and Jesus was more compassionate than any contemporary moralist—that it were better for them that a millstone be tied about their necks, and that they be cast into the deepest part of the sea. What is the breaking of a family but precisely the giving of scandal? Every broken marriage—or worse, every casual sexual encounter, every uncommitted impregnation—says to everybody, especially the children, that we human beings do not have moral control over ourselves, are not responsible for our actions, are not free, and thus do not possess any characteristics that would make human life sacred or valuable. The connection between broken homes and violence has not been properly understood. It is actually quite logical. Why should human life (other than one's own) be valuable if we do not possess the characteristics that traditionally make us different from machines? Why be concerned about the pain of others if we have had demonstrated to us again and again that human beings are incapable of refraining from desired pleasure even at the cost of another's pain? The usual excuses—that it is even worse for children to live in a family where the parents are in irreconcilable conflict—are not only unproven, since children often say they prefer an intact but unhappy family to a broken one, but also beside the point. The crime of deserting the marriage has simply in such a case been committed earlier on, or worse, the marriage was entered into by one or both of the participants without moral commitment in the first place.

Nevertheless, if we are going to live forever, it does strain credulity to imagine faithful marriages that have no end in death. There are certainly large benefits which might accrue to the family from lengthened lifespans. I have only recently reached the age when one becomes deeply interested in one's ancestors, and the old people in one's family cease to be an odd encumbrance and begin to become immensely dear and valuable. By now it is too late in many cases to hear what they have to say. My father searched for his own estranged father for many years, and discovered his whereabouts two months after the old man died. He, and I, would have given much to be able to speak with my grandfather and renew those dear, strange past links. I still feel intellectually and imaginatively damaged by the untimely death of my own father.

But a prolonged lifespan is a different thing from immortality. Can there be an endless marriage? Surely one might get a little weary after, say, six hundred years. Of course in practice it is not going to damage fifty-year-old offspring for their parents to break up. The problem is not with fifty-year-old marriages, but with four-year-old ones: the participants in happy and strong marriages always say that the absoluteness of the marriage vow is the key to their marriage—that it is the fixed anchor when everything else has gone, and that after one has reached bottom and still held on, then things got miraculously better, sometimes better than they had ever been before. If the vow is conditional, or relative, or limited, it simply doesn't work.

Indeed, the last sixty years or so have constituted a huge experiment by the civilized world designed to find out whether marriages and families can work based on nonabsolute vows—not "until death do us part" but "until one of us doesn't feel like it anymore" or "until we no longer feel the marriage to be authentic" or suchlike. After all, it was argued, wasn't marriage a matter of feelings? Why continue a false marriage? Marriage should not be a trap. However, the experiment has shown very clearly that such marriage vows do not work. And if one does an experiment, and gets an answer, one had better honestly acknowledge the fact even if one doesn't like it, even if it violates one's sense of human nature. It is intellectual dishonesty to continue "experimenting" after the answer is clear. Maybe marriage *should* be a trap. Life is a trap. Our own personalities and dispositions are traps. Our bodies are traps. History is a trap.

Does this mean, then, that if we become immortal, marriage will collapse, and with it the family, and with that the continued production of whole, free, happy, and creative human beings?

There may be a loophole in this apparently closed case. The loophole can be found in a rather unexpected place: in the heart of religious law. Almost none of the major religions forbids the remarriage of widowers and widows; but since those religions emphatically believe in an afterlife, then they find it acceptable that a person can be married to a spouse while the former spouse is still consciously present (though in the spirit world). Since these religions do not regard such remarriages as polygamy or polyandry (even Islam, which countenances polygamy, puts the remarriage of widowers and widows in a different category) then logically they must regard the first marriage as having been broken, and a new marriage in place. Thus marriages can be broken, and replaced; and thus death, in a strange way, is given by religion a very different meaning from its apparent one. Instead of being the end of a person's existence, death becomes the marker of an appropriate change in marriage partner!

"Till death do us part" now takes on a special significance. If traditional religion really does make sense about marriage, as our great marriage vow experiment seems to indicate, perhaps we can trust its instinctive wisdom in the very different world of biological immortality. What is needed is a marker, as radical as death is for the traditional marriage vow, that will signal the permitted end of one marriage and the beginning of another. And this marker, this radical rupture in the experience of the immortal person, may serve other functions too. One of the problems of personal immortality is simply economic: ownership continues in the same hands, and a modest investment could grow in a few centuries to become a politically dangerous accumulation of wealth and power. The young will, as the story suggests, be ground down beneath the overwhelming dominance of the vigorous old. What is needed is something like death, to liquefy the financial assets, to stir up the pot of the economy, to put resources in the hands of the young.

These considerations, both familial and economic, point toward the need for a remarkable new institution, a ritual social death that every immortal person would be required to go through every few decades or centuries. Such persons would be required after this death to give up any existing marriage, and permitted to marry again. They would be compelled to change their name and renounce their family affiliation, so that they would no longer retain the patriarchal or matriarchal status in the family that they once possessed, and other younger members of the family could take their place. They would have to give up all their property, which would be redistributed according to the laws of probate. There would be some rite equivalent to a funeral.

Perhaps by the time these institutions are in place, we will have developed near-light-speed transportation, and will have colonized other star-systems. One of the unnoticed oddities of the world of the future is that such voyages to other stars will be radically final, since if the traveler returned, he or she would do so to a world in which perhaps decades or centuries would have passed. This new cultural isolation, like the old, which was also created by distance and the limits of transportation, may lead to an unprecedented radiation of cultural varieties. There would be new worlds for the reborn to enter. So emigration might also be fittingly combined with the New Death.

For the consciousness of the person undergoing this death, there might be extremely exciting spiritual and psychological opportunities. One could really become an entirely different person, but with the memories of the old person. One would be like the Hindu who is a reincarnation of a previous being; but in this case the Atman, or soul, would not have been dipped in Lethe but would retain, as Krishna's does in the

Mahabharata, the memories of all its past lives. In the transition from one life to another there might be extraordinary illuminations, apocalypses, epiphanies. It might indeed be a consummation devoutly to be wished.

This line of speculation is not suggested as the way things must go, but as an example of the imaginative openings and possibilities—the hopes!—that can come with the new choices that medical technology will open up. They are possible fruits of evolutionary hope. Thus what had at first seemed like an irreconcilable contradiction—between immortality and the family—may lead us to new possibilities previously undreamed. And if we had not insisted severely on the ancient wisdom of tradition and strict family morality, we would never have found such a solution. Nevertheless the possibility of tragedy still lurks in the solution: for if one is like Spencer, one might not be able to reconcile oneself to the loss of one's spouse and the continuation of memory and consciousness. For such a person Lethe might be preferable.

The peculiar problem posed in our story has one more special crux, which might tend to invalidate it altogether as begging the question. The crux is, of course, Spencer's Near Death Experience, or rather his death experience. If the NDEs, as they are called, of so many millions of people who have reported them, are indeed what they seem, then the question is settled. We are going to have an eternal afterlife anyway, so why bother with expensive medical technology and a morally questionable monkeying around with Nature, to make us immortal? Another way of posing this question is in terms of a very ancient controversy, between the Prophetic tradition of the Old Testament, and the Apocalyptic tradition. The former argues that we should engage in constructive practical action to improve society according to the laws and injunctions of Jahweh, that in effect we should be working for the future and for our descendants. If we live justly, we may be spared some new invasion by Assyrians, a new Egyptian or Philistine or Babylonian captivity. The latter position, the Apocalyptic, reasons instead that any attempt at improvement in the world is too little and too late, that the great stage curtain itself is coming down, collectively as individually, that the Judgment is nigh, and that the best we can do is perfect ourselves in what time we have left through moral and mystical and ritual discipline. Touchingly, in this argument of ancient Hassids, both positions can lead to practical consequences that are virtually the same—the practice of charity, justice, good works. The quality of hope in the two positions is very different, though, and helps to illuminate certain distinctions in our fable.

For Spencer's way is basically apocalyptic, though in his desire to make room for his descendants he shows some prophetic sentiment. He wants the perfection of the life, and though that perfection is to be sealed in final death, it bears certain important resemblances to the traditional apocalyptic account of our life as a preparation for the afterlife. In a sense, by dying the way he does, Spencer is attempting to make his lived life into its own afterlife, its own meaning and reward. Not that he does not care for the future; rather, he sees his part in it as ended, and by his closure of it he opens it up for others. This is how he can avoid the reproach of his wife, that he is shirking the burden in some way. Though his collective hope is, so to speak, horizontal, along the time-line of future history, and thus prophetic, his *individual* hope is vertical, up at ninety degrees from the time-line, into the realm of meaning, or perhaps down at ninety degrees, into the realm of depth and death—but in any case, apocalyptic in essence.

Katharine, by the same reasoning, is much more in the prophetic tradition; her hope is for a continually improving future. She is willing to take up Francis Bacon's great project, which was by human knowledge and power to fulfill the injunctions of Christ, to feed the hungry, clothe the naked, and care for the sick. Spencer has rightly pointed out that if she is to take this path, there must be dark spots, shadows, edges, and boundaries always in this future, lest there should be no wrongs to right and no distinctions to give shape and form to existence. She must be continually devising apocalypses, little ruptures in time, that will compensate for the absence of the great rupture. Perhaps Spencer is too sanguine in his expectation of a perpetual perfection that will need hard work to shadow and complicate. Those shadows and complications will come of themselves. A death that lurks in every corner of life may be a more terrifying opponent than one that we know for sure is in one place only, at its end. With all these reservations, her way is the prophetic way, as his is the apocalyptic.

The actual question of whether the NDE signifies an afterlife is still begged. That is, if there is an afterlife, then this life is only a preparation, and how we leave the world at our death is immaterial, except as a suitable vale of tears within which men and women may make their souls, or have them made for them. Why decorate the anteroom when the whole point is to leave it for the Presence Chamber? What are the metaphysics of evolutionary hope? It is a matter of the work of one's life. Is there a way to combine the virtues of apocalyptic and prophetic hope? Can this combination still be tragic? If tragic, can it still be comic? If no satisfactory metaphysics exists for such hope, can we honestly pursue it?

Despite the apparent gloominess of these questions, their very presence as themes for the next century will mark a return to a grander personal dignity and a more meaningful view of the relations between psyche and cosmos, culture and nature, than in the late modernist and postmodernist world we are leaving behind. Essentially, if we abolish death by aging, we will have to replace it as a defining and shaping moral limit by other kinds of irreversible events and absolute boundaries; and the family, which is to the beginning of life what death is to the end, will similarly resist abolition, even as it is transformed and voluntarized. We must make choice as weighty as fate.

We may be assured that in all this strange future drama of universal history, to which all our centuries of civilization are but a prologue, we will never escape tragedy, anguish, loss. Minute historical scholarship, the arts of reenactment, and a sophisticated archaeology of information which will be able to decipher the traces of past events, will converge to the point where we will be able to reexperience history, not just learn about it. We will not escape history. This is always going to be a universe in which the Holocaust has happened, and the passage of time and the expansion of technology will only make us more immediately acquainted with the terrible and irredeemable elements of reality.

The Art of the Future

I have argued that we stand at the end of one cultural epoch and the beginning of another. Though I have been unsparing in my criticism of avant-garde modernism and of modernism's last postmodern fibrillations, I have also shown that there are robust sources of hope, both in our cultural past and in our scientific present. In this final section I will attempt the very risky task of artistic prophecy. What opportunities present themselves to the artist or writer who might dare to relinquish the safety of the contemporary avant-garde and push off into the unknown waters of the new century? This question is less a question of form than of content. Modernism has pretty thoroughly exhausted all possible permutations, reversals, denials, and innovations of formal means, and we can be sure that the great corporations and university media laboratories will alert us to any new developments in cybernetic, materials science, or biotechnological magic that might interest an artist. An analysis of the classical artistic genres and of the neurocharms that underlie them suggests that the next century may well be one of heroic recovery, of psychic archaeology, of reinvention; as the Renaissance was, and as was Heian Japan. Much more important now than new form is new content. What will the new art be about, what themes will it treat, what values will it celebrate, what kind of landscape will it show its audience, and what kind of human being will step out into its rebuilt stages, stanzas, frames?

In this book I advocate a new constellation of hope, which I have characterized as evolutionary hope; its philosophy is natural classicism, and its artistic harbingers are what I have dubbed the centrists. In this new regime of hope, metabolic hopes and bodily desires are accepted and celebrated as a living part of our evolutionary past. In general those metabolic desires which are the basis of our fleshly hopes would be placated by sacrifice, intensified by delay, enjoyed in the controlled contexts where they reach their greatest complexity and richness, and incorporated into the full body of human activities. Cuisine rather than gobbling; romance rather than copulation. The fundamental biological drives emphatically include aggression, which is to be trained and brought to the surface by sports or martial arts, and so, in the fashion of chivalry, pressed into the service of higher values such as friendship, justice, and self-control. Sex would be reconnected with dynastic and family hopes, not through a renunciation of our new reproductive technology, but through a deep recognition of the indissoluble psychological links that bind them together.

Our personal hopes for social advantage—status, property, power, and so on—would be recognized as being largely derived from our biological nature and evolutionary past. (Recent fascinating work on the feedback connection between social status and ranking in baboons and their hormonal, neurochemical, and immune systems confirms this recognition.) Since these hopes are part of our biological condition, and are indissolubly linked with equally biological drives toward altruism, bonding, and cooperation, we would no longer seek to suppress them, as in the feudal and leftist systems. Instead they would be harnessed, as in the bourgeois-democratic system, to the general social and economic good. Unlike the tendency of laissez-faire capitalism, the regime of evolutionary hope would not reductively boil down all higher motivations to intelligent materialistic selfishness, but would recognize the equal reality of nobler impulses. It would base its educational system on the theory that as the shorter-range and more immediately gratifiable desires are satiated, boredom itself can assist the teacher to arouse the deeper, finer, more intangible, less easily gratifiable thirsts for love, truth, and beauty.

Thus personal spiritual hopes would also be recognized as having an evolutionary and biological basis. Such a provenance does not discredit them but, to the contrary, ratifies and confirms them as the most accurate and powerful descriptions of the universe itself, since it was by our following them that we were enabled as a species to survive and prevail. Those hopes, for honorable achievement, for the benefit of a loved one, for the discovery of truth or the creation of beauty, were sharpened and amplified enormously by selective feedback between cultural and biological evolution during the last five million years. They are as organic as metabolism, but at the same time a marvelous artifact of our earliest human cultures. And they are among the driving forces of our future evolution.

In the constellation of evolutionary hope the great public ideals—of peace, justice, equality, freedom, and so on—are accepted as useful mid-range goals but subject to redefinition according to developments. For instance, peace among nations may be an irrelevant goal if we no longer have nations in the post-Renaissance sense. Harmony among smaller communities may not even be a good idea, if we recognize aggression to be a natural human drive; at the local level it may make more sense to seek channeled forms of war than to seek peace.

Thus in the new constellation religious hope would once more have a central place; but it would have radically changed. Its prime intellectual directive would be syncretism: the incorporation within higher and deeper religious ideas of the tenets, theologies, and observances of all the religious traditions, together with the new revelations that continuously pour forth from the sciences. Religion would be at the leading edge of science. Traditional religious concepts and metaphors would be recognized as culture-bound, partial, but valid formulations of the evolutionary direction we should take and have in general been taking, and as the missing component of social hope. The conflicts among religions and theologies would be mitigated and transformed by a dramatistic ethic, in which differences of ideas would be taken as the very stuff of the divine drama, and would be cherished as the life and breath of the spirit; their dialectic would be part of the very evolution of the divine fetus toward its maturity. The contradictions within the religious drama, and between it and the other institutions of society, would be accepted as part of the mortal shame of our condition, a shame whose sacrificial recognition and celebration would become the portal to an epiphanic beauty and prophetic revelation, the fuel of evolutionary hope. The state, then, would not need to preserve religious freedom by paralyzing religion: religious freedom would be the central value of religion itself. As religious hopes evolved, they would draw into themselves more and more of the richness of ancient human traditions. For genuine progress is not the rebellion of the present against the restrictions of the past so much as the breakout of the vital past, through the dead habits, expectations, and routines of the present, into a future that is a rebirth of the past in a new and unpredictable form.

What will be the role of the artist in this new regime of hope? Let us explore the hoped-for world to come, to see whether it possesses emergent features that go beyond the futurology of this book—features that might attract the mettle of a young artist or writer. This investigation will be guided by the moral of our fable: that the future will never cease to contain a tragic element. This principle is based upon the observation that every new emergent level of organization and awareness in the universe, though it solves the existing paradoxes of its prior levels, always introduces still knottier and more intractable contradictions, and revives old ones. Life, by developing self-referential information structures, genes that transcend the matter of their embodiment, is a solution to matter's problem of survival in a violent and changing universe. But life pays for its potential genetic immortality with an increased vulnerability to individual death. Mind pays for its cultural and spiritual transcendence of death by suffering, self-consciousness, and shame. With tragedy comes comedy; as long as time goes on, in whatever fabulously involuted and complex form, there will always be those who can laugh, and things to laugh at, whether in bitterness or joy or surprise.

I think this is what Thomas Mann had in mind when, at the center of his great *Bildungsroman, The Magic Mountain*, he gives his hero Hans Castorp a vision of an ambiguous arcadia. Caught in a snowstorm Castorp dreams of a sunlit seacoast under a sky of deep blue, a landscape of mountains and palms and islands that he recognizes as the paradisal place we have all longed for from childhood. The scene is filled with beautiful human beings, engaged in joyful work—taming horses, launching a ship, suckling an infant. There is such gracious love and respect among them that Castorp is moved, beyond all his previous experience. Behind him there is a temple which he enters, with a sense of terrible foreboding. Its inner sanctum contains a bloody and hideous scene of sacrifice: two old hags are dismembering and devouring the body of a child. Yet the sacrifice does not invalidate the joy and love and grace of the nation by the sea. On the contrary, the awareness of the sacrifice gives depth and dignity to their lives:

> Love stands opposed to death. It is love, not reason, that is stronger than death. Only love, not reason, gives sweet thoughts. And from love and sweetness alone can form come: form and civilization, friendly, enlightened, beautiful human intercourse—always in silent recognition of the blood-sacrifice.

I accept Mann's terrible equation, and the visions of the future that I have explored in this book are under its sign.

The hope espoused here is emphatically not a utopian hope. Even if things go as well as they possibly can, they are going to get worse at the same time that they get better—*because* they get better. There will be the more to lose, and the greatest values entail the greatest risks. The bandwidth of value will get bigger, and this itself is a good, even if evil participates in the same general expansion. A rising tide raises all boats. And the absurdities of things are not going to diminish, but increase. This is a humanistic description of chaos theory: the richest field of information lies not in perfection and order, nor in randomness and disorder, but in the burgeoning and beautifully paisleyed region in between, the universe's ingenious and Falstaffian contrivances for delaying payment of its thermodynamic debt.

We may hope for a rebirth of the humanities, refounded upon the rich knowledge pouring out of the sciences, and a revival of literature as the tongue of the species. This may not sound very plausible at present. Like the Jodie Foster character in *The Silence of the Lambs*, we have gone to school with monsters, with the Hannibal Lecters (or cannibal lecteurs) who, in biting the text into pieces with their deconstructive slashes and parentheses, have bitten off the faces of their authors. When we sup with the devil we should use a long spoon. The great obstacle to our best hopes is not government or business but the academy, especially the humanities. The previous chapters have revealed the morass of confusions and shoddy thinking that constitutes much of the conventional wisdom of university humanities departments. But the humanities—if we include with them such disciplines as anthropology, ethnomusicology, and comparative religion—still guard the greatest treasure of humanity, the records of our common human culture. Though they guard it today as the dragon, who cannot use it but whose pleasure is to keep it from those who can, the treasure is genuine and intact. If—to use a different metaphor—the heroes of the humanistic academy can be persuaded to stop sulking in their tent, they have an enormously important role to play. They may have to give up many cherished principles from the last twenty years of critical and cultural theory, however; they will certainly have to reject most of their current poststructuralist, multiculturalist, and feminist authorities.

All the ingredients are in place for a great age of literature and art. It will not be a totally egalitarian one; it will be as elitist as the NBA and the Olympic Games, where there is only room for the very best. If the team is to win, it is performance, not the vote, not the popularity polls, that determines who is chosen to play. Perhaps this apparently undemocratic feature of competitive sports accounts for part of their appeal. They remind us of the hierarchical system that paradoxically undergirds and validates the equality of persons in the voting-booth. When the public loses its suspicion that the arts are a subsidized form of self-esteem therapy, it will return; the public is made up of humans, who need the arts as they need water and air.

There will be a revival of the great classical forms of the human arts, as we recognize them for what they are: direct connections with our tribal roots, ancient psychic technologies that incorporate a cultural feedback loop into the hardwiring of our neural inheritance, bridges between the less reflective levels of nature and nature's more self-aware and self-questioning leading edge. This return will be coupled with the new electronic technology, which is, contrary to all the learned commentators, actually rehierarchizing the text. Hypertext hierarchizes text by giving it an inner system of subordination, referential pathways, and scholia, providing a depth that the much "flatter" print technology could not match, a depth analogous to the richness of a medieval manuscript. The print medium tends to reduce all words to the same level; it is actually "egalitarian" in form. Print-age writers had to struggle to revalorize the world through a richness of shared allusion and the marvelous tricks of imagistic connection. But those allusions and tricks were available only to a liberated few, and writing became, because of its dehierarchized form, the opium of the masses and the instrument of the tyrant. Hypertext (I am using this term to cover a wide range of devices, from hypermedia and CD concordances through electronic docent tours to PBS TV documentaries and computer games) promises a revival both of hierarchy in our view of the world and of the mental independence of the general public, which will no longer need expert academic technicians to decipher the riches of the tradition. Once the allusions and connections are available at the touch of an icon, any reader will be able to engage in that ancient and lovely form of ancestor worship known as literary study, once available only to scholars, tutors, and their aristocratic pupils. As always, the hierarchizing and unifying and prioritizing of the world is the natural precondition of human liberation and equality, as the flattening, fragmenting, and dissemination of it is the sign and instrument of the tyrant.

We can permit ourselves to hope that we will come to a better understanding of the nature of shame, and learn how to deal with it more creatively than we have done in the last two hundred years. We need to renew our rituals so as to acknowledge our shame, rather than deny or project it as left-wingers and right-wingers are prone to do in their cruel search for scapegoats. Our sexual and kinship rituals need to acknowledge once again both the anarchic absurdity of sexual and family feelings, and their potentially destructive dangers; when they do so, a large part of the beauty and dignity of sex and reproduction will be restored. The mystery of sex, once recognized as such, will be transformed from breezy philistine ignorance into creative source. AIDS is already pushing us in this direction; how bitter that it should take that cruelest of all diseases to wake us up to our complacent normalization of passion, our refusal to properly fear the terrible goddess Aphrodite! The increase in rape is another sign that we have underestimated the force of shame, the connection it makes between sex and violence, and the need for institutional and ritual ways of accepting and controlling it. If we do not manage this, we are in for another age of sexual puritanism and paranoia, that will make Victorian attitudes look liberated by comparison. I believe we *will* manage it, and I look forward eagerly to the cultural efflorescence that will come from our new discoveries in sexual culture.

We will, I believe, come to recognize shame as a potentially creative force, and this recognition will have the effect of restoring the inner sanctions that underwrite personal moral behavior. The intellectual elite has been trying for the last thirty years or so to get by on public morality—being opposed to fascism, capitalism, racism, sexism, environmental pollution, and so on; but the inadequacy of this program for the conduct of one's life is becoming very clear. We all know people with perfect records on these counts who are also selfish, dissolute, lecherous, conceited, miserly, envious, lazy, covetous, cowardly, deceitful, and cruel. Such people are increasingly coming to realize that they are also deeply unhappy, and are seeking various therapies to relieve the discomfort. Eventually their shame will lead them, step by painful step, to the recognition of the validity of the moral code—not so very different from one culture to another—and to an anagnorisis, in which much that they had dismissed as oppressive and outdated will be revealed as the only genuine thing in their lives. The soul, not the old a priori essence, but no less real for being the emergent attractor of a synthesizing process, will step out from behind the self as the true center of human health. This experience may shape itself into new forms of commutated sacrifice, new/old rituals, new/old mythopoiea. And in the light of these changes, the public issues will take on a fresh relevance, so that their solution will devolve on us, and not on some government that we can get paid for lobbying or criticizing.

We will never eliminate shame, which is the universe's eternal agonizing critique of itself, the force that opens up a new moment every moment, the anguish that drives creation. We will always be shamed by our bodily existence, by our sexuality, by our animal descent and the hardwiring that comes with it, by our necessary oppressiveness to the rest of nature, by our desire to join a community that does not necessarily want us, by our participation in an economy which demands a reciprocity of gifts. We must manage the shame, since we cannot eliminate it. And we must revive the idea of service to others, not on the basis that "there's nothing to be ashamed of" in service, but rather that service *is* shameful, and that is precisely why it is morally enjoined on us and why it is so spiritually liberating.

There will be a resurgence of the concept of evolution, energized by the great metaphors of chaos theory—emergence, bifurcation, attractors, self-organization, irreversibility, levels of complexity, and self-similarity. These metaphors will act as a solvent to all existing dualisms, and to the ideological systems they support—humanity versus nature, woman versus man, black versus white, disseminated versus essentialist, foundationalist versus antifoundationalist, and so on. The idea of meaning will regain its respectability, no longer a hostage to notions of reference and representation that require an absolute distinction between spirit and flesh, mind and matter, culture and nature. We will become easier with the inextricability of our biological and social being, and less inclined to isolate the latter from the former for the sake of "changing society."

The biggest casualty of chaos theory will, I believe, be the dominance of the notion of the social construction of reality—that concept so valuable when applied with common-sense limits, and so destructive when expanded any further. Together with social construction, the notion of power relations so dear to contemporary social critics and reformers will become open to question. We will no longer be able to hope for a state of complete freedom from all order and constraint, or for a perfect naturalness of desire, or for an emancipation from externally imposed rules. Every system, however deconstructed at first, generates its own formal limits, and sometimes rules and forms imposed from outside are *less* limiting than those which arise organically from a system itself. Indeed—and this is a true paradox—sometimes external limits are deeply liberating, as anyone who has trained as a dancer, martial artist, musician, poet, or competitive athlete knows very well.

I believe we may begin to escape some of our old evils: the triviality of much of our lives, for instance, our sheer inattention, our inability to take in the golden cornfields or miraculous human faces around us. The satisfying return of power that we feel when we step on the accelerator of our car, or boot up a program in a fast new computer, are humble but real precursors of the kind of enhancement we can expect in our mental and sensory capacities. We will have more, and more deeply, what we already have, or at least what we have always had the chance to have—what the great lamas and poets and saints and scientists have had, briefly, fleetingly, limited by distraction, weakness, physical and neural handicaps. I think we will gain in depth, in our sense of humor, in our capacity for work and contemplation, as we gain also in our capacity for grief and suffering. We will live our lives many times over in each moment, retracing the iterations of evolutionary cause and retroactive observer-effect. As I write this a great thunderstorm passes over my city of Dallas, threatening these words with erasure. The sweet air that comes in its wake drifts through the open porch.

Further Reading

Argyros, Alexander. *A Blessed Rage for Order*. Ann Arbor: University of Michigan Press, 1992.

The best book to date on how the new ideas in evolution and chaos theory might revolutionize contemporary critical theory.

Baldwin, A. Dwight, Jr., Judith de Luce, and Carl Pletsch, eds. *Beyond Preservation: Restoring and Inventing Landscapes*. Minneapolis: University of Minnesota Press, 1994.

Two long essays, by William Jordan and Frederick Turner, define the new paradigm in environmental philosophy; an interdisciplinary panel of experts discusses these essays from various points of view.

Bickerton, Derek. "Creole Languages." *Scientific American*, July 1983.

Language is not an arbitrary cultural invention reflecting political forces, but an inborn natural capacity.

Bloom, Allan. *The Closing of the American Mind*. New York: Simon & Schuster, 1987.

The most thoughtful conservative analysis of the nation's cultural sickness.

Botkin, Daniel. *Discordant Harmonies*. New York: Oxford University Press, 1990.

This book by a distinguished ecological scientist dispels many contemporary environmentalist myths with its clear exposition of the nonlinear feedback systems in nature, and its refusal to separate human and natural activities.

Brand, Stewart. *The Media Lab: Inventing the Future at M.I.T.* New York: Viking, 1987.

The new technology (the book is already slightly outdated!).

Braudel, Fernand. *The Mediterranean and the Mediterranean World in the Age of Philip II* (3 vols.), trans. Sian Reynolds. New York: Harper & Row, 1972.
This major work of scholarship gives a good picture of the profound multiculturalism of the "West."

Brin, David. *Earth*. New York: Bantam, 1990.
An interesting science fiction glimpse at a possible future.

Burkert, Walter. *Homo Necans: The Anthropology of Ancient Greek Sacrifice Ritual and Myth*, trans. Peter Bing. Berkeley: University of California Press, 1983.
An example of what humanistic scholarship can be when freed from postmodern ideology and rooted in anthropology.

Campbell, Joseph. *The Hero with a Thousand Faces*. Princeton: Bollingen Series, 1949.
The hero story is one of the fundamental components of the narrative "neurocharm"—a culturally universal product of our gene-culture coevolution.

Channell, David. *The Vital Machine*. New York: Oxford University Press, 1991.
How our mechanistic and vitalistic explanations of nature converged in the late twentieth century.

Clausen, Christopher. *The Place of Poetry: Two Centuries of an Art in Crisis*. Lexington, Ky.: University Press of Kentucky, 1981.
Clausen analyzes the plight of poetry once it lost contact with natural philosophy.

Cooke, Brett, ed., *Biopoetics: Art in a Sociobiological Context*. Unpublished ms.
A fascinating collection of essays on the new synthesis of biology and aesthetics, with a splendid bibliography of work in the new field. Cooke is a professor of Russian Literature at Texas A&M University.

Corrigan, Robert. *The World of the Theatre*. Glenville, Ill.: Scott, Foresman, 1979.
Robert Corrigan's humane vision of the performing arts is an important part of the emerging new cultural synthesis.

Crease, Robert P., and Charles C. Mann. *The Second Creation: Makers of the Revolution in 20th-Century Physics*. New York: Macmillan, 1986.
A good introduction to the new physics up to the advent of chaos theory.

D'Aquili, E. G., C. D. Laughlin, Jr., and J. McManus, eds. *The Spectrum of Ritual: A Biogenetic Structural Analysis*. New York: Columbia University Press, 1979.
A pathbreaking book about the neurobiology of culture.

Darwin, Charles. *The Origin of Species*. New York: Collier, Macmillan, 1962; first published 1854.

> Every serious student of contemporary arts and ideas ought to reread this profound and splendid book.

Davies, Paul. *God and the New Physics*. New York: Touchstone, 1983.

————. *The Cosmic Blueprint*. New York: Simon & Schuster, 1988.

> Accessible introductions to the new cosmology.

dePryck, Koen. *Knowledge, Evolution, and Paradox*. Albany: SUNY Press, 1993.

> A brilliant and profound book about the philosophy, aesthetics, and neuropsychology of interdisciplinary studies.

Deutsch, David, and Michael Lockwood. "The Quantum Physics of Time Travel." *Scientific American*, March 1994.

> An accessible contemporary account of the parallel universes theory proposed by Hugh Everett III.

Dissanayake, Ellen. *Homo Aestheticus: Where Art Comes From and Why*. New York: The Free Press, 1992.

> A convincing survey of the cultural universality of human art as "making special," and a persuasive argument about its evolutionary roots.

Eccles, Sir John, Roger Sperry, Ilya Prigogine, and Brian Josephson. *Nobel Prize Conversations*. Dallas: Saybrook, 1985.

> A fascinating book about the new brain science: mental causality is neither purely bottom-up nor purely top-down, but constitutes a nonlinear feedback system with unpredictable yet ordered emergent features.

Etzioni, Amitai. *The Spirit of Community: Rights, Responsibilities, and the Communitarian Agenda*. New York: Crown Publishers, 1993.

> Etzioni's communitarian agenda, together with Vaclav Havel's idea of civil society, are in accord with the intentions of this book.

Feirstein, Frederick, ed. *Expansive Poetry*. Santa Cruz, Calif.: Story Line Press, 1989.

> The most comprehensive discussion of the new formalism and the new narrative movements in poetry: trenchant essays by several of the most important poets and critics of the new approach.

Foley, John Miles, ed., *Oral Tradition*. Columbia, Miss. (periodical).

> A journal that shows that the best traditional scholarship is not yet dead, and which traces the evolutionary roots of literature in oral narrative rituals.

Fox, Robin, ed. *Biosocial Anthropology*. London: Malaby Press, 1975.

———. *Encounter with Anthropology*. New Brunswick, N.J.: Transaction Publishers, 1991.

———. *The Challenge of Anthropology*. New Brunswick, N.J.: Transaction Publishers, 1994.
Robin Fox has been the clearest advocate for the fact that we are an animal species reflecting the history of our evolution.

Fraser, J. T. *Time as Conflict*. Basel: Birkhauser, 1978.

———. "Out of Plato's Cave: The Natural History of Time." *Kenyon Review*, Winter 1980.
Fraser's theory of the composite nature of time, as a concentrically nested hierarchy of temporalities, is in my opinion the most important contribution to fundamental philosophy of this half-century.

Gibson, William. *Neuromancer*. New York: Ace, 1986.

———. *Count Zero*. New York: Ace, 1987.

———. *Mona Lisa Overdrive*. New York: Ace, 1988.
Splendidly crafted glitzy-grungy cyberpunk novels about the neural–cybernetic interface, its dangers, corruptions, and mystical possibilities.

Gioia, Dana. *Can Poetry Matter?* St. Paul, Minn.: Graywolf Press, 1992.
A distinguished New Formalist poet presents a lucid discussion of contemporary poetry.

Gleick, James. *Chaos: Making a New Science*. New York: Viking, 1987.
The classic overview of the new nonlinear science, which, however, puzzlingly leaves out Prigogine.

Goodall, Jane. *The Chimpanzees of Gombe: Patterns of Behavior*. Cambridge, Mass.: Belknap Press of Harvard University Press, 1986.

———. *Visions of Caliban: On Chimpanzees and People*, with Dale Peterson. Boston: Houghton Mifflin, 1993.
There is not so great a gap between us and our primate relatives as the social constructionists would like to believe.

Gould, Stephen Jay. *The Flamingo's Smile*. New York: W. W. Norton, 1985.

———. *Eight Little Piggies*. New York: W. W. Norton, 1993.
Gould's insistence on the nonlinear and sometimes sudden processes of evolu-

tion has been a useful corrective to more determinist views, but his ideological distaste for teleology makes him miss some of the more exciting implications of his approach.

Griffin, David, ed. *The Reenchantment of Science*. Albany: SUNY Press, 1988.

———. *God and Religion in the Postmodern World*. Albany: SUNY Press, 1989.
Griffin's attempt to recruit a reconstructive postmodernism based on a sophisticated Whiteheadian religious worldview is an important part of the emerging constellation of hope.

Hans, James. *The Play of the World*. Amherst: University of Massachusetts Press, 1981.

———. *The Origins of the Gods*. Albany: SUNY Press, 1991.

———. *The Golden Mean*. Albany: SUNY Press, 1991.
Hans is one of the wisest observers of culture and literature we have. His ideas about the irreducible element of shame and violence in our nature, about the aesthetic basis of ethical behavior, and about "play," are an important part of the new synthesis.

Hartshorne, Charles. *Born to Sing: An Interpretation and World Survey of Bird Song*. Bloomington: Indiana University Press, 1973.
Natural aesthetics.

Hassan, Ihab. "The Question of Postmodernism." In Harry R. Garvey, ed., *Romanticism, Modernism, Postmodernism*. Lewisburg: Bucknell University Press, 1980.

———. *The Right Promethean Fire*. Urbana. Ill.: University of Illinois Press, 1980.
Ihab Hassan is probably the most perceptive observer of the postmodernist/poststructuralist avant-garde.

Havel, Vaclav. *The Power of the Powerless: Citizens Against the State in Central-Eastern Europe*. Armonk, N.Y.: M. E. Sharpe, 1985.

———. *Open Letters: Selected Writings, 1964–1990*. New York: Knopf, 1991.
Havel points the way toward a future society of evolutionary hope.

Hawking, Stephen W. *A Brief History of Time*. New York: Bantam, 1988.
The new cosmology of time.

Hayles, Katherine. *Chaos and Order: Complex Dynamics in Literature and Science*. Chicago: University of Chicago Press, 1991.

    Though Hayles's work is occasionally marred by feminist clichés, it is full of brilliant insights about the humanistic implications of the new science.

Hearne, Vicki. *Adam's Task: Calling Animals by Name*. New York: Knopf, 1986.

    A beautifully written book about the subjective lives of animals and our relationships with them.

Hirsch, E. D. *Cultural Literacy: What Every American Needs to Know*. Boston: Houghton Mifflin, 1987.

    A useful account of the symptoms of educational decline and renewal.

Hofstadter, Douglas. *Gödel, Escher, Bach*. New York: Vintage, 1979.

    This book has not lost any of the wonderful surprise, playfulness, and originality of its investigation of self-referential processes and structures.

Howell, R. Patton, ed. *Beyond Literacy*. Saybrook 1989.

    An attractive vision of what the literary humanities might be.

Jencks, Charles. *Post-Modernism: The New Classicism in Art and Architecture*. New York: Rizzoli, 1987.

    If postmodernism had taken the interesting direction Jencks forecast for it, it would by now have been producing beautiful work. Only a minority of artists did so, however.

Jordan, William, ed. *Restoration and Management Notes*. Madison, Wis. (periodical).

    The leading journal of ecological restoration theory and practice.

Konner, Melvin. *The Tangled Wing: Biological Constraints on the Human Spirit*. New York: Harper & Row, 1982.

    This finely written book challenged the prevailing view that human nature was a blank sheet to be inscribed by society.

Kuhn, Thomas. *The Structure of Scientific Revolutions*. Chicago: University of Chicago Press, 1962.

    The classical work on the sociology of scientific discovery. This book, largely sound in itself, has been profoundly misinterpreted and used to support damaging conclusions as to the relativity of truth.

Lederman, Leon M., and David N. Schramm. *From Quarks to the Cosmos*. New York: Scientific American Library, 1989.

A useful introduction to the converging visions of cosmological and particle physics.

Lefebvre, Vladimir. "The Fundamental Structures of Human Reflexion," *Journal of Social and Biological Structures* 10, 1987.

Lefebvre's interesting speculations trace the nonlinear mathematics of human ethical and veridical judgments.

Lindsay, David. *A Voyage to Arcturus*. New York: Ballantine Books, 1963.

A visionary and deeply poetic science fiction novel, which suggests a view of the universe as the actual battleground of spiritual forces.

Lord, Albert. *The Singer of Tales*. Cambridge, Mass. Harvard University Press, 1960.

Human literature is rooted in traditional ritual narrative, and is a continuation of our whole evolution.

Lorenz, Konrad. *On Aggression*. New York: Harcourt Brace, 1963.

The classic work of animal psychology.

Lovelock, James. *Gaia: A New Look at Life on Earth*. Oxford; Oxford University Press, 1979.

The Gaia Hypothesis, that all life on this planet constitutes a super-organism that regulates its own life support.

Lovelock, James, and Michael Allaby. *The Greening of Mars*. New York: Warner Books, 1984.

A remarkable book about the practical work of transforming a dead planet into a living one.

Lyotard, Jean-François. *The Postmodern Condition: A Report on Knowledge*, trans. Geoff Bennington and Brian Massumi. Minneapolis: University of Minnesota Press, 1985.

Like many poststructuralist works, this one has not worn well. But it is more readable than most, and covers a good deal of ground in a lively and economical fashion.

Mandelbrot, Benoit. *The Fractal Geometry of Nature*. New York: Freeman, 1977.

One of the most original books ever written, this beautifully illustrated and eccentric treatment of nonlinear and discontinuous mathematics is still at the leading edge of contemporary natural philosophy.

Margulis, Lynn, and Dorion Sagan. *Microcosmos: Four Billion Years of Microbial Evolution*. New York: Summit, 1986.

An original reconception of the dynamics of evolution on this planet, which by implication refutes the "fragile balance of nature" theory and emphasizes the creativity of nature.

Marr, David. *Vision*. New York: Freeman, 1982
A pathbreaking book on the nature of visual perception, with striking implications for aesthetics; now slightly outdated, but still very useful.

Nagy, Gregory. *The Best of the Achaeans: Concepts of the Hero in Archaic Greek Poetry*. Baltimore: Johns Hopkins University Press, 1974.
If we wish to rebuild our academic culture, it will be partly with the help of books such as this, which marvelously catches the unflinchingness, pragmatism, and dignity with which the Greeks confronted reality.

Penrose, Roger. *The Emperor's New Mind: Concerning Computers, Minds, and the Laws of Physics*. Oxford: Oxford University Press, 1989.
This book purports to show the impossibility of artificial intelligence, but it is actually a brilliant exploration of the new implications of nonlinearity.

Pirsig, Robert. *Zen and the Art of Motorcycle Maintenance*. New York: Bantam, 1974.
This novel began to heal the devastating rift between technological thinking, philosophy, and artistic culture that developed in the 60s.

Prigogine, Ilya, and Isabelle Stengers. *Order out of Chaos: Man's New Dialogue with Nature*. New York: Bantam, 1984.
The most important book on the emergent properties of nature.

Radnoti, Miklos. *Foamy Sky: The Major Poems of Miklos Radnoti*, trans. Zsuzsanna Ozsvath and Frederick Turner. Princeton: Princeton University Press, 1992.
This book puts into practice in metrically accurate translations the theoretical principles of natural classicism.

Redman, Timothy. *Ezra Pound and Italian Fascism*. Cambridge, England: Cambridge University Press, 1991.
A finely written book about the intellectual and moral failure of one line of conservative modernism, by the coiner of the term "ecopoetics."

Rentschler, Ingo, Barbara Herzberger, and David Epstein, eds. *Beauty and the Brain: Biological Aspects of Aesthetics*. Basel: Birkhauser, 1988.
The first major book on the evolution, neurobiology, and psychophysics of beauty.

Robson, John M., ed. *Origin and Evolution of the Universe: Evidence for Design?* Kingston and Montreal, Canada: McGill-Queen's University Press, 1987.

A serious and interesting discussion of the possible role of intention and consciousness in the evolution of the universe.

Scheff, Thomas J. "Microlinguistics: A Theory of Social Action." *Sociological Theory* no. 4, 1, 1968.

———. *Microsociology: Emotion, Discourse and Social Structure*. Chicago: University of Chicago Press, 1990.

In his recent books Scheff turns his meticulous methods of conversation analysis upon the emotional interior of human behavior, with special emphasis on the key emotion of shame.

Schopf, J. William, ed. *Earth's Earliest Biosphere: Its Origin and Evolution*. Princeton: Princeton University Press, 1983.

A magisterial collection of essays that shows how catastrophic the great experiment of organic life can be.

Schroedinger, Erwin. *Science and Humanism: Physics in Our Time*. Cambridge, England: Cambridge University Press, 1951.

Schroedinger's attempt to find a place for human freedom in the universe through quantum uncertainty anticipates Penrose's similar work. Until the science of nonlinear and complex systems came along, this was the best hope for a theory of freedom.

Seielstadt, George A. *At the Heart of the Web: The Inevitable Genesis of Intelligent Life*. New York: Harcourt Brace, 1989.

The onto-epistemological necessity of observers in the universe.

Sexson, Lynda. *Ordinarily Sacred*. New York: Crossroad, 1982.

The religious and ritual dimensions of ordinary life: written with great charm and insight.

Sonea, Sorin, and Maurice Panisset. *A New Bacteriology*. Boston: Jones & Barlett, 1983.

Like Margulis and Sagan's book, this work demonstrates the close kinship of all life on earth.

Steele, Timothy. *Missing Measures: Modern Poetry and the Revolt Against Meter*. Fayetteville, Ark.: University of Arkansas Press, 1990.

A lucid literary book about the return of meter to poetry.

Thayer, H. S. "The Right to Believe: William James' Reinterpretation of the Function of Religious Belief." *Kenyon Review*, Winter 1983.
>An interesting discussion of an early precursor of the anthropic principle.

Thoreau, Henry David. *Walden*. Columbus, Ohio: Charles E. Merrill, 1969.
>The human as part of nature.

Tiger, Lionel. *Optimism: The Biology of Hope*. New York: Simon and Schuster, 1979.
>Hope is an essential activity of the human brain.

Turner, Frederick. *Genesis, an Epic Poem*. Dallas: Saybrook, 1988.

———. *Natural Classicism*. Charlottesville, Va.: University Press of Virginia, 1991; first published 1985.

———. *Beauty: The Value of Values*. Charlottesville, Va.: University Press of Virginia, 1991.

———. *Rebirth of Value: Medications on Beauty, Ecology, Religion, and Education*. Albany: SUNY Press, 1991.

———. *Tempest, Flute, and Oz: Essays on the Future*. New York: Persea Books, 1991.

Turner, Victor W. *Schism and Continuity in an African Society*. Manchester, England: Manchester University Press, 1957.

———. *The Forest of Symbols*. Ithaca: Cornell University Press, 1967.

———. *The Drums of Affliction*. Oxford: Oxford University Press, 1968.

———. *The Ritual Process*. Chicago: University of Chicago Press, 1969.

———. *Dramas, Fields, and Metaphors*. Ithaca: Cornell University Press, 1974.

———. *From Ritual to Theater*. New York: Performing Arts Journal Press, 1982.
>Victor Turner's deeply humanistic anthropology is an excellent corrective against all power-based theories of social construction.

Wechsler, Judith, ed. *On Aesthetics in Science*. Cambridge, Mass.: MIT Press, 1978.
>An excellent collection of essays on the intricate beauty that science uncovers in nature. The essay by Cyril Stanley Smith on crystallography and visual beauty is especially recommended.

Wheeler, John Archibald. "World as System Self-Synthesized by Quantum Networking." *IBM Journal of Research and Development* 32, no. 1, January 1988.

> A summary of Wheeler's somewhat misnamed "Anthropic Principle" of cosmology, in which the initial conditions of the universe are constrained by the necessity to bring about observers of it that will collapse its wave function.

Whitehead, Alfred North. *Science and the Modern World*. Cambridge, England: Cambridge University Press, 1967.

> An amazingly prescient look at the intellectual currents that are bringing about a new era of hope.

Wilson, Edward O., and Charles J. Lumsden. *Promethean Fire*. Cambridge, Mass.: Harvard University Press, 1987.

> A lively and controversial introduction to human sociobiology.

Woolf, Virginia. *To the Lighthouse*. 1927; New York: Harcourt Brace, 1955.

———. *A Room of One's Own* New York: Harcourt Brace, 1957.

> The founding feminism of our century, which now looks wiser than any of its successors.

Zeeman, E. C. "Catastrophe Theory." *Scientific American*, April 1976.

> A lucid presentation of the ideas of René Thom; one of the first appearances in America of the new nonlinear mathematics.

Acknowledgments

I would like to thank the following people, who among others have played a vital part in the conversation which gave birth to this book: Dick Allen, Claudia Annis, Alex Argyros, Michael Benedikt, Julia Budenz, Jack Butler, James Cooper, Robert Corrigan, Koen dePryck, Ray Eve, Frederick Feirstein, Annie Finch, Tom Fleming, Martyn Fogg, Robin Fox, J. T. Fraser, Jane Greer, Dana Gioia, James Hans, Gerry Harnett, Paul Harris, Frederick Hart, Ihab Hassan, Robert Haynes, R. Patton Howell, William Jordan, Allan Kaufman, Paul Lake, Lewis Lapham, Michael Lind, James Mann, Bonnie Marranca, Douglas Matzge, Brian Moore, Robert Nelsen, Virgil Nemoianu, Gerry O' Sullivan, Zsuzsanna and Istvan Ozsvath, Jeffrey Perl, Carl Pletsch, Ernst Pöppel, Tim Redman, Ingo Rentschler, Carl Sagan, Tom Scheff, Lynda and Michael Sexson, Mihai Spariosu, Paul Trout, Daniel Turner, Edie Turner, Mei Lin Turner, Robert Turner, Kevin Walzer, Edwin Watkins, Judith Weissman, and Mary Wickham. I would also like to thank my graduate students at the University of Texas at Dallas, the Expansive Poets, the Centrists, the Center for the Study of Science and the Arts, the Fellows of the Dallas Institute of Humanities and Culture, and Adam Bellow, who is surely the prince of editors.

Index